Artists are the diaries of our time. If we go back thousands of years ago, and look at Chinese culture, Egyptian culture, Mayan culture, Eskimo culture, we look at artifacts of what artists have done. Art serves a unique function in society. It can bring people together regardless of political, religious, social, or economical backgrounds. If we don't support art and culture we won't have it. If we lose it, we lose our memory. Stan Lai's book on creativity is foundational support for arts and culture and will enhance the hopes that we keep our memory.

—*Robert Wilson, The World's Foremost Vanguard Theater Artist (New York Times)*

Stan Lai masterfully shows us how sudden bursts of limitless creativity do not emerge from nowhere; rather, they are the blossoms of a lifelong process of maturation, which crystallize into something self-evident and awe-inspiring that can then be translated into art through the seamless union of wisdom and method. Stan Lai teaches us how to see and how to do.

—*Matthieu Ricard, author of Notebooks of a Wandering Monk*

I've always looked up to Stan Lai as an inspiration, in both his playwriting and his life as an artist. How he has managed to create one iconic work after another over many decades, achieving a stature second to none among world dramatists? Now I have some answers. His classic book *Creativitry*, long revered in China by artists and business leaders alike, has finally been published in English. As one of the world's leading artists (as well as a longtime practitioner of Buddhism), Stan Lai gives us an invaluable and practical guide for anyone who seeks to live a richer, deeper, more realized life.

—*David Henry Hwang, Tony Award–winning playwright*

Stan Lai is an exceptional creative artist, who also has rich teaching experience, and deep spiritual training in Buddhism. In this book, he shares his creative experience to help us remove the barrier of knowledge, to activate the wisdom energy, to give us a look at the mystery of creativity.

—*Ang Lee, Academy Award–winning director*

Entrepreneurs need the imagination of artists. You must read Stan Lai's *Creativitry*. It will help you open your creative mind, making it agile and full of magic.

—*Jack Ma, founder, Alibaba Group*

There are few people in this world who are as ideally placed as Stan Lai to discuss the vast concept of creativity. His vision is rooted in the ancient traditions of the East, but it has reached the skies of Western culture. He is a Buddhist and a personality of the twenty-first century, at once. He is both a playwright and director. More than all that, he is a creative spirit for whom no boundaries exist. This book is not a manual, but a statement of belief, an enduring message about how each of us can go beyond our limits. In times when new technologies seem to threaten the uniqueness of our species, it reminds everyone who reads it that the essence of who we are resides in our most precious talent. That is, our ability to create. It is a divine gift, simply because it makes us human.

—*Octavian Saiu, founder and president, International Association of Theatre Leaders*

The main difference between Stan Lai's *Creativitry* and the many other books on this subject available is that the author is a major heavyweight creative artist. From his own experience, Stan talks about the source of creativity, about how to develop from motivation and transform materials to the finished product. Each and every point is ruthlessly explained. Stan does not provide quick answers, because he understands that true creativity must come from one's practice in life.

—*Lin Hwai-min, founder and artistic director, Cloud Gate Dance Company*

At a time when the widespread use of the word "creativity" dilutes its significance, Stan Lai restores the meaning of creativity, along with its magic and complexity. A must-read from an internationally renowned artist.

—*Shannon Jackson, Chair, History of Art Department; director, Environmental Arts and Humanities Initiative, U.C. Berkeley*

This is a path to artistic creativity; it is also a soul's self-discovery into a life of creativity.

—*Feng Lun, founder and chairman, Vantone Holdings and Real Estate*

Creativitry is a revelation! In this extraordinary work Artist/Shaman, Stan Lai, guides us to the center of the creative moment and the ultimate unity of the spiritual and physical worlds.

—*Travis Preston, founding artistic director of the CalArts Center for New Performance, former dean of the School of Theater, California Institute of the Arts*

Mankind perpetually seeks to rid itself of the state of non-creativity, but unfortunately, such methods are not at all creative. This is the great tragedy of humanity: the essence of life is creation, but life itself has swallowed up creativity. Fortunately, throughout history there have always emerged masters who come forth with compassion to inspire people to avoid being swallowed up. The master of our times is Stan Lai, who, with years of practice and training, tells people that creativity is a kind of mental process that can be traced, and that after a series of effective training, many people can enter a state of constant creativity.

—*Yu Qiuyu, China's most prominent prose writer*

CREATIVITRY

CREATIVITRY

Asia's Iconic Playwright Reveals
the Art of Creativity

BY STAN LAI

ANTHEM PRESS

Anthem Press
An imprint of Wimbledon Publishing Company
www.anthempress.com

This edition first published in UK and USA 2026
by ANTHEM PRESS
75–76 Blackfriars Road, London SE1 8HA, UK
or PO Box 9779, London SW19 7ZG, UK
and
244 Madison Ave #116, New York, NY 10016, USA

© 2026 Stan Lai

The author asserts the moral right to be identified as the author of this work.

All rights reserved. Without limiting the rights under copyright reserved above, no part of this publication may be reproduced, stored or introduced into a retrieval system, or transmitted, in any form or by any means (electronic, mechanical, photocopying, recording or otherwise), without the prior written permission of both the copyright owner and the above publisher of this book.

British Library Cataloguing-in-Publication Data
A catalogue record for this book is available from the British Library.

Library of Congress Cataloging-in-Publication Data: 2025933784
A catalog record for this book has been requested.

ISBN-13: 978-1-83999-395-4 (Pbk)
ISBN-10: 1-83999-395-2 (Pbk)

Cover Design by tight.nyc

Photo by Li Jiaxin

Illustration by Stan Lai

This title is also available as an eBook.

CONTENTS

Acknowledgments	xvii
List of Figures	xix
Foreword	xxi
Preface	xxiii
Creativitry	xxv

PART ONE: IS CREATIVITY LEARNABLE? 1

Chapter One **How Amazing It Is That We Lack This Amazing Thing** 3
What Exactly Is Creativity? 4
We Teach to Be More Creative, But Can We First Teach How to Be Creative? 5
The Accidental Playwright 6
Breakthroughs as an Artist Are Not Breakthroughs as a Teacher 7

PART TWO: AN ANATOMY OF INSPIRATION 9

Chapter Two **Infusion or Extraction?** 11
Finding Museland 11
Inspiration Captured in Slow Motion 12
Extraction, Not Infusion 15
Visualizing A New Kind of Performance 17
Instant Replay 18
The Anatomy of Inspiration 19
Exercises and Further Thoughts 20

ix

Chapter Three	**What Makes You Not Creative?**	**21**
	Be Safe, Don't Create	21
	Exercises and Further Thoughts	24

PART THREE: A GENERAL THEORY OF CREATIVITY — 25

Chapter Four	**The Two Parts of Creativity**	**27**
	On a Rickshaw in Bodh Gaya, India, with Matthieu Ricard	27
	Fingers and Music	29
	A Dance, in Two Acts	30
	Exercises and Further Thoughts	32
Chapter Five	**A Map for Creativity**	**35**
	The Short Guide	35
	Being and Doing	36
	A Path	37
	Exercises and Further Thoughts	37

PART FOUR: CREATIVE WISDOM — 39

Chapter Six	**The Curious Disappearance of Wisdom**	**41**
	Training in Being	41
	Life, Unexamined	42
	Lost in Definition	44
	The Threat of Wisdom	45
	Center and Periphery	46
	Wisdom = Knowing	47
	Learning to Question	48
	To Know What You Don't Know	50
	Exercises and Further Thoughts	52
Chapter Seven	**Wisdom Starts with Why**	**53**
	Why Create?	53
	Why Not?	54
	A Freeway to Creativity	55
	Artists, in Bali?	56
	Gift or Garbage?	57
	Offering or Destruction?	59
	The Spectrum of Why	61
	Shakespeare's Passions, Michelangelo's Contracts	62

	My Lesson in Motivation	64
	Exercises and Further Thoughts	66
Chapter Eight	**How to See**	**67**
	Cleaning the Doors of Perception	68
	What Don't We See?	68
	Creativity Is a Process of Discovery	70
	The Magical Paradox	71
	Creativity 101	72
	Exercises and Further Thoughts	73
Chapter Nine	**Inspiration's Warehouse**	**75**
	A Storage Space for Creative Files	75
	What's in You?	76
	Creativity Is Like Memory	76
	The Pliable Tissue of Concern	77
	How Do We File Experience?	78
	The Equality of Things	79
	Seeing Is a Habit	81
	A Sharp Blur	82
	Exercises and Further Thoughts	82
Chapter Ten	**De-labeling**	**87**
	The Liberation of Objects	87
	An Ancient Theory of Relativity	87
	Mind the Gap!	88
	Wisdom Is Space	91
	Creativity As Is	91
	A Crack in the Ground	93
	Exercises and Further Thoughts	94
Chapter Eleven	**Three Views**	**97**
	World View	97
	The Floating World	99
	Cause-and-Effect View	99
	A Kettle Boils	102
	Mind Reading	102
	Not-So-Instant Karma	103
	Effect without Cause	103
	As It Is	104

	Flowing	104
	Your Personal Lie Detector	106
	Let Go and Hold Everything	107
	Q&A sans Q	107
	Exercises and Further Thoughts	108
Chapter Twelve	**Motivation Re-examined**	**111**
	Is Creativity a Chronic Illness?	111
	Awards Rehearsal	113
	Wisdom without Method	113
	Relax!	114
	Exercises and Further Thoughts	115

PART FIVE: THE SOURCE — 117

Chapter Thirteen	**The Tao Is a Well**	**119**
	Connecting the Personal to the Collective	119
	The Source is Chaos	120
	What is Blocking Us?	121
	Breaching the Barrier	122
	The Clutter	123
	Upgrading Experience	124
	Exercises and Further Thoughts	126

PART SIX: CREATIVE METHOD — 127

Chapter Fourteen	**Doing**	**129**
	The Wisdom of Method	129
	What Works?	130
	Playing Without Rules	131
	How Your Work Works	133
	Working with Time	134
	A Toolbox for Method	135
	A Tool Named Curiosity	136
	Conceptual Gear	137
	The Paradox of My Toolbox	138
	Exercises and Further Thoughts	141
Chapter Fifteen	**How Things Work**	**143**
	Being Encyclopedic	143
	The Past Is a Long Prologue	144

	Being an Expert	146
	Exercises and Further Thoughts	148
Chapter Sixteen	**The Practice of Practice**	**149**
	To Learn How to Do, You Need to Do	149
	The Other Shore	150
	The Engine Room	151
	Slowing It All Down	152
	Getting Dunked on, by Art	154
	Apprenticeship	155
	Pushing a Burned-out Car Over a Cliff	156
	My 10,000	158
	Diligence	160
	Exercises and Further Thoughts	161
Chapter Seventeen	**Crafting Structure**	**163**
	The Key to How Things Work	163
	The Urge for Unity	164
	Searching for Rules	166
	Deconstruction in a Shanghai Café	167
	X-Ray Vision	167
	The Numerology of Creativity	169
	To Make a Flower Bloom	171
	Two Primal Choices	171
	Proportion	173
	Arc and Triangle	173
	The Primordial Pattern	175
	Seeing the Forest While Working on the Trees	176
	Exercises and Further Thoughts	180

PART SEVEN: YOUR CREATIVE APP — 181

Chapter Eighteen	**Activating Your App**	**183**
	Showtime!	183
	The Fast Track: Being Space	185
	The Blank Canvas in Your Mind	187
	The Analytical Path	189
	Catch the Wind	190
	Toolbox Full, Mind Open	191
	Exercises and Further Thoughts	191

Chapter Nineteen	**Putting It All Together**	**193**
	Melding Style to Substance	193
	The 99 Percent	194
	Satisfying the Devil	195
	Schedules, Schedules	197
	Keeping Sanity	199
	Setting a Zone	200
	Retreat	201
	Eccentricity Is the Norm	202
	When Stuck	203
	How to Plan a Breakthrough	205
	Compromise Can Be a Blessing	206
	Notes on Giving Notes	207
	Holistic Creative Healing	208
	Exercises and Further Thoughts	209
Chapter Twenty	**Wild Cards**	**211**
	A Theory of Talent	211
	Luck	213
	Personality	213
	Sense and Sensitivity	214
	Perseverance	215
	The Kung-Fu of Improvisation	216
	The Grand Conspiracy	219
	Exercises and Further Thoughts	220
Chapter Twenty-One	**Completion**	**221**
	Seeing the Mountain	221
	The Dreaded Bell	222
	Spell Weavers	223
	Seamlessness	223
	Harvest	224
	Exercises and Further Thoughts	225
PART EIGHT: JOURNEY TO TRANSFORMATION		**227**
Chapter Twenty-Two	**From Where to Where?**	**229**
	The Journey	229
	The Efficacy of Art	230
	The Accidental Arsonist	230

	Pain, Healing, and Sharing	231
	To Forget or Remember?	232
	Destination: Beyond	233
	A Circle	234
	Listen, Contemplate, Act	234
	The Language of the Soul	235
	Sincerity and Humility	236
	Passion and Compassion	237
	Exercises and Further Thoughts	237
Chapter Twenty-Three	**Further Thoughts on the Creative Act**	**239**
	Is Creativity Innately Selfish?	239
	Practice and Window	240
	Artistic License	241
	Is Art Spelled with a Capital "A"?	242
	The Curse of Originality	242
	Exercises and Further Thoughts	243
Chapter Twenty-Four	**My Personal Journey**	**245**
	Some References	245
	Surprise: Success	246
	Lost Noodles	247
	The Encore, and Beyond	248
	Creativity Is a Steamed Bun	249
	An Olympic-sized Elephant	251
	New Horizons	253
	Exercises and Further Thoughts	254
Closing Thoughts		**255**
Afterword by Eugenio Barba		**257**
References		259
Index		267

ACKNOWLEDGMENTS

To my mother, Lingling Lai, the true artist who never had the opportunity to train as one.

Sincere thanks to all my teachers, colleagues, students, friends, and strangers throughout my life, West and East, in all walks of life, for everything they have taught me about creativity.

Thanks to my colleagues at Performance Workshop, Taipei, and Theatre Above, Shanghai, for assistance with this manuscript and graphics. Thanks to Octavian Saiu, who suggested that I work with Anthem, and my friends at Anthem for their care with this publication. Thanks to dear friend Judy Shih, for being a most acute and eloquent sounding board for drafts of this book. Thanks to Suzan Ting for her generous and brilliant cover design.

I would also like to thank my daughters and their beautiful families, who provide me with constant inspiration.

Finally, I could so easily forget to thank my most important source of inspiration, my life companion Nai-chu, for she is so much a part of me, but here I have not.

Thank you.

LIST OF FIGURES

4.1	Initial thoughts of the creative path, on a postcard, 2000	28
5.1	The Creative Map, basic version	34
6.1	Center and periphery	47
6.2	Pathways to and from the center	48
10.1	Expanded Map of Creativity	84
13.1	The Source with barrier surrounding	124
13.2	The Source with the barrier removed	125
17.1	The well-made play	174
17.2	The elaborately well-made play	175
17.3	Progression chart for *Secret Love in Peach Blossom Land*, using 2 minutes as a unit	178
17.4	Progression chart for *Secret Love in Peach Blossom Land*, annotated	179

FOREWORD

On the face of it, the majority of us go through life by merely interacting with what has already been created. We don't ask questions like, who created everything, how did they do it, and when. We simply take it all for granted. We are not even curious about how the things we see around us work, let alone astonished by the human ingenuity that, for example, came up with the idea that by carving an elegant wooden box, adding a long, thin ebony neck, and then stretching four strings of different thicknesses over the two, would create a violin, bringing the joy of music to millions.

There are, however, some who for various reasons—it could be curiosity, necessity, or the search for truth—are not content with and settling for what we have and yearn to want to go beyond the surface of what we see to uncover what lies behind it. We not only want to explore all aspects of creativity, but we also want to know the creator, little suspecting that the very fact of a creator is just another amazing creation of the human mind.

In recent times, for whatever reason—it could be a quest for a creative climax, or it could be an enterprise to make money—from Hanoi to Hollywood, everyone wants to be "creative," everyone wants to be a small god, "a creator." Of course, creative people can earn a great deal of money, and so inevitably, perhaps, many of us suffer and struggle to find and develop our creativity. This explosion of creative endeavor has opened all kinds of doors for truly creative individuals to be able to express their ideas fully and, often, to be able to enrich our society. At the same time, there are those who only want to make money and who reduce creativity to yet another commercial commodity that caters to the consumer society and, in the process, corrupts creativity itself.

Whichever creative world you belong to, one way or another you will need to find and learn to work with your own creativity. In other words, you will need feedback to know that what you are doing is creative, and guidance on how to develop your ideas—basically, you will need an indicator of some kind.

Of course, whether something is creative or not is subjective, and it's very difficult to teach someone how to be creative. But I assume that you can make a creative map by encouraging people to be courageous so that they can be free from what is redundant or clichéd. And it is this courage or bravery that I personally have seen in Stan Lai's work. In particular, I can see that Mr. Lai's book, *Creativitry*, is like a creative map that will help you choose the direction you should take, or simply encourage you to lose yourself for a while, knowing that either way you will always have his map to help you should you need it.

Dzongsar Jamyang Khyentse

Dzongsar Jamyang Khyentse is one of the most prominent Buddhist masters of our time, and filmmaker, author of What Makes You Not a Buddhist.

PREFACE

I sit in my writing retreat in the Xixi wetlands in ancient Hangzhou, surrounded by gentle lotus ponds and persimmon trees. It is raining. The breeze blows ripples across the pond, and the leaves sway in soft rhythm as part of the ongoing dance. I am immersed. In creativity. Every instant, each moment reveals itself to me in a never-ending display of amazing.

Art and life both depend on creativity. Creativity itself is an art, that comes from life. Life is an art. This book is a guide for you to bring forth your creative being through the art that is your life.

I feel very blessed to have led a long and fruitful creative life, and more so to be able to explain and impart what I have learned along the path. Though my 40-odd plays have been performed under my direction in over 100 cities in Asia and the West (mostly Chinese-speaking), my films have been shown in festivals around the world, and I have taught for decades while founding three theater festivals, I still feel humbled by the boundless power of creativity and stand reverent before it. I therefore do not assume any authority in writing this book. I have merely organized and set forth what I have seen and learned over the years, in the hope that it may be of use to you.

This book is based on my book in Chinese on creativity, *Chuangyixue*, which was published in Taipei and Beijing in 2006,[1] and has found a steady and loyal readership in many fields outside of the arts, including sciences, tech, business, and education. It is a total rewrite of that work, not a translation. Creativity is an intensely personal subject, and each of us must find our own way to access it. This book is not so much about clever techniques to enhance your creativity, but more about working on yourself, to become the creative being you were meant

---

1 Stan Lai (Lai Shengchuan), *Chuangyixue* (Taipei: Commonwealth, 2006; Beijing: CITIC, 2006; Guangxi Normal University Press, 2007). Over one million copies have been sold.

to be. Working on yourself is never easy. You have to grow to like it and want it, like working out at the gym, and you have to learn to persevere, to seek creative breakthroughs when you often don't even know what the problem is.

In rewriting, I found it important to re-vision and rephrase everything for a Western readership. I went back to my notes for a class I taught at Stanford before my book was published in Chinese. In that class, 35 students from a wide swathe of disciplines were inspired by this unique view of creativity. In the almost two decades since the original Chinese book was published, through continual creative work and lectures on the subject, my insight into the creative act has also grown. These insights were included in a class I taught at Berkeley in 2019, and I share them with you here.

I sincerely hope that whatever your calling is, this book can help you discover your creative self and gain ever more from your creative journey.

Stan Lai, 2025

Creativitry

Doesn't exist as a word.
Just as all creative things do not exist
Until they do.
Rhymes with "Artistry" and "Chemistry."
And "Sorcery."
"The know-how, practice and mastery of creativity."

PART ONE
Is Creativity Learnable?

CHAPTER ONE

HOW AMAZING IT IS THAT WE LACK THIS AMAZING THING

The best things in life are free. Love is perhaps the greatest freebie, with creativity coming in at a close second, but both are not really "free," because they are free to learn, but once learned, they are used to give. They are not gifts to be taken, but to be given. And neither is easy to learn.

Creative ideas are in the public domain, in the air, touching everything, sitting on your blank piece of paper, perched next to your kitchen stove, connecting invisible lines in the sky. They are pressing against your eyes and ears, shouting out for you to use them. But strangely, most of us are not aware. That is because there is a mechanism within you that needs to be turned on. Once activated, your world is permeated by this wondrous thing. Unfortunately, it is not a simple switch that you can just flip on and off.

We are all born with immense creative power that emanates from the source of life itself. The problem is, this power has been obstructed from most of us, hidden not in some external place, but somewhere deep within ourselves. To access our unlimited creative power, we need to regain many abilities that we have lost. To this end, we must *un-learn* many things that we were taught and thought were important, and *re-learn* how to see and think about how we experience life and the world.

Ironically, though creativity is the wellspring of life, it is life itself, living, that creates the barrier between us and creativity. This barrier is erected early in childhood, and as adults, we often unwittingly contribute to the construction of the barriers in our own children. Family, school, society, all play a part in most of us growing up into what I call a "non-creative mode," whereas we could and should naturally become highly creative beings.

What Exactly Is Creativity?

We as a species have counted on creativity since time immemorial, but what actually is it? We know so little about it that we even suppose it is not something that can be learned. The common sentiment is that those who have it, have it, and those who don't, don't. It is true that creative inspiration often comes in a flash that happens too quickly to analyze, and therefore those who often gain such flashes are seen as the privileged few. The ensuing process of actually making a creative work is often then long and drawn out, so complex and personal that it also seems impossible to describe in one-size-fits-all terms. On the other hand, the word seems to have become devalued in its overuse today. People are called "Creators" just if they provide digital content to online platforms. This further confuses our understanding of what creativity is.

> Creativity (n.)
> the ability to produce or use original and unusual ideas.
> —*Cambridge Dictionary*[1]

One would assume that dictionaries know what they are saying. Unfortunately, this misleading definition represents what most people understand. It emphasizes the ability to generate ideas, which to me is only a small part of what creativity is. People set up exercises to "think outside the box" to come up with creative ideas, but once they are done, they go back into the safety of the box. This is actually wrong and disrespectful to creativity, as if the "box" were some clean, safe place, and outside it lies a dangerous zone that can be tapped for benefit, after which one must quickly get out and return to the disinfected air of the box. Science fiction indeed.

Once at a forum in Beijing, I was sitting next to John Hawkins, the man who coined the term "Creative Cultural Industries," the buzzword behind the creative policies of many countries. I asked him what the words actually meant. He confessed to me, albeit jokingly, that he didn't know. The term came to him as he was filling out a form for a film grant from the British Council.[2]

Then what is it? A power? An energy? A talent? Apparently, the corporate world seems to consider it a skill. The Partnership for 21st Century Skills—a

---

1 dictionary.cambridge.org/dictionary/english/creativity
2 Personal conversation at Xinjingbao 2012 Economic Forum, International Hotel, Beijing, November 30, 2011.

collective of 250 researchers at 60 educational institutions—listed creativity as the most important skill for children to thrive in the future.[3] A recent article in *Forbes* is titled "70% of Employers Say Creative Thinking is Most In-Demand Skill in 2024."[4]

Wait a minute. Creativity is a skill? For career development? If creativity is a skill, it should be easy for those of us who are fluent in it to simply write a manual, and anyone can train from it, like swimming, cooking, or learning how to strengthen lower back muscles. But no such manual for creativity exists. Is it possible that all these esteemed organizations are endorsing something they don't really understand?

Consider the writing of *Hamlet*. A "skill"? There is no denying that Shakespeare, da Vinci, Eileen Chang, Lennon and McCartney, to think randomly of some creative geniuses, were all skilled at a beyond-amazing level, but the word can obviously only describe part of what they do. For Tang Xianzu to write *The Peony Pavilion*, he would have needed a *collection* of skills—classical Chinese poetry, lyrical songwriting, storytelling, and a mastery of *kunqu* musical patterns. However, even if we consider the writing of his masterpiece to be a package of skills, we still miss an entirely unnamed aspect that he and all the artists above share. This is it. Creativity.

We Teach to Be More Creative, But Can We First Teach How to Be Creative?

My personal creative journey has spanned over four decades, starting in Taiwan and continuing throughout the Chinese-speaking world, where I have created what are considered some of the more notable works of contemporary Chinese language theater. For over two decades, I also taught creative disciplines, so I have always considered creativity from both sides of teaching and practice. Like all of my own teachers, I taught actors to act and directors to direct. I never thought that creativity *itself* could, or even should be taught.

The common understanding is that creativity is in a special domain for certain geniuses only. Yet training in creativity has become common now in art institutes as well as the corporate and science worlds. Is this really training in creativity

---

[3] Jennifer Henderson, "Developing Students' Creative Skills for 21st Century Success," www.ascd.org/el/articles/developing-students-creative-skills-for-21st-century-success
[4] Rachel Wells, www.forbes.com/sites/rachelwells/2024/01/28/70-of-employers-say-creative-thinking-is-most-in-demand-skill-in-2024/?sh=4192aa7d391d

itself? Exercises like brainstorming or alternative thinking can be employed during a creative project, but are they creativity *itself*? Teaching creativity *itself* was never part of my job description. Though it means everything to the curriculum, it oddly is not part of it. It seems we teach parts of the whole, without knowing exactly what the whole is.

The Accidental Playwright

If we are either born creative or not, that means that no one could *become* creative. But I did, just as I am sure many others have—through a traceable process, become the creative artist I now am.

I recall my first bumbling attempts at creativity. After I completed my PhD in Dramatic Art at U.C. Berkeley, I went back to my home in Taipei, Taiwan, in 1983, to teach at a newly established school for the arts, the National Institute. Those were repressive times, and I often wonder why I made the choice to go back to a place that was under martial law, where pervasive censorship had stunted artistic expression and free thought throughout my adolescent years. But there was a feeling that things were changing. The establishment of this new school was one of them. I also held the naïve conviction that under the poorest of circumstances lie the greatest possibilities.

I was not trained to be a playwright, nor was it my intention to be one when studying at Berkeley. The problem was, when I arrived back in Taiwan, I could not find any teaching materials to teach with! To teach acting or directing, you need scenes from plays for students to practice with. But due to decades of artistic suppression, very few new plays had been written in Taiwan or in China that were not propagandist in nature. Taiwan didn't even have a proper (in Western terms) functioning theater. The development of modern theater in the Chinese-speaking world had been thoroughly suppressed, creating a vacuum for over thirty years. I did come across some older translations of Shakespeare, and a few Ibsens and Chekhovs of questionable reliability. But to train and perform using these translations—was that the path we, as a burgeoning modern Asian culture, wanted to take? My gut feeling was no. Though Pinter and Stoppard were exemplary, what would it say about our cultural identity if we staged only Western plays? We needed to figure out for ourselves what our own theater was.

And so I abandoned my Western training in order to devise an effective way of teaching. Perhaps it was this letting go that opened the doors to my own creativity. I decided to use improvisation for actor training. This was a way to start with as few preconceptions about acting and about theater as possible. Working with my students' life experiences, we began to create scenes and build stories through improvisation that grew into plays. Actor training was achieved in the process. Without the need of ready-made texts, we fulfilled the task of constructing plays to be performed for the public (part of my job description). And so I became in charge of "composing" these new works for a new theater. I stopped worrying about classical or contemporary playwriting theory, about what was playing in London, New York, or Tokyo. We explored stories that came from our hearts, then figured out how to tell them on the stage.[5]

Together with my students, and later with amateur actors and professional TV actors, with only our inner selves to guide us, we succeeded in creating original new works for an audience who in general had never experienced modern theater. In an unexpected twist, these experimental works became popular. Just as a new generation of theater artists emerged from our training, each new production served as a catalyst for a vibrant creative theater culture that developed in Taiwan, and later influenced theater in mainland China.[6]

Breakthroughs as an Artist Are Not Breakthroughs as a Teacher

My breakthroughs as an artist came in gradual steps, in those first few years of writing and directing new plays using improvisation as my major creative tool. This was a time of political and social upheaval that transformed Taiwan into a democracy. At the dizzying pace of creating and performing an average of two new full-length plays a year, I struggled with everything to do with creativity and playwriting: What is this play about? Why am I telling this story? Where to start? What goes where, and why? Basically, through relentless practice, slowly and incrementally, I began to understand how to assemble all the diverse pieces into a cohesive whole and create a work of theater.

Since I was writing for a society that had no tradition of modern theater, there were no conventions or rules that applied to me. Yet I understood deep down that yes, there were rules. I was making the rules, but they came from organic and intrinsic needs. Each new play grew through its own conditions, and had rules of its own built into its existence. This logic needed to be discovered, or as it felt, uncovered. Without a mentor, I would make breakthroughs and say, "Ah, I get

---

[5] See "How I 'Wright' Plays," in Stan Lai, *Selected Plays of Stan Lai, Vol. 1*, ed. Lissa Tyler Renaud (Ann Arbor: University of Michigan Press, 2022), 1–6.

[6] Further reading on my career and its creative challenges is in Chapter Twenty-Four of this book: "My Personal Journey," and elsewhere in this book as well, where pertinent to the discussion.

it." And as I got "it" more and more, smaller realizations developed and expanded into grander *satori*s about the creative act, and within a few years, I started to recognize the face of creativity and got to know it better, until I came to a point where I had broken through as an artist. It is a point I am sure many artists have experienced, where you can say with confidence that you know what you're doing, and how to do it.

Unfortunately, breaking through as an artist does not translate into breaking through as a teacher. At school, I continued to teach as I always did, seeking to inspire my students to find their own paths, never thinking that I would be able to teach them directly what I had now understood.

Why? Maybe I wanted them to find their own way, just as I had found mine. But the path was so hard! It was like knowing the answer to a question that you didn't think should have a standard answer, so you never gave your answer.

I now believe that we do not consider creativity teachable because we don't really understand what actually happens in the process of the creative act. Can we slow down the instantaneous moment in the mind when inspiration comes and see what actually occurs? If so, we may have a window into how creativity happens and start to see how we may train in it.

PART TWO
An Anatomy of Inspiration

*"And one day they taught Hesiod glorious song
while he was shepherding his lambs under holy Helicon [...]"*[1]

---
1 Hesiod, *Theogeny*, trans. H. G. Evelyn-White, www.theoi.com/Text/HesiodTheogony.html

CHAPTER TWO

INFUSION OR EXTRACTION?

Finding Museland

Are there actual muses who exist to visit the chosen few? Or is there some rationale, some principle, a path that we can pin down and follow to attain creativity? There are many colorful accounts of creative inspiration throughout history, from creative luminaries themselves:

> I myself do nothing. The Holy Spirit accomplishes all through me.[1]
> —*William Blake*

> The music for this opera was dictated to me directly by God. I only served the function of putting down the notes on paper, to be shared with the public.[2]
> —*Puccini, on the composing of* Madame Butterfly

Blake and Puccini describe divine intervention. Lorca spoke of the "Duende," a being/force neither angelic nor demonic, that instills the artist with inspiration.[3] A. E. Housman describes how the evocative concluding poem (LXIII) in his collection *A Shropshire Lad* came to be:

> Two of the stanzas, I do not say which, came into my head, just as they are printed, while I was crossing the corner of Hampstead Heath between the Spaniard's Inn and the footpath to Temple Fortune. A third stanza came with

---

[1] www.goodreads.com/quotes/87548-i-myself-do-nothing-the-holy-spirit-accomplishes-all-through
[2] www.youroperadaily.com/p/opera-daily-madame-butterfly-the
[3] Frederico Garcia Lorca, "Theory and Play of the Duende," www.poetryintranslation.com/PITBR/Spanish/LorcaDuende.php

a little coaxing after tea. One more was needed, but it did not come: I had to turn to and compose it myself, and that was laborious business. I wrote it thirteen times, and it was more than a twelvemonth before I got it right.[4]

All these narratives suggest that inspiration is something external that comes from without, and this is in line with popular sentiment. If this is so, we should consider stopping right here. That is not something I or anyone can teach. If inspiration is a gift from above, and those selected to receive it cannot choose when and where, or what its contents may be, then it is totally random, and we can only wait for it to happen, like snow.

How discouraging. We put so much effort into training skills associated with the creative act, but are not able to count on that thing called inspiration. You get a contract to write a new film script. Then you wait. You aspire to compose a new symphony. It's not coming. You are commissioned to build a vehicle for time travel. You pray. You wake up with some vague notions. Maybe the Muses visited you, but you didn't recognize or understand them.

And what about lousy inspiration? Where does that come from? Do the Muses have off days? Or is there a separate set of Muses who aren't particularly talented, or those who specialize in failed inspiration?

The central question is coming into focus:

Does inspiration come from within or without?

Inspiration Captured in Slow Motion

What did Housman mean when he said that stanzas "came into" his head? From where? Is there a storehouse of stories, poems, music, art, inventions, and ideas somewhere in space that some of us have access to, sometimes, and others, like Shakespeare or Miles Davis, can draw from anytime, or even live inside it? How does it come in? Through the breath? Through thoughts? Through pressure points? If possible, can we slow down that seemingly divine moment called "inspiration," real slow, for a better look from all angles?

---

4 A. E. Housman, *The Name and Nature of Poetry: The Leslie Stephen Lecture Delivered at Cambridge, 9 May 1933* (Cambridge: Cambridge University Press, 1933), 50.

What gushed on to the paper were characters and events that had accumulated in my mind over a long period of time.⁵
—*Stan Lai, on the inspiration for* A Dream Like a Dream

I do not consider myself a particularly narcissistic artist. I try to stay objective about all my works. This brief dissenting explanation of inspiration is recounted here because it is pertinent and, moreover, firsthand, leaving no guesswork about what happened in the artist's mind.

A Dream Like a Dream, first performed in 2000, is an eight-hour play that I wrote and directed, which has been called many things, even "the greatest Chinese language play since time immemorial."⁶ I'm not sure about that one. I mention it to emphasize that *Dream* is a serious and complex work with a pioneering staging format. The audience is in the center of the auditorium. The performance circles around them. There are seven intersecting storylines, five main characters, and over 100 minor characters, spanning over 80 years in time and two continents in space.⁷

The inspiration for this epic and complex work came into my mind all at once in a single moment. I recall the instant vividly:

I was in Bodh Gaya, India, in November 1999, attending a Buddhist seminar. Back home at the National Institute in Taipei, where I had been teaching for 15 years, it was my turn to direct a new play for the public. The faculty requested that I create a new piece. A class had been set up to create the work with students in fall 1999, to be performed the coming spring. When the semester started, I had no idea what I was going to do. I designed the class for 12 actors to form an ensemble, but on the first day, 60 students showed up! I don't know why I didn't hold auditions and kick out 48 of them, but I didn't. (I am a great believer, you will see, in serendipity and the simple belief that things happen for a reason.) The weeks went by with no inspiration, so I couldn't get started on composing the piece to be performed. I taught fundamental improvisation techniques to this large group to buy time while I agonized. During a break, I traveled to India to attend this seminar.

Bodh Gaya is a place of special majesty and energy, and in my experience, creativity. My days were spent attending profound dharma teachings and in

---

5 Stan Lai, "Director's Notes," in *Rumengzhimeng* [*A Dream Like a Dream Theatre Program*] (Hong Kong: Hong Kong Repertory Theatre, 2002), 6.
6 Raymond Zhou, "Cosmic Dream Drama," *China Daily*, April 15, 2013.
7 See Stan Lai, *A Dream Like a Dream. Selected Plays of Stan Lai, Vol. 3*, ed. Lissa Tyler Renaud (Ann Arbor: University of Michigan Press, 2022).

activities around the grand Mahabodhi Stupa, next to the pippala tree under which Shakyamuni meditated and attained enlightenment 2,500 years ago. We lit 100,000 butter lamps in prayer for the recent victims of a devastating Taiwan earthquake, and like all visitors to this holy spot, we circumambulated the stupa.

It was a quiet evening after teachings and dinner. I was in my simple hostel room reading the book I had randomly grabbed off my bookshelf at home in Taipei as I rushed out to the airport. It was Sogyal Rinpoche's *The Tibetan Book of Living and Dying*, which I had already read. No matter, it was nice to re-read.

I sat on my cot, poring over a page about a doctor in London who was in shock when several of her patients died on her first day in the ward. I didn't recall reading this passage the first time around, as is sometimes the case when you re-read a book. She asked the author for advice on how to better care for dying patients, particularly one man in particular who died frightened and alone. The author said, "I would have sat by his side, held his hand, and let him talk."[8] By letting the patient talk about his life at the end of his life, the author said, the patient may say things with surprising depth. "Everyone has their own life wisdom, and when you let a person talk you allow this life wisdom to emerge."[9]

In the moment I read this, the complex structure and content of *A Dream Like a Dream* came into my mind, vividly, in a rush, complete.

I paused and closed my eyes for a moment to take it all in, a bit overwhelmed by the enormity of the concept—stories within stories, dreams within stories, stories within dreams, cyclical patterns of violence, present to past to present, Asia to Europe to Asia …

I jotted down a few key words on a slip of paper and was content to let the "wholeness" of it sink in and solidify in my mind. Then I went to sleep.

The content revealed to me in that moment was a series of interlocking stories and dreams that started with a doctor and her dying patient. The creative premise was that, if we want to truly make sense of a person's life story, we may need to make a diversion into the story of *another* person, and so on and so forth. The interweaving of stories will create a tapestry that will tell a greater story. From the story of the patient, who was dying from an undiagnosed disease, came the story of an art student from Beijing in Paris, and the patient's relationship with her, which segued into the story of an old lady in Shanghai and her youth in Shanghai and Paris, which involved a French aristocrat and his chateau in Brittany. From

---

8 Sogyal Rinpoche, *The Tibetan Book of Living and Dying* (San Francisco: Harper, 1992), 210.
9 Ibid., 211.

contemporary Taipei, the stories and characters moved around two continents for 80 years. Seemingly unrelated, all the lines wove together at the end.

What happened in that moment? It surely was fast, truly a flash. How could so much be revealed in a mind's moment? After the fact, on careful examination, by singling out all the people and places that fell into place in that moment, I found I knew all of them. Everything that came together was traceable to people or events or news stories or ideas that I had seen or heard or experienced or thought about in the decade or so leading up to that moment, some earlier, that were dormant in my brain. In other words, I recognized all the individual elements contained in the inspired moment. They were already parked somewhere in my mind, and before the moment of inspiration, had not yet been introduced to each other.

The moment of inspiration that I experienced was not an infusion, but an extraction.

Extraction, Not Infusion

The extraction that pulled all the random things together worked under a certain hidden logic that had been brewing inside my brain for a long time: It was 1990. At an art exhibition at the Palazzo delle Esposizioni in Rome, I stood before Jan Brueghel the Elder's *Allegory of Sight and Smell*, a painting about—paintings. There were paintings on the walls, on the floor, everywhere in that painting. In that moment the "paintings within a painting" concept registered in me, and I pulled out a notebook (which I always keep handy) and wrote the following words:

"In a story, someone had a dream; in that dream, someone told a story."

This was my literal way of interpreting this visual work. That particular notebook was later tucked into a drawer in Taipei and forgotten about. Little did I suspect that it would be essential to a play that was to be written 10 years later!

Images that came together in that moment of inspiration in the Indian night came from different and seemingly random sources: staying at my friend the cinematographer Christopher Doyle's tiny seventh floor flat in Paris in the 1980s, which featured a circular staircase with a light bulb that went out every 30 seconds, so you had to run up as fast as you could before it went pitch dark; an intricately structured dream about my own death on a beach camping trip in northern Taiwan when I was 17; a dream about frying eggs that my American friend Peter Dratz told me by a lake in Montana; staying in a stately chateau in Brittany in 1999 that had a beautiful lake behind it, where I saw in the drawing room a portrait of its former owner, a diplomat (coincidentally the same profession as my father); perching myself on a rock in Bhutan in 1991, over the mystical "Burning Lake" where supposedly one can "see yourself" (did not see anything but water); news clippings from the *International Herald Tribune* about a patient with an undiagnosable terminal disease (what?) and the fatal Paddington train wreck in London where many travelers left the chaotic scene uninjured but did *not* go home or call home (most eventually did, but another big "what?" in my mind).

I did not write down any of these things when I encountered them, although they obviously made an impression on me and stayed in my mind somewhere.

Other relevant scattered things that popped into my mind that night in India had to do with meeting an old Chinese lady in Lyon, my studies of the French avant-garde when I was a student at Berkeley, and a short story I wrote in college about an ancient Chinese poet who escaped execution by disappearing into a dream he had constructed. I also had been thinking of a friend who had passed away at the age of 36. I was wondering how karma worked, and whether a single lifetime is long enough to gauge the workings of cause-and-effect. Providing an umbrella to all these thoughts and experiences was my life-long infatuation with cultural diversity and culture shock, born from the trials and tribulations of my own bi-cultural upbringing, as well as all of the things I normally think about—basically, *who I am*.

It was in that moment while reading the *Tibetan Book*, that all these unrelated things, plus many more, inexplicitly, it seemed, arose in my mind and assembled together in a complex order. They all fit into a coherent whole, a complex puzzle of interlocking stories that became *A Dream Like a Dream*.

Though the *Tibetan Book* was an external source, it did not function as a muse-like conferral. It was an external catalyst that triggered the inspiration, which gathered and combined things extracted from within. Through roads in the brain were opened, lines of communication activated, and essential connections made. The concept of "paintings within a painting"/stories within stories from Rome had not occupied my conscious thoughts for the better part of a decade, but the concept leaped out that evening, providing a conceptual frame where all the unrelated elements and characters suddenly came alive, as if extracted from where they had been stored. They adhered to the frame and interacted.

Aside from artistic considerations, this eventually solved my practical predicament of needing to create a work for a group of 60!

The point: All of these characters, events, and thoughts had their origins somewhere in my life, and somehow they were stored somewhere in the cavernous files of my mind. In that moment, the stress of the practical need to create a work for 60 students interacted with the deeper and more abiding concerns in my mind about life, war, love, injustice, cultural misrepresentation, cause-and-effect, and recurring patterns of violence. Through some inner mechanism, stories, people, and dreams that were dormant in my mind assembled on to a framework made of the deeper concerns of who I am. Everything joined together into an interconnected web, like strangers who were all brought into the same room and actually made perfect sense together.

Visualizing A New Kind of Performance

The next afternoon, I sat on one of the small hills facing the sacred stupa and wrote out an outline from my mind on a single piece of A4 paper, which was all I had with me. While I wrote, the afternoon unfolded before me. The grand stupa, with its mandala form and constant flow of circumambulating pilgrims, provided the backdrop to my writing. Buddhist pilgrims circumambulate a holy object in a clockwise direction. What is the holy object in the theater, I wondered? My immediate answer was: the audience, for it is for the audience that our work exists. Could we put the audience in the center and circle it? This novel staging configuration came to me naturally from being within the sweep of the swirling movement at the site, and as I wrote the outline, I thought of how each new scene would unfold before the audience in a clockwise direction, with the audience turning in unison to watch. As opposed to the window box proscenium configuration that has dominated theater for centuries, this way of staging brought theater back to its original ritual functions, which was what *Dream* was built to do.

Thus, content and form, script, and directing strategy for *A Dream Like a Dream* were conceived simultaneously, organically, that afternoon by the sacred stupa in Bodh Gaya.

A spirited inspiration is just the start. After that revelatory moment in Bodh Gaya, it took six months of intensive work in the rehearsal studio with actors, in meetings with designers, in solitude contemplating, and on the computer writing and editing, to bring *A Dream Like a Dream* to an actual physical form in the theater. In the process, 32 actors, a live band, and the rest of the 60 students fell into place working as assistants and crew. Since then, the play has had seven incarnations, performing throughout cities in the Chinese-speaking world, including Taipei, Hong Kong, Singapore, Beijing, Shanghai, Shenzhen, to name a few, to surprisingly sold-out houses. It opened the inaugural Wuzhen Theatre Festival in 2013. Part of the audience interest, aside from the eight-hour length and the novel staging configuration, is that I have been fortunate to work with some of the brightest film stars in China, like Hu Ge and Ni Ni, and the pop star Li Yuchun, to name a few, who are happy to perform in this marathon work. As for the audience, there is even a club of *Dream* fans who have seen the play over 10 times. I am told they meet once a year and use *Dream* as a reference point to talk about their lives.

All from that one spark in that one moment—a kernel from which has sprouted limitless potential.

That night in Bodh Gaya, a mechanism within me had been triggered, accessing all sorts of seemingly random things inside me, transforming them from the ordinary into the creative. Who did this? What did this?

Instant Replay

OK. I have slowed down a complex moment of inspiration. I believe we can take a few important lessons from it. Firstly, the answer to our question is that although inspiration is often triggered by some external elements, it is something that comes from within, and we must capture it as it arises.

"Inspiration" in my case was the identifying, extracting, and combining of previously unrelated elements that were stored somewhere in my mind. These elements were not in someone else's mind, nor were they floating around in the air or whispered to me by some mysterious being. However random their association seemed, they were all traceable to places and people, thoughts in my life, some close, some distant. The common factor was that they all had once made some sort of impact on me. At the same time, some apparatus in my mind had the capability to draw these diverse elements together and knew that they could coexist and flourish together as a unified story. This is not genius in the traditional sense of solutions appearing in mid-air but a traceable process from which we can analyze all the parts.

What then can we say about the statements of Blake and Puccini above, and other artists and scientists who have felt that their work is not even theirs, but controlled by a divine power? It is hard for us to know. Maybe if they could run their inspirational experiences through instant replay, slow everything down frame by frame, they might also be able to see what actually happened. I don't believe the replay will reveal the appearance and intrusion of some divine being. It should show how all of the elements in the work they had created came from somewhere in their own minds. Creativity scholar Albert Rothenberg explains this strange phenomenon that occurs when artists complete a monumental work:

> They themselves are often awestruck by the immensity of their accomplishment and, standing back or introspecting, they too adopt the mythic view. In such cases, a view of the accomplishment as both inexplicable and arising virtually full grown from an unknown or outside source seems somehow

valid; such a view is at least more comfortable than fully bearing the otherwise weighty pride and responsibility.[10]

Using my own example, can we say that experience is stored in our minds like files, then extracted at the moment of inspiration? If so, we should start exploring the process of how these files are saved, organized, deleted or disregarded. Who is in charge? These files are the materials for our creativity. Can we control how they are selected and stored?

Next: we need to start exploring what the apparatus is inside us that knows how to pull different files and connect them together into new files. Can this apparatus be nurtured and customized?

We move closer to the crux of the matter. As Arthur Koestler says,

> The creative act does not create something out of nothing, like the God of the Old Testament; it combines, reshuffles and relates already existing but hitherto separate ideas, facts, frames of perception, associative contexts.[11]

The Anatomy of Inspiration

In summary, through the example of *A Dream Like a Dream*, we see that when catalytic moments of inspiration are slowed down, what seems to happen is that there is an "app" in our mind that is triggered by some external or internal catalyst. This "app" extracts files from our storehouse of thoughts, feelings, stories, images, concepts, and even fragments of all of the above floating around in our subconscious, and it combines these files into a new file that becomes the creative project.

Before that happens, the mind must first save and store files somewhere in its memory system. This is an everyday job that seems to happen automatically without our knowing.

In the catalytic moment when the mind is triggered into the creative act, it essentially does two amazing things—the app activates, goes to work to search for files, pulls them, and then assembles them together into a new file, which becomes the foundation for a creative work.

This is the anatomy of creative inspiration.

---

10 Albert Rothenberg, *The Emerging Goddess: The Creative Process in Art, Science, and Other Fields* (Chicago: University of Chicago Press, 1979), 2.
11 Arthur Koestler, *The Act of Creation* (New York: Macmillan, 1964), 120.

Exercises and Further Thoughts

1. Think back to any recent moment of personal inspiration. It doesn't have to be artistic or scientific, but can be very ordinary, like figuring out how to fix a toaster or scheduling kids' pickup—breakthroughs that lead to solutions. Can you see what actually happened in that moment?
2. Examine the solutions that come from these inspirations. Are they composed of anything that wasn't already in your mind?
3. Think back to any creative project you have been inspired to do. What actually happened in that moment of inspiration? Run it back, slow it down, and think about it. Can you see that the inspiration you gained was an assembly of different elements in your mind? Do you agree that this is what happened? If so, can you start exploring how you did it?
4. Have you ever received inspiration from a source totally outside of yourself? If so, can you slow down the moment and make sure the inspiration came from an external/foreign/alien source? Make sure to differentiate between an external conferral of inspiration and an external event that acts as a catalyst to trigger internal inspiration. If indeed your inspiration came from some external infusion, can you identify the entity bestowing it? Are you able to call for this entity when needed?

CHAPTER THREE

WHAT MAKES YOU NOT CREATIVE?[1]

Be Safe, Don't Create

To learn to be creative, it might be good to first explore why we aren't.

I live and work in Asia, where societies in general are programmed to be non-creative. I believe this is part of a default general outlook that is a strange but lethal combination of Confucianism plus Capitalism. Confucianism installed an elaborate social structure in which everyone has their set place in the cosmology. Capitalism has embedded a value system that is well served by this order, which has replaced emperors and royalty with a new ruling class of corporations.

If you have ever lived in Asia, you can understand how the sheer mass of people crowded into dense living areas creates the need for some sort of order. When 3.5 million people go through a train station in one day, like in Shinjuku, Tokyo, or over 2,000 patients a day crowd an emergency room in a Shanghai hospital, conformity becomes the natural path. Children in Asia are usually not encouraged to think outside the order, or I guess we should call it the heavily fortified box. Everything they learn teaches them to keep the box tidy and organized, and to stay inside. Creative activities are like dessert to "serious" studies. They should never become the main course.

As the novelist Amy Tan, who grew up in California the daughter of Chinese immigrants put it:

> My parents told me I would become a doctor and then in my spare time I would become a concert pianist. So, both my day job and my spare time were sort of taken care of.[2]

---

[1] Borrowing from and in homage to Dzongsar Jamyang Khyentse, *What Makes You Not a Buddhist* (Shambhala, 2008).

[2] Quoted in *medium.com*, www.quotesandsayings.medium.com/the-best-20-amy-tan-quotes

The denigration of creativity is a pity, given the amazing creative legacy that our Asian ancestors have left us in all facets of life.

To be in the non-creative mode is quite simple. Just see things the way everyone sees them, and do what everyone does. Don't try to change anything, or you will get in trouble. Non-creative mode is the safe mode. The reason you are not creative may be that your default mode of existence is to be safe. That is a rather dangerous assumption.

Here are a few stories from my personal experience, illustrating how strong a grip the non-creative mode has on us:

A child on the street, a dog in the sky

One bright sunny day I was walking on the streets of Shanghai. Coming toward me were a mother and her young boy, around five years old. The boy stopped, gazed at the sky, and pointed at one of the clouds, saying, "Mama, look at the dog!" What happened next quite shocked me. The mother slapped the child on the shoulder and said sternly, "That's a cloud."

Stunned, I watched with deep sadness as they disappeared in the distance. "Wow ... there goes another," I sighed to myself. That boy will never dare see a dog in the sky again.

"My Father"

One year, my daughter, in sixth grade, competed in a speech competition in Taiwan. The topic was, "My Father." A few days before the contest, there was an essay published in a popular newspaper for children,[3] titled "My Father." On the day of the contest, not one, *but two* of the contestants memorized and used this essay, word for word, as the content of their speech.

Unbelievable? It happened. I asked my daughter what was the situation with these kids' fathers. She said she had no idea, but apparently they did have fathers.

---

3 The well-loved and now defunct *Guoyuribao* or *Mandarin Daily* that all elementary school classrooms subscribed to, as well as many households in Taiwan.

Bound hands

One year in a European metropolis, I met a wealthy Chinese couple who ran three successful Chinese restaurants. Their son was a five-year-old who loved to draw. The parents were adamantly against this, to the cruel point where they would tie up his hands whenever he wanted to draw. I was frankly appalled by this behavior, which I considered abusive, but they considered loving. Not knowing them well, I could not just reprimand them. I treaded carefully, asking the wife, "Why are you doing this?" She said, "Because our son is going to grow up to be a businessman." I said, "How can you be sure?" With all confidence, she answered, "Because my husband and I are both talented in business, so will he be, and he will take over the family business."

Speechless, I searched for something to say in a language they could understand. I found the words, "Do you know who makes the most money these days?" I asked them to check out how much successful artists make. It worked. They stopped binding his hands.

This is a very, very sad story, but true. I never saw this family again. I do hope it turned out OK for the boy and all of them.

A Theatre, Above

In 2015, I was designing a new theater in Shanghai, dedicated to the performances of my works. This was a great honor that is not bestowed on many playwrights that are living. The site was on the top floor of a busy shopping mall. I decided to name it Theatre Above, the perfect name, I thought, as did all of my colleagues, because it was literally above, upstairs, and the word "above," "*shang*" in Chinese, is the same word as the first word in "Shang"-hai. So, a theater in Shanghai, that is above, physically and aspirationally. The word can also be a verb, which means "to go." So "Theatre Above" also means "go to the theatre!" Perfect all around. Right?

I received a phone call from a top official in the district government who had veto power over the name. With all good intentions, he asked me to reconsider. He told me, "You cannot name a theatre with just one word, *shang*." I asked, "Why not?" He said because people just don't do that. Theaters always have two words in their name, like "Da-hua" ("Great China") or "Mei-qi" ("Majestic"). He said Shanghai people are very chic, so if I liked the sound of the word, there is a homonym that means "chic." His suggestion was "Theatre Chic."

I was at a total loss for words. Everything we had worked so hard for was encapsulated in this simple and perfect name that I had gained the inspiration to coin. There was a silence of about 5 seconds on the phone. Suddenly, I said,

"With due respect, throughout my career, I have never followed anybody to do anything. But," I continued, "the record shows that once we choose to name something, people follow us." Another 5 seconds of silence. Suddenly, he said decisively, "Understood, go for it." And he hung up.

I was amazed that he could process so much so quickly. As it turned out, just as the titles of many of my plays have been copied, modified, and used in popular culture, theaters all over China started using one word in their title. Theatre South, Theatre East, and so on. Theatre Above later survived the pandemic and has become a cultural landmark in Shanghai.

Exercises and Further Thoughts

1. Are you in creative or non-creative mode? Evaluate.
2. Do you prefer order or disorder? Do you believe order must be violated to be creative?
3. Have you been encouraged to think freely, or to conform to what everyone says and does? Are there moments in your life where you felt your creativity was being stifled? Have you felt confined in general as a result?
4. If you are a parent or teacher, have you ever stifled the creativity of your child or student? If so, did you do so knowingly or inadvertently?
5. Can you see how being creative demands a certain amount of courage, particularly for people living in societies that advocate conformity? Assess the amount of courage you would need to embark on a creative career.

PART THREE
A General Theory of Creativity

Creativity is not just the property of special people but a special property of all people.*
—*Ronald Carter*

---
* Ronald Carter, interviewed in *Interalia*, July 2016, www.interaliamag.org/interviews/ronald-carter/

CHAPTER FOUR

THE TWO PARTS OF CREATIVITY

On a Rickshaw in Bodh Gaya, India, with Matthieu Ricard

My breakthrough in understanding how to teach creativity came in 2000 when I returned to the Buddhist studies seminar in Bodh Gaya, India, one year after I was inspired at that same place to write *A Dream Like a Dream*.

One afternoon during a break from the teachings, my good friend, the Buddhist monk and author Matthieu Ricard, beckoned me to hop on a rickshaw with him to go to a nearby temple where a Buddhist relic was being displayed. On the ride, we discussed how practice on the spiritual path stresses the equal importance of wisdom and method. In the words of the eleventh-century master Atisha:

The practitioner should continually cultivate
The perfection of wisdom with skillful means.
Wisdom without skillful means
And skillful means, too, without wisdom
Are referred to as bondage.
Therefore do not give up either.[1]

I had been reminded over the years how wisdom and method needed to work hand in hand for progress in Buddhist practice. Suddenly I realized: Isn't this true for creativity? To be an artist, you need to have skills. At the same time, you must have the wisdom to know what to use those skills for. Method and Wisdom.

If this was true, I reflected, our education in the arts, creativity, and actually most everything, was missing one half!

---

1 Atisha Dipamkarashrijnana (982–1054), *Atisha's Lamp for the Path to Enlightenment* (New York: Snow Lion Publications, 1997), Chapter 4, verses 42–43.

On that rickshaw I had gained a new insight into the question of teaching creativity. I jotted down on a postcard a simple chart that reflected my thoughts, splitting the card vertically into two halves (see Figure 4.1). I saw how education in creative fields (and in fact, all fields) takes place these days, logically, in its own domain—wherever you learn your skills as an artist. I called it the domain of "Art," where we learn "Method," or "skillful means" in Atisha's terms—the technical side of it. But essential learning in creativity has to do with things *outside* of your own skill field, through which you can begin to approach the *knowing* that is necessary to true creativity. The wisdom needed to complete the training does not happen in "Art." It's in a place called "Life." The two things have to be learned in two separate domains.

I pondered a strange possibility: Have we only been teaching in one of two required domains?

My breakthrough simply was:

Learning in creativity has to happen in two different domains, Method in Art, Wisdom in Life.

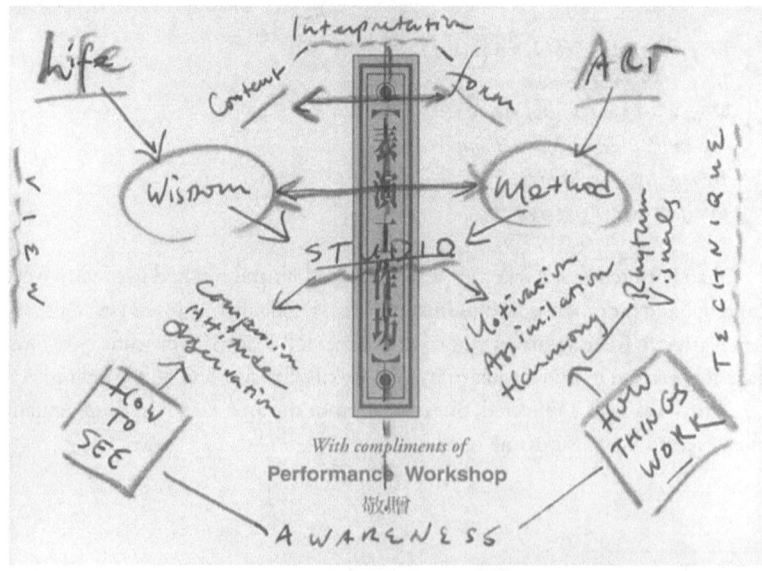

FIGURE 4.1 Initial thoughts of the creative path, on a postcard, 2000.

The more I thought about it, the more I saw that we truly were spending all our resources teaching "method," and little or nothing on "wisdom." I taught my students the techniques of playwriting and directing so they could become skillfully proficient writers and directors. But who was in charge of teaching the wisdom part of it? Me? I guess so. Who else? But how? Was I even qualified? Or was my artistic wisdom supposed to just sort of be transmitted to them, through the air? If I was a lousy artist then, wouldn't that be more like transmitting germs?

The postcard started to evolve into a system for training in creativity. Its simplest essence is: To be able to succeed creatively, we need wisdom, and we need method. It doesn't work if we lack either. But schools and conservatories can only guarantee training in method. To learn both is to learn in two separate domains, Art and Life.

I recently explained this in a talk at Princeton, held in Einstein's former office. I playfully but in homage and deep respect called it my General Theory of Creativity.[2]

Fingers and Music

I recall a conversation I had one year with my friend, the late classical pianist Fou Ts'ong (1934–2020), who told me he had been off the concert touring trail, working as a juror for international piano competitions while getting acupuncture for arthritis in his hands. We spoke in Chinese. I asked him how the up-and-coming young pianists were. He said, "Their fingers are incredible, far beyond what we could ever imagine." I said, "That's good." Then he suddenly broke into English and said slowly, in an impassioned voice, "But—where is the music?"

Fou Ts'ong accurately described proficiency in method but lack of wisdom in the field, music. This equation is plain to see. It applies not just to artists but to all endeavors. You can have an MBA but not really understand business. A doctor is certified to practice, but he may not have the wisdom of healing. On the other side of the equation, a Buddhist theoretician may be able to speak of the deeper points of Buddhist philosophy, but if she never does any meditation or other actual practice, it is doubtful how far her true realization will go. Even in everyday life, we can see how one may have an encyclopedia of techniques for raising children, but not really understand the essence of parenthood. Recipes are great for "method," but without the wisdom of cooking, you probably won't cook a great meal.

---

[2] Stan Lai, "General Theory of Creativity," talk at Jones Hall, Princeton University, April 20, 2025.

I have seen many theatrical productions that were technically stunning but lacked a soul and wound up being quite boring—method lacking wisdom. I think of visionary artists such as Antonin Artaud, whose theories of theater were so profound that he or anyone after him had little chance of actualizing them—wisdom lacking method. I thought of the great Charlie Parker, who said about bebop, the trailblazing jazz style he invented, "I could hear it sometimes but I couldn't play it."[3] After years of hearing this revolutionary sound in his mind, one day, he figured out how to actually manifest it. His method caught up with his wisdom, and music has never been the same.

A Dance, in Two Acts

Teresa Amabile of Harvard Business School once gave a simple definition of creativity as "Novelty that works."[4] I like it because it points out that creativity is not just some wild thinking. It needs a purpose to think wildly, and it has to work. Wisdom + Method. Robert Sternberg, another leading scholar in the field, defines creativity as:

> The ability to produce work that is both novel (i.e., original, unexpected) and appropriate (i.e., useful, adaptive concerning task constraints).[5]

This hits the key points. Creativity must address a purpose, and must produce work. It does not happen in one movement, but two. Wisdom + Method. Creativity is the posing of a problem, then the solving of the problem. "Inspiration" must be followed by "execution," "conceptualizing" by "actualizing," "content" must find "form." Creativity has two aspects that must be learned in two different domains.

Another way of posing the equation "Wisdom + Method" is to say that creativity is a process of discovering the question, then discovering its answer. Who poses the problem to be solved? Sometimes we are contracted to do a creative project, sometimes it is assigned by a teacher or boss. Usually for the artist

---

3 Quoted in Nat Hentoff and Nat Shapiro, ed., *Hear Me Talkin' to Ya* (Garden City, NY: Dover Press, 1966), 354.
4 Teresa Amabile, "Freakonomics Radio Podcast," www.wnyc.org/widgets/ondemand_player/freakonomics/#file=json/906997
5 Robert J. Sternberg and Todd I. Lubart, "The Concept of Creativity: Prospects and Paradigms," in *Handbook of Creativity*, ed. Robert J. Sternberg (Cambridge: Cambridge University Press, 1999), 3.

or inventor, it is ourselves. Einstein was not commissioned by anyone to find a Theory of Relativity. The problem was something that must have gnawed at him from deep inside, a profound urge to explain the universe. Shakyamuni left the palace at Kapilavastu and all its resplendent luxury to seek the answer to a question that tormented his soul, the truth of existence. What questions! That's why it took Buddha six years of constant reflection to come up with his answer, and Einstein ten.

We create our own problem, then find its solution. Two parts. Wisdom/ Method. The chances for a creative project to succeed are often in inverse proportion to the difficulty of the question. Simple questions create simple challenges; complex and profound questions drive the creator to complex and profound solutions. We can use an old cookie box to stash stray tennis balls. That counts as a simple solution to a simple question. Einstein and Shakyamuni dreamt up and challenged themselves with the most profound questions imaginable, and changed the way we think and live on this earth.

On her deathbed, Gertrude Stein famously asked Alice Toklas, "What is the answer?" After a long silence, Stein continued, "In that case, what is the question?"[6] Often we spend as much time, or more, seeking the question as the answer. The refined, well-thought-out question is bursting at the seams with answers. The healthy creative project starts with a solid and worthy question.

Wisdom is the knowing that nurtures life, and informs our craft. There is wisdom to everything small and large. There is wisdom to making coffee, to asking questions to AI, to organizing a journey, to launching a rocket, to exploring the meaning of your art and life. The cultivation of wisdom moves us to higher levels of awareness, which in turn enriches our knowing. Method is the acquisition and perfecting of skills used to create things. From frying rice to directing a musical, if you lack wisdom in what you are doing, your work will lack weight. If you lack method, your work will be messy. Lacking both, you cannot possibly succeed. Lacking either, things somehow just won't fit together properly. Working in tandem, they can create beautiful and transformative things.

After returning home to Taipei from India, I spent two afternoons imparting my newfound ideas to a small group of graduate students at a quiet Taipei teahouse over oolong and biscuits. They responded with enthusiasm, eyes beaming with a newfound way of seeing the creative act. Thereafter, a group of students who had graduated many years before requested to meet with me regularly for "continuing" training and I offered to impart to them my new and expanding

---

6 Alice B. Toklas, *What is Remembered* (New York: Holt, Rinehart and Winston, 1963), 173.

understanding of the creative act. These classes, held in my home, gave me the chance to develop and expand my original thoughts, and afterward, to my joy, saw how the teaching affected the students in a positive way.

The simple postcard began to evolve into the map (see Figure 5.1, page 34) that became the foundation for all my later teachings in the field and is the basis for this book.

Exercises and Further Thoughts

1. Re-read Atisha's quote on page 27 and give it deeper thought.
2. Examine the aspects of your profession. What do you need to be good at method? What do you need to be good at wisdom? Can you define the wisdom of your profession?
3. Think of some work of art, a film, or a popular song, that moves you profoundly. Can you separately see the method and wisdom aspects of the work? Can you see how both are needed for the work to have its moving quality?
4. Think of other professions outside of your own. What is the method aspect and what is the wisdom aspect of those professions? For example: Chef, lawyer, critic, waiter, pilot, cleaner, nanny, accountant …

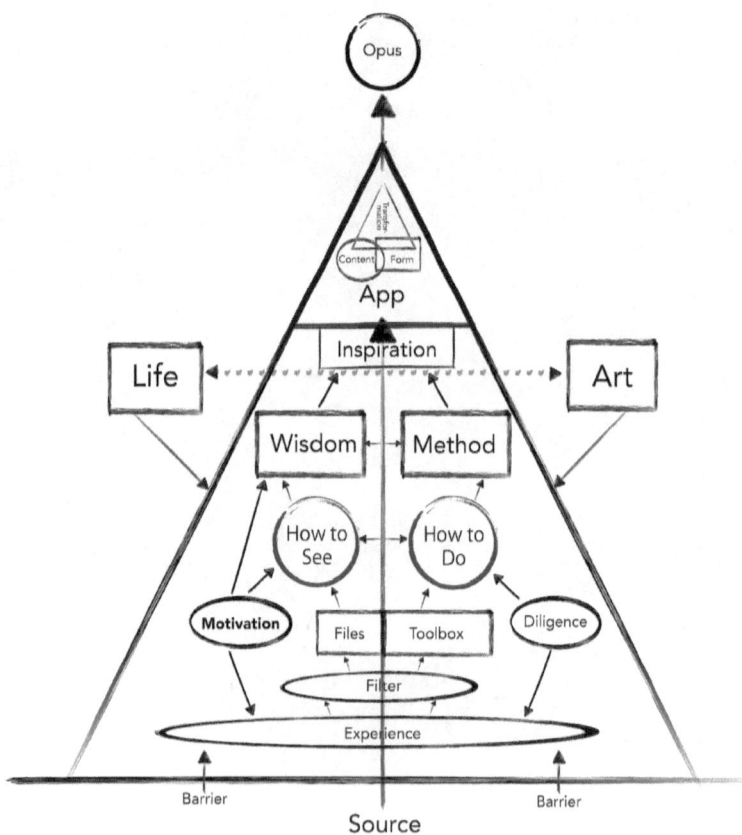

FIGURE 5.1 The Creative Map, basic version.

CHAPTER FIVE

A MAP FOR CREATIVITY

From the simple postcard on that rickshaw in India, which laid out the concept that learning in creativity needs to happen in two separate domains, my thinking expanded over time into a complete path for the learning of creativity, which is charted in this, a map for creativity. This is the basic version that should work for most. The expanded version is on page 84, which contains many more details that I have laid out in the text. The map was not designed to feel intimidating, so I hope it isn't. On the contrary, it is meant to render a complex and difficult topic accessible and understandable for all. I will do my best to explain everything in an easy way.

The Short Guide

The map is a path. It is split into two sides, left and right, and horizontally also into two sides, below and above. Our journey starts from the bottom up, progressing gradually to the final creative product at the top.

On the left, we work on our selves in the realm of Life. It is a path of being.
On the right, we work on our craft in the realm of Art. It is a path of doing.

Experience is gained from life as well as art. On the left side, there is a filter that decides what images or memories from everyday experience are kept in our minds. These become the files in our file warehouse that, in the moment of inspiration, are pulled into the creative app. They provide content. On the right side, there is also a filter that decides what tools go into our toolbox, which are used to craft our creative project.

On the bottom is the Source, of creative energy, which is always there, available universally, but is sealed off partially or totally to most people. A fuzzy bar runs horizontally through the bottom. This is the Barrier, which is an internal barricade that blocks us from the Source. Our task is to break down the Barrier and gain access to the energy of the Source, releasing it into both the left and right sides of the map. To those who have broken down the barrier, the wellsprings of creativity are available at any moment, like the air, permeating our existence. It is air moist with creative energy that sees and connects. Without it, we are enclosed by barrenness that blocks off connectivity and possibility.

Near the top is a triangle which is called the "App." The real creative work on a project happens inside that triangle. Everything else is preparation.

Being and Doing

As explained, learning in creativity needs to happen in two domains. On the left is the path of Wisdom, to be learned and trained in the domain of Life. It is the path of becoming, of developing one's own personal wisdom, of being. On the right is the path of Method, to be learned and trained in the domain of Art, which can be a rehearsal room if one is a theater director, actor, or choreographer, a laptop computer if one is a novelist, playwright, or screenwriter, the classroom if one is a teacher, a laboratory if one is a scientist, or the corporate office if one is a manager. It is the place where the creative idea ferments and is then actualized. It is the path of making, of doing.

Your task, as you journey up the map, is to gain awareness and mastery of both sides. The left side can be seen as where you develop the wisdom that informs content; the right side is where you develop the method that molds the content into form. You can call it the generation of ideas and their transformation into a physical product. Sometimes, you will feel progress on one side only, sometimes the other, but you work on both sides simultaneously. As you progress on one side, you may find what you have learned helps you progress on the other.

In the end, for the accomplished master, there is no left and right. Wisdom and method are not two things, but one. Creativity comes and forms naturally.

For now, we need to be patient and find out where we are on either side.

The map illustrates the age-old adage that opportunity comes to one who is prepared. Inspiration cannot come to one whose warehouse is empty. One cannot craft inspiration into form without tools. Creativity may call at any moment in the day. You may get a wonderful contract to create a dream work, but if you are not prepared, in Wisdom or Method or both, you will find yourself hopelessly inadequate for the challenge. If you are ready, your bags are packed, and you're set to go on the journey with passion and confidence.

A Path

The Creative Map reflects my thinking on the path to creativity and contains the essential concepts and components of this book. Everything is interdependent in this map. The key is to understand the symbiotic relationship between wisdom and method. They work together as parts of a whole, and they are part of one another. There is method to wisdom, and wisdom to any method. As we gain deeper knowledge and proficiency in each of the components, the two sides start to interplay and merge, until they are one.

The map resembles a triangle or a mountain. Or you could call it a tree, which draws its resources from the earth below, however you wish to visualize it. The triangle funnels all the learning, practice, and resources toward the center line, resulting in the final product. I do hope you personalize it to your own vision. A pyramid, which you climb to the top, or simply a roadmap, a guide to get you from where you are to where you want to be.

The path is not easy, nor did I promise it would be, because it depends as much on working on your self as on your craft, and your self is a pretty stubborn stone to sculpt. If it is any consolation, I learned long ago that anything easy probably isn't worth doing.

Exercises and Further Thoughts

1. Study the map. Give some thought to each component. Evaluate how you are positioned on either side of it.

PART FOUR
Creative Wisdom

After changes upon changes
We are more or less the same.

-- Paul Simon[1]

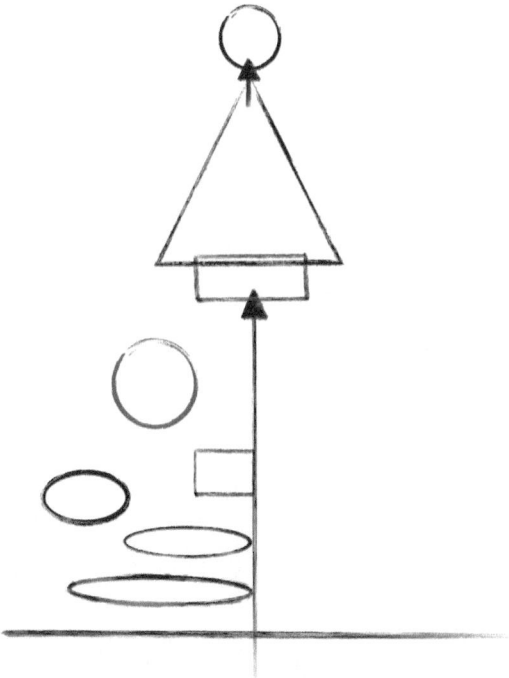

---

1 Paul Simon, from "The Boxer," *Paul Simon in Concert: Live Rhymin'*, Columbia, 1974.

CHAPTER SIX

THE CURIOUS DISAPPEARANCE OF WISDOM

We are used to training in all sorts of things, except life.

Training in Being

Without skills, you can't make anything. But without ideas, there is nothing to make. For creativity, you need method, and you need wisdom, and they have to work together. This seems obvious. Method is tangible. There is training for every kind of skill. But what about wisdom? Where do we teach and learn it?

Where art is the domain in which we learn method, life is the domain where we acquire wisdom. But no, we are not used to the concept of training in life itself. We bring our kids to learn all sorts of things after school. There are classes for everything imaginable, except "life." Where's the MA or PhD in "Life"? I guess it's something that is easily neglected because ... Good question.

Life is a continual work in process. The most important part of that process is to find yourself, to know yourself, to be yourself. We are so wrapped up in doing that we often neglect the doer. While we learn so many techniques to upgrade how we do things, wouldn't it make sense to first upgrade the doer himself?

Corporations are more and more choosing workshops outside of their own realm of expertise to train personnel, sending high-level executives into survival courses in the jungle, or to skydive, or for an intensive acting course. There seems to be some tacit acknowledgment that training in their own field is no longer sufficient.

The profession of "Life Coaching" and "Wellness Coaching" has risen in recent years. I am sure it is helpful to individuals. But from what little I know, these trainings seem to be geared toward so-called personal development and personal fulfillment, which are often, in the end, career-oriented, with the goal of maximizing gain, helping the individual figure out what she wants to *do* instead of *be*. The odd reality in this day and age is, we are defined by what we do, not who we are.

If our map represents a complete path to creativity, then something serious has been missing. Bodybuilders have developed ways to build different muscles to contour different body shapes, but we rarely consider that the mind itself can be built or shaped. Yet it is the mind that holds the capacity for knowing, for wisdom, for creativity. Is there a way to train to be, to know, to be wise?

Training in method is everywhere. But where is the training for wisdom? So, let's see—hmmm. What is wisdom? Where can I learn wisdom?

Life, Unexamined

I would trade all my technology for an afternoon with Socrates.[1]

—*Steve Jobs*

The unexamined life is not worth living.[2]

—*Socrates*

If we agree with Atisha, wisdom and method are the two things necessary to be successful in the practice of almost everything. Then why has an entire half of the equation been neglected? It is hard to believe that we are unaware of the importance of wisdom in education, but from kindergarten through graduate school, is there a course with its name? I know of no institute of higher education in the world that has a College or Department of Wisdom. Does Cambridge offer "Beginning Wisdom"? If so, there should also be "Intermediate" and "Advanced Wisdom," and perhaps a Graduate Seminar in Wisdom would be required across the board.

Modern education systems seem to vaguely understand that the ultimate goal of education is to impart wisdom. If so, they seem to assume that this essential thing is somehow embedded into the curriculum. When students read classics, it

---

1 Quoted in www.goodreads.com/quotes/455762-i-would-trade-all-of-my-technology-for-an-afternoon
2 Quoted from Plato's *Apology*, 38a 5-6 in *Wikipedia*, en.wikipedia.org/wiki/The_unexamined_life_is_not_worth_living

is assumed that the "wisdom" contained therein will more or less be imparted to them. Yet curricula these days at higher education institutions have strayed far away from what were previously acknowledged as standard definitions of "classic." How does a student integrate the wisdom of, say, Sappho, with that of, say, Malcolm X and Suehiro Maruo, who could conceivably occupy the same reading list for a required humanities course?

As we progress from generation to generation, reading lists compiled by teachers at all levels continue to be regulated by whatever the teacher thinks is—important? Significant? Cool? To whom? For what? By what standard? There are abundant lists of "75 Things You Must Know" or "100 Books You Must Read" in this lifetime. This is all fine and well meaning, I am sure, but if you asked the authors of these lists why? For what purpose? Why must I read these books? To become smarter? To know more? To become better? At what? The word "wisdom" may supply a clue, but it might be too broad or obscure to discuss with any coherence. In ancient China, there would be no question about a reading list. You would start with the *Four Books and Five Classics*,[3] and go from there. Every scholar would read basically the same things. I am not endorsing this, just pointing out how times have changed, and how in the not-too-recent past, required reading lists at major universities in the West looked quite similar. As we seemingly move into a post-diversity age, what will educators require students to learn, and for what?

The next inconvenient question is: If our students are supposed to gain their wisdom from their teachers, how do our teachers qualify to teach wisdom? Where can they train? There are IQ and EQ exams. There is even an AQ test for artistic potential. But as far as I know, there is nothing called "WQ." Someone or some organization that is recognized and accredited as wise would have to figure out a form of accreditation! And we would need to take a qualifying exam for wisdom. This sounds rather terrifying.

Modern systems are able to produce productive and intellectual individuals to fill the needs of our do-driven society. But how often do we see a highly competent, well-educated professional ace the "do" but fail the "be"? If "the unexamined life is not worth living," Socrates has painted a bleak picture of worthless lives. To be fair, the fact that wisdom is inexplicitly missing in action leaves most of us unaware that the crucial examination is not taking place.

What happened?

---

3 Referring to *The Great Learning, Doctrine of the Mean, Analects of Confucius, Analects of Mencius*, and the *Classic of Poetry, The Book of Documents, Book of Rites, I Ching (Book of Changes)* and *the Spring and Autumn Annals*.

Lost in Definition

A problem which actually is more of a clue, is that there no longer seems to be a standard definition of the term. I went to Webster's Dictionary, which in its great authority gave me this surprising definition:

wis·dom (wzdm) *n.*
The quality of being wise [...] [4]

Hold on a moment. This didn't look like a legitimate dictionary entry. It was like defining "beauty" as "the quality of being beautiful." Can you do that? I decided I should at least crosscheck the word "wise" to see if Webster's was actually cheating. What I found was:

wise, *adj.*,
1 a: characterized by wisdom [...][5]

Was this an honest slip on the part of the editor? Or was it too difficult a concept to define? Or had it been so long neglected that its definition was no longer known? Could wisdom be extinct, and most everything we have learned in school since we were kids is method?

I turned to my friend Lin Huo-wang, Chair of the Philosophy Department at National Taiwan University, and asked him about this curious finding. Was wisdom undefinable? His thoughtful answer was yes, but not because we can't. His view was that in free societies, "wisdom" is increasingly left to the individual to define. He quoted John Stuart Mill in explaining to me that in a democracy, the pursuit of happiness is dependent on one's personal definition of what "happiness" is. This is inextricably linked to "wisdom." In a democracy, it is not only one's right, but one's obligation to define the word. The problem is, many of us have failed to fulfill this responsibility. In fact, few of us understand that the obligation exists.

And so it seems possible that because of the failure to personalize this concept for oneself, the meaning of the word "wisdom" has eroded. Missing in the maze of living. Lost in definition.

---

4 *Webster's New Universal Unabridged Dictionary* (New York: Barnes and Noble, 2003), or see entry: www.gutenberg.org/files/669/669-h/669-h.htm
5 Ibid. Also see www.merriam-webster.com/dictionary/wise

The Threat of Wisdom

Recently I was delighted to come across the book *Wisdom: From Philosophy to Neuroscience* by Stephen S. Hall, one of the few books I have found dealing exclusively with the topic. Part One of the book is titled "Wisdom Defined (Sort of)," and it is the "Sort of" that made me feel a camaraderie with the author. Hall quotes Sternberg, who said, "To understand wisdom fully and correctly probably requires more wisdom than any of us have."[6]

Hall gives another reason why wisdom may be de-emphasized, even hiding—because it is perceived as dangerous. "In many cultures the wise man is also a marked man."[7] In writing of the trial of Socrates, Hall asks "When was the last time a 'trial of the century,' in any century, devoted so much public discussion to the meaning of wisdom?"[8] Could it be that after 399 BC, when Socrates was condemned to death for "corrupting" the young people of Athens with his thoughts (wisdom?), the concept and definition of wisdom died with him?

The death of Socrates ended an era where sages such as he, Laozi (also spelled Lao Tzu or Lao Zi), the Buddha, and Confucius roamed the earth. Within this golden century and a half, disciples East and West dedicated their lives to follow these sages, for the one course they taught, which if forced to have a name, would be called "Wisdom."

We have drifted far away from the master/disciple model of teaching/learning of 2,500 years ago, where there was no degree to confer, no course description, syllabus, or even topic. Today if a course titled "Wisdom 101" existed at Berkeley, it could only possibly be some sort of historical overview of knowledge systems. The reading list would probably be a hybrid of Philosophy, Religious Studies, and New Age Spirituality. The lecturer probably would not define wisdom, nor could she teach what that thing would be. If she did, she probably would not dare ask the students to actually practice her definition of this "thing," for fear of litigation, or of being accused of creating a cult.

If these masters were around today, they sadly would probably not enjoy the sage status that they deserve. Precisely because of the erosion of wisdom, their expertise would not be seen as particularly useful or relevant. You might

---

6 Stephen S. Hall, *Wisdom: From Philosophy to Neuroscience* (New York: Alfred A. Knopf, 2010), 9.
7 Ibid., 12.
8 Ibid., 23.

encounter them at a lecture on campus, among five other interesting speakers you would want to hear that evening. Consider if Socrates, Confucius, or Shakyamuni were lecturing some evening at Harvard. What edge would they have in the minds of the attendee over, say, Greta Thunberg or Jensen Huang? In today's jungle of information, how would you even begin to understand that you need to be looking for this thing that can no longer be clearly defined?

In the flatness of the post-post-modern world, we find it hard to prioritize this thing called wisdom. To teach it assumes teaching how to live, how to act, what to believe in. In this increasingly diverse world, how could there be such a thing? Only in authoritarian regimes could one dictate what time to get up, what morning exercises to do, and so on, to the masses. As Lin pointed out to me, the modern democratic government cannot tell you what to do. It can only, through the legal system, tell you what you can't do.

So, who teaches you what to do these days? How to live your life? Family? School? Friends? Coworkers? TikTok? If you are not part of some organized religion, you are pretty much left to yourself. We seem to accept this.

Center and Periphery

Without a clear definition or way of teaching wisdom, education in all fields since the Industrial Revolution has emphasized method. Though my map places wisdom and method left and right, we can also look at wisdom as the center of our being. If all is functioning correctly, all of your thoughts and activities should funnel out from this center. This puts method on the outer circle, or periphery. Sadly, center and periphery are often in a state of disconnection in the modern mind. We live, learn, think, and do on the outer ring.

Learning on the periphery, without knowledge of the center, is like driving on a metropolitan ring road where exits to the center are all blocked. We wander in the outer ring, learning peripheral skills without realizing that they need to be connected to the center in order to have meaning (see Figure 6.1). With our current neglect of the center, we are like an ancient city that has declined to ruins, while the urban sprawl continues to develop uncontrolled on the outskirts.

We need a strong center that has web-like connections to the periphery. Without a center, life has no base, no core, no soul. Creativity becomes something with which to doodle or just to show off some skills. When center and periphery are both strong and connected, we have a fluid inner ecology, with wisdom connected to method, conducive to creativity (see Figure 6.2).

FIGURE 6.1 Center and periphery.

Wisdom = Knowing

In the context of creativity, wisdom is a *knowing*. A knowing of what creative question to pose, and how to creatively assemble the answer. It is knowing what notes to play in the throes of improvisation, what colors to use when painting an expressionist garden. It is also knowing whether a story is worthy of becoming a feature film or not, and which actor you should cast for a role.

It is also a knowing that in itself is something so encompassing that it is almost impossible to define. Hall gives us a nice working definition:

> One of the hallmarks of wisdom, what distinguishes it so sharply from "mere" intelligence, is the ability to exercise good judgment in the face of imperfect knowledge.[9]

---

9 Hall, 4.

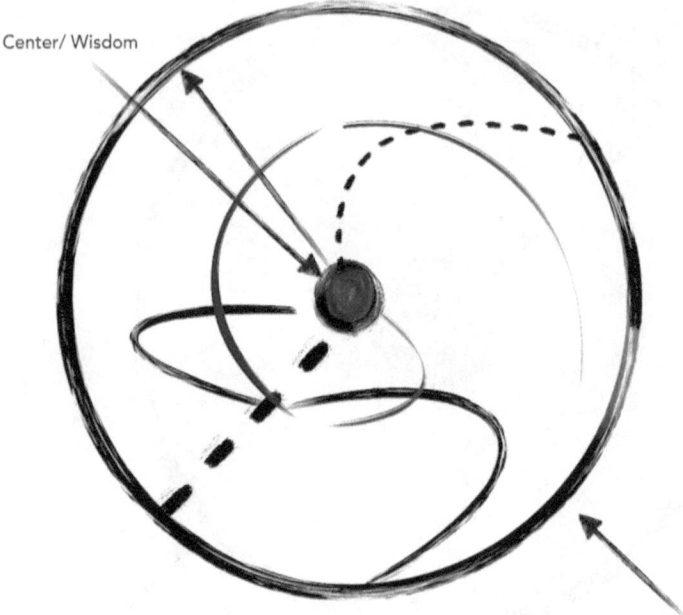

FIGURE 6.2 Pathways to and from the center.

If knowledge of what we are doing is perfect, making decisions would be easy. In creative work, that is never the case. This leads all creative work into a predicament: How do we make necessary decisions when they are called for, knowing that these decisions will not necessarily lead to answers, but only to further questions that push the nebulous process of creativity forward? Even when knowledge is close to perfect, like in data-saturated NFL drafts, without wisdom, you hit and miss. In hindsight, all is clear. But in the moment, which quarterback should be chosen first? It often seems that in these cases, a coin toss, or a hunch, even divination from a medium, may be as reliable a decision as a data-based opinion.

Learning to Question

Wisdom works on many levels. It starts with knowing what questions to ask. The Chinese word for knowledge, which infers wisdom, is *"xuewen,"* literally "learn to ask." You can't possibly get the right answers if you don't know the right questions. Wisdom is learning to ask. It is the same for creativity. Creative thinking doesn't assume the answer to a problem, nor does it jump to conclusions. Creative thinking seeks to find the question and to continually refine it, until the answer appears. Instead of demanding an instant answer, you need to continually refine the question. It is that simple, yet that difficult.

You don't need to have a high level of wisdom to pose the question to write a limerick for a school project, but you do if you want to write *One Hundred Years of Solitude*. Your level of wisdom drives you to undertake a project at that level of wisdom. Your wisdom may also tell you that a project you envision is undoable, or not worth the effort.

The wisdom of method allows you to visualize what your project looks like, how it all fits together, what goes where. This is the knowing of structure. For beginners, a creative project is intimidating indeed, because you can't get a grip on the whole thing. You don't know how large it is, how many parts it is made of, or how many compartments it has. You can barely see a leaf on a branch of a tree; how can you possibly fathom the whole forest that you have aspired to create?

From the beginner, who doesn't know whether to draw a mountain here or to use red there, to the master who knows exactly where everything goes, wisdom extends to all the details of the creative project. The playwright knows to put a pause here, not there, for optimal dramatic effect. The film director knows that a certain shot should be a pan, not a zoom. The cook knows that the dumplings go in after the water is boiling, not before. There is less and less guesswork. It is a knowing that functions on all levels, from the minute details to the building up and ultimate revelation of grand themes.

You may think that one of the charms of creativity is that the possibilities are limitless, and it is so much fun exploring it all. But in actuality, as your wisdom develops, you find that there aren't that many options to make things right. To want to keep exploring is often because you enjoy the fun of it. Once creative decisions need to be made, that is when the beginner is most challenged. As the Zen master Shunryū Suzuki says, "In the beginner's mind there are many possibilities, but in the expert's there are few."[10]

Wisdom is knowing. What do we know? A good way to start is to first understand what we don't know.

---

10 Shunryū Suzuki, *Zen Mind, Beginner's Mind: Informal Talks on Zen Meditation and Practice* (Trumble, CT: Weatherhill, 1970), 2.

To Know What You Don't Know

I am not a big fan of Confucius, whose teachings present how one should behave/live *within* the "box." His vast influence over the centuries is one of the reasons why Asian cultures have had a long way to catch up in creativity. However, I do have a favorite quote from him, which is: "To know what you know, and to know what you don't know, that is wisdom."[11]

If you are training in the arts, it is fortuitous to be able to attend a master class, receiving direct tutorship from a master in your field. My master class came unscheduled, with my mentor, Shireen Strooker (1935–2018), when I was finishing my studies at Berkeley. This Dutch director/devisor/poet/playwright/actress was a master in the art of forming plays through improvisation, and had been doing it for over a decade with her innovative group, the Amsterdam Werkteater.[12] I learned this difficult art through assisting her when she was visiting at Berkeley in 1983, during the creation of a work based on Jean Anouilh's *Ondine*. Every day in the rehearsal studio, working with the student cast, Shireen would transform text from the original play into powerful scenes with poetic dialogue and music. How she pulled different elements together into a layered and poetic whole seemed like magic to all present. We were mesmerized by her artistic powers, and her uncanny ability to bring out the best and deepest in all of us.

When she had completed composing the entire work, we knew we had something special. Shireen had to go to New York for a week for a prior commitment, leaving the production in what she thought were my capable hands. As Assistant Director, I only needed to lead rehearsals and caretake, but I overstepped my authority, trying to replicate the brilliance that I had been seeing and learning from my mentor every day that was so inspiring, and looked so easy and cool. Within a week, with me in the director's seat, I basically destroyed the performance! Under my "guidance," the play had lost all its magic.

Shireen came back to a depressed ensemble and asked why we all looked so glum. I confided, "I think I screwed up. The whole thing is wrong now." She said, "Let's see." She sat down in the middle of the theater and beckoned me to sit beside her. We began a run-through. Those were the most excruciating 100 minutes of my life in the theater. I grimaced at every wrong moment that appeared on stage, which was pretty much every moment. Where once was magic, everything

---

11 Confucius, *The Analects*. Chapter 2, Verse 17, Chinese Text Project, ctext.org/analects/wei-zheng. My translation.

12 Stan Lai, *Selected Plays*, Vol 1, 1–6.

had become ordinary. I would glance at her whenever a once sublime moment had been lost, but her gaze was intently on what was happening, like a hawk. I knew that we were in deep trouble.

The run-through ended. Everyone was silent. Without looking at me, without any statement on what went wrong, without pointing fingers, Shireen suddenly said, "Let's get to work." And so we started from the top, again. When we got to each and every moment that was wrong, she halted everyone, and fixed it. She basically undid everything that I had changed, which was a lot. After every directive she gave to the actors, I sat there going in my mind, "Wow, right, yeah … why the hell did I change that? What was I thinking? … How did she find that one?"

After two hours without a break, the ship had been righted, the magic had been restored, the production was back on its feet. Everyone was happy. As the actors gathered their things to go, I turned to Shireen, who was still sitting next to me in the auditorium, staring at the stage. I asked her the stupidest question anyone could ask at that moment. I said, "How did you do that?"

Shireen turned to me slowly, and said, "Stan, I know what you can do, and what you can't."

That was it. That was my master class for life.

To know what I didn't know.

And I didn't. What Shireen accomplished in front of me in those two hours was way beyond my poor powers of comprehension. It was a *tour de force* of directing where she was like a surgeon, performing comprehensive surgery on multi-levels, slicing away everything extraneous that had been added by me, and restoring the beauty of the production. This beauty could not be broken down and analyzed in pieces. It was a grand vision where everything interlocked together and coalesced into something magical. How could anyone do that?

My master class wasn't learning how to do it, but simply to learn that I couldn't do it, and the grand chasm between being able and not being able was first and foremost in knowing what worked and what didn't. I also understood that to be able to know what works, you have to be able to do what works. My skills were simply not at that level. It is so easy to make wrong decisions when your skills aren't at a certain level of proficiency. I made a vow to work hard, to one day be able to say those exact words to someone else! For in those words was true wisdom, an acknowledgment that the master had the *knowing* of the art of theater. I had to admit, painfully, that my years of studying theater amounted to nothing. I was still an outsider.

We went on to wow audiences with a spellbinding performance that was unlike any other contemporary theater work around, because it was so seamless and organic. I realized that Shireen had a sorcerer-like ability to connect the deepest inner impulses of the actors to their roles. This connection in turn connected the audience to the performance at a profound level. By showing me how to do it, she was also showing me what qualities I lacked. I may have studied a lot of theater, and was on the verge of attaining a PhD, but she showed me the intangibles, the invisible qualities that made her a sorcerer, a healer, one who could share the healing, one who can transform, and trigger transformation.

I spent many years working to get inside, to become a sorcerer. To know what you don't know is actually pretty hard, and a brutal process. In fact it is a paradox. But in admitting what you don't know, you open the door to wisdom. Your journey begins. "Not knowing" and "knowing" are both parts of the mysterious process. If you don't start from knowing what you don't know, you may waste precious years swimming around in an ocean of what you think is knowing.

Creativity is like alchemy, making something amazing from things otherwise unremarkable. But before things can be transformed, the sorcerer-to-be must first be transformed. The non-creative mode must be transformed into the creative mode.

Exercises and Further Thoughts

1. What is your definition of wisdom? Have you ever given it a thought? Can there be one singular definition? Can you define it for your own purposes?
2. Who do you consider wise in your life? What is this person's wisdom composed of? What do you value most about this person's wisdom? Is this person happy?
3. Think of a creative work you have recently seen, and analyze it in terms of the ratio between wisdom and method.
4. Are you aware of what you don't know in your field? Make a list of the things you need to work on. Split it into a list of things you don't know how to do, and conceptual things you don't understand.

CHAPTER SEVEN

WISDOM STARTS WITH WHY

The fastest way to change your path is to change your destination.[1]
—*Jigme Khyentse Rinpoche*

Let's assume that wisdom is something that can be learned. Without that assumption, life becomes very random. There is no way we can regulate how we react or feel to the "slings and arrows of outrageous fortune" that shoot at us in life. There is no way we can control what goes into our creative projects. By affirming this assumption, we can get down to work, on creativity, on life. But we must first concede that it won't come easily, because wisdom is not information that can be looked up online. Perhaps AI may serve as a support to our learning, but AI is artificial *intelligence*, not wisdom itself. Wisdom utilizes and manages intelligence and knowledge. It is self-knowledge, knowing, judgmental ability, that must be nurtured from within, using tools from life itself.

Why Create?

The Dunning-Kruger effect refers to a sort of catch-22 wherein incompetent people don't have the skills to recognize their own incompetence.[2] Unfortunately, this also seems to be true for wisdom. How can we know how wise we are if we aren't wise in the first place? How can we get to the point where we are able to judge our wisdom quotient? How can we read the right books, find the right teachings, do the right exercises, if we don't understand what the goal is?

---

[1] Public teaching, Taipei, Taiwan, December 3, 2005.
[2] See "Dunning–Kruger effect," *Wikipedia*, en.wikipedia.org/wiki/Dunning%E2%80%93Kruger_effect

So let's start with the goal. What is our goal? In life? In creativity? If we don't know what's there at the top of the mountain of wisdom, we need to know why we are going to attempt the climb. Otherwise, we may easily go up the wrong mountain. The strange paradox is, our goal in itself, for instance, "success," "wealth," "fame," "greatness" ... may unwittingly not be conducive to the attainment of it.

We are too wrapped up in defining the what, and then figuring out how to attain that what, to the point where we seldomly think about the why. This seems natural. When we learn anything, we first learn what and how. This is true for arithmatic, doing laundry, as well as playing the violin. We usually bypass the why, because it is either totally obvious, or strangely, we are oblivious to it.

Why we want to be creative isn't something we usually ask ourselves, because we assume the entitlement. Why do you need to express yourself? Why create? We are not used to asking such questions, because we can't really see anything wrong or dangerous with what we are doing, and contemporary society encourages creativity. But truly wanting to be creative hooks into deep desires within ourselves, of wanting to be seen and heard, of wanting to transcend, of wanting to express, to become, to share that becoming. If we start to ask "why," we start to peel away the layers of motivation that can bring us face to face with our naked selves. This is a bit intimidating, and unusual for most people. It can be a long process, and usually is not very comfortable. But on the way, we may discover some very revealing things about ourselves, or we may find to our disappointment that the reasons we want to undertake a creative career are not very good. Either way, understanding the "why" is the foundation for our creativity, as well as our personal wisdom.

Why Not?

To many artists, there is no "why," nor is there a need to ask. They just do what they do. The desire in itself is not something to be examined. This seems totally reasonable. Should we question why Beethoven composed music, or why Li Po wrote poetry? Maybe it would only be revealing to ask, "why not?" if they didn't. To question their motive for creating seems to go against every romantic notion of the creative genius. But not to ask is leaving out perhaps the most essential question in the creative process. It is the same for a businessman. You would not question why a billionaire purchases a yacht. It's what they do. Perhaps if they thought about it, they wouldn't do it. In fact, certain individuals in different professions get to a point where they think very deeply about why they are doing what they do, and then decide to give up all of it. This is how the "why" connects to judgmental ability, to wisdom.

How do we start any creative project? Usually the beginning is the most difficult, enough to drive one crazy. To understand how to start, it would be a great benefit to understand why we want to start. Paul Cezanne said, "A work of art which did not begin in emotion is not art."[3] Certainly passion is a prerequisite. But where did the passion come from? Why is the passion sufficient justification for undertaking a creative project? We usually ask "How to start?" The better question is, "Why start?"

Critics usually deal with the "what" and "how" of a creative work, because the "why" isn't something that can be readily seen or modified. But the true engine behind a work is its motive for being. The original motivation permeates everything and informs everything. The initial passion for the project is the "why." To understand the motivation is to understand the wellspring. If something is wrong at the wellspring, it is hard to fix downstream, because the stream has been polluted from the spring. You need to fix the spring to fix the stream. You need to start from the why.

Wisdom starts with asking why, and grows through the honest process of learning why.

A Freeway to Creativity

On our Map of Creativity, "Motivation" is placed on the Wisdom side, on the left, connected to "How to See," but it has a straight line that leads directly to wisdom. Motivation is a little-explored freeway to creativity. To examine your motivation is to start to explore your "Why." We approach this self-examination on two levels: the motivation for undertaking a certain creative project, like the one you are doing now, which we can call your "micro-why," and your overall motivation for doing creative work, which we can call your "macro-why." To examine and understand deeply these whys is to understand your initial motivation to create. This is of ultimate importance because the micro-why is the spark that drives your project, and the macro-why is what drives your whole existence. There is no way to disconnect the relationship between the two.

Motivation can be as simple as a paycheck for a gig. It can also be a deep reconciliation with one's life after learning one has a terminal disease. It often is unknown, hidden, secret. The artist often works and thrives on these hidden motivations, and knowing too much may destroy the creative spell. Do we really want or need to know why? My view is, if you don't understand the deeper reasons

---

3 Paul Cezanne, quoted in https://www.brainyquote.com/quotes/paul_cezanne_134682

why you are doing something, you are at a disadvantage as the project unfolds because the deeper motivation is controlling the inner mechanism of your creative project all the way, whether you know it or not. We can and must jumpstart our creative wisdom by delving into why we want to create.

Artists, in Bali?

When Europeans discovered the island of Bali in the early twentieth century, they felt they had stumbled upon some hidden paradise. Not only was the island bestowed with great natural beauty, but more importantly, every single person living on the island was an artist! This certainly was some sublime utopia that Miguel Covarrubias championed in his *Island of Bali*,[4] and Margaret Mead and Walter Spies described as "an enchanted land of aesthetes at peace with themselves and nature."[5]

Every person was an artist! This villager was a musician, that one a dancer, this one a supreme silversmith, that one a weaver of exquisite fabrics. Bali gained legendary status as a place where art was a way of life, every object a work of art, every person an artist.

The slight problem with this idyllic scenario was: the people of Bali did not quite think of themselves in these terms. Certainly, the objects they made were beautiful, the music exquisite, the dances magnificent. These seem to define them as artists. Yet if we examine the motives behind making the work, there seems to be something that comes before "art." Before they were "artists," they were villagers, part of a society, each with civic responsibilities to sustain and forward the communal life. This includes farming for physical sustenance, as well as the successful carrying forth of all the rituals vital to the inner well-being of the society, like elaborate funeral rites and ritual performances to the gods to safeguard the society.

Exquisite figurines that take months for villagers to make are not made to be sold to tourists but burned at a funeral for a deceased villager. People unaware of the cultural context would be shocked to see that such intricate objects had been created to be destroyed. Yet to the Balinese, the reason why the figurine was beautiful was the same reason why the ritual performance was so powerful: it had to be, in order to work. If someone made a mistake during the performance of *Barong*, or was not able to enter the trance state this ritual is famous for, there

---

4 Miguel Covarrubias, *Island of Bali* (New York: Alfred Knopf, 1937).
5 Quoted in "History of Bali," *Wikipedia*, en.wikipedia.org/wiki/History_of_Bali

would be consequences for the society at large. No one would want to be responsible for a year of famine or disease. Through the correct execution of the ritual, the community is purified. The witch Rangda is driven back to the forest, into the shadows, till next year.

Artists? Judging by artistry, certainly. But first and foremost, the motivation for the performance was the welfare of the community. Perhaps we should more rightfully consider them ordinary citizens, living their lives, fulfilling their civic duties.

Could it be that on Bali, there are no works of art, and there are no artists? Could it be that in Bali, precisely because there are individuals who are able to create things at the skill level that contemporary society considers "art," all of them are therefore artists? What if they don't agree with or care about such a label? Could it be that because of their original motivation, which was not to create "art," there is no art in these places, and none of them are artists?

Different motives create different work. If the Balinese craftsman's motivation was to sell his handicraft to a dealer in Paris, the final product would not look or feel the same. When genuine, these works touch us deeply not only because their shapes are aesthetically pleasing but more so because of a sense of purity, something sacred that is infused within the object. This was installed at the outset, part of the motivation to make the work.

Art? Going by the motivation, no. Going by effect, yes. By this measure, we can also gauge why artworks in boutiques often do not move us. Perhaps the motivation was not to make art but to make a commercial product.

Gift or Garbage?

Hip-hop artists take open revenge on their exes or rivals through explicit song lyrics, and in the excitement generated by the ensuing gossip, they are seldom challenged about the why. Are they producing such songs because of the calculated lucrative earnings? Or are they truly so passionately in hate against their ex? If the latter, would they need to vent their hatred publicly? Why do we consider their motivation legitimate, and become complicit in their feud? Do we control our passions, or are we controlled by them? In life? In creativity?

In the spectrum of artist motivation, shocking viewers has long been a valid endeavor for the work of modern artists. Manet's *The Luncheon on the Grass* (*Le Dejeuner sur l'Herbe*, 1863) is often considered the earliest attempt in the modern era to shock and create controversy in a work of art. The composition looks totally normal—two men and a woman seated for a pastoral picnic—except the woman is totally naked. What was Manet's initial motivation for this painting? Along with perfect craftsmanship, he also wanted to shock. Shock who? Why?

A 2004 Berlin production of Mozart's opera *Die Einführung aus dem Serail* directed by the Spanish director Calixto Bieito included liberal use of nudity and actual prostitutes urinating on stage. The *Financial Times* opera critic said:

> Food packaging now informs in advance of what we are about to eat. Perhaps it's time for honesty in opera labelling. "Calixto Bieito: an evening of sex and violence, background music by Mozart" might have been a fair title. Then those shocked by the disservice to Mozart's opera would have only themselves to blame.[6]

I am not passing judgment on this production, which I did not see. I have seen plenty of provocative works at the Wuzhen Theatre Festival, which I co-founded. The provocation comes from some desire in the artist to provoke. But for what? Who gains from the provocation, audience or author? Is your passion to gain pleasure from my pain? Or am I benefiting from you torturing me? Does the artist himself know? If not, what is he doing, and for whom?

The contemporary Chinese painter Zhang Xiaogang said, "I'm just a simple painter, I just paint what appeals to me."[7] It's easy to explain one's motivation in this non-controversial way, and so we hear this sentiment from many artists. But what "appeals" to an artist? Dismembered bodies appealed to Bacon, dark rectangles to Rothko. Why? One playwright's work is totally autobiographical; another only adapts classics. Gangs and sex appeal to a hip-hop artist. Another singer is infatuated with medieval Irish ballads. You can take it all for granted, but to examine why you are attracted to certain things enough to do a creative project about it is an opportunity to cut inside your soul and see what's going on in there.

I have viewed theater performances that connected me deeply to a greater humanity. I have also seen theater works where I felt vomited upon. You can give the audience a gift, or you can throw your garbage out at them. The choice is yours. Being conscious of the choice changes the way you work and the way you look at your work.

You can use the theater, an art gallery, or a concert hall as a place of offering, or you can use it as waste disposal. Pollution is easy to produce. But offering a gift

---

6 Shirley Apthorp, "Shock Tactics Getting Dirtier," *Financial Times*, July 3/4, 2004.
7 David Barboza, "Painting that Hints at Past Turbulence," *International Herald Tribune*, September 5, 2005.

is not so easy. If we have little means (including talent), then the gift we offer may be very humble and simple. But the sincere offering of a simple gift may be worth much more to the person who receives it than intricate and elaborate garbage, which may be fascinating to look at but, in the end is, ultimately, garbage.

Offering or Destruction?

To use an extreme example, one day on an international flight, in the days when they still offered newspapers and magazines, I thumbed through a copy of *Newsweek*, and came across the following random passage of which I did not know the context:

> They are the real warriors. They are the ones with the intellectual and operational sophistication to stage simultaneous events.[8]

I was wondering what performing arts piece was being reviewed here. When I turned the page, I was shocked to see a photo of the Twin Towers under siege. The quote was from terrorism expert Bruce Hoffman, who was describing the 9-11 ringleaders!

Indeed, in the aftermath of 9-11, when I met artist friends, we looked each other in the eye, mournfully, then raised a finger to our lips. Shh. The composer Karlheinz Stockhausen said what we dared not express out loud, that the terrorist attacks on New York and Washington that day should be considered *creative*. He went so far as to call the deed "the greatest work of art imaginable for the whole cosmos."[9] Though his words were taken out of context and not meant to glorify the deed, they understandably created shock and outrage. Stockhausen was vilified, his concerts canceled, his reputation shattered. It took a whole year for someone to come to his defense, when the visual artist Damien Hirst said, "this controversial quote remains the most interesting, challenging, and indeed instructive analysis of the events to date."[10] Only after almost two decades could there be scholar/artists such as Richard Schechner coming to the forefront to

---

8 From *Newsweek* Special Edition "Issues 2004," December 2003, 14.
9 Quoted in Julia Spinola, "Monstrous Art," *Frankfurter Allgemeine Zeitung*, Sept. 25, 2001.
10 Damien Hirst, quoted in *The Guardian*. www.theguardian.com/uk/2002/sep/11/arts.september11

voice the previously unthinkable question in an academic journal: "9/11 as Avant Garde Art?"[11]

These thoughts, with absolutely no disrespect to the memories of the victims intended whatsoever, and even less thought to exalting the despicable criminals, deal with how the horrifying events of that day resembled a complex performance piece, and the "director" had a toolbox of formidable skills. The difference between this and some enlightening site-specific performance artwork you might see at BAM or Wuzhen starts in the motivation, the initial passion behind the project.

We shouldn't shy away from labeling 9-11 as a creative act, just as we mustn't shy away from considering the atomic bomb an incredible piece of creativity and Oppenheimer and his colleagues as dedicated artists. Only in this way can we see that the difference is completely in the initial motivation. All the components that we normally work with as artists on a performance piece were present in the horrifying act of 9-11: performers, performer training, audience, intricate timing, cues, props, suspense, spectacle ...

I am sorry if this is disturbing to you, but the point I am making is that creativity in itself is a power, an energy, a tool. It is not innately good or bad or righteous or evil. Whoever wields the talent and power decides how to use it. Generals are lauded for their creative strategies on the bloody warfront. The infamous "Top Ten" torture techniques used in the Qing Dynasty of China are diabolically creative. Indeed, the usage of explosives in pagers by Israel in Lebanon in 2024 was called "Gruesome Creativity" by the *New York Times*:

> [...] it is in the modern era that assassinations—now often whitewashed as "extrajudicial killings"—have become instruments of state and have harnessed cutting-edge science and inventiveness [...] ingenuity is still prized for the toughest targets.[12]

Once I visited the Renaissance painter Fra Angelico's monastery in Florence. I was overwhelmed by the *Annunciation*, probably his most well-known work, which hung in the entrance. I stood there, mesmerized, lost in the sublime silence of

---

11 Richard Schechner, "9/11 as Avant Garde Art?" Published online by Cambridge University Press, October 23, 2020. www.cambridge.org/core/journals/pmla/article/abs/9-11-as-avantgarde-art
12 Serge Schmermann, "The Gruesome Creativity of Assassinations Enters a New Phase," *New York Times*, September 18, 2024.

the painting for I do not know how long. I traced the sightline of the angel, who is looking at Mary. I traced the sightline of Mary, which disappears mysteriously into space. It moved me beyond words or concepts.

Vasari, biographer and contemporary of the Renaissance masters, wrote that Fra Angelico "spent every minute of his life in the service of God and in benefiting both the world and his neighbor." Vasari notes he "never set his hand to a brush without first saying a prayer. He never painted a Crucifix without the tears streaming down his cheeks."[13]

This is a description of an artist's motivation to make art, which was the basis for the profoundly moving quality of his work. Fra Angelico didn't paint for the primary purpose of making a great painting, and certainly not for money (he considered possessions to be burdens), but as a gesture of devotion. All else follows from that. In making his art, Fra Angelico thought zero of himself, but 100 percent of the world, and his God. All of his paintings were gifts to the world. This aspect overshadows any other aspect of his work: style, colors, composition, and so on.

Fra Angelico and Osama bin Laden may seem heavens and hells apart. But they both check most of the boxes in our creative map. What separates them is, in essence, the difference in their motivation. The angel and the devil have similar skills and capabilities. They diverge at the very fount, the initial motivation for what they do.

Gift or garbage? Offering or destruction? Creativity can do both, and certainly has over time. It is the "why" that decides, more than any technique you can learn for any art.

The Spectrum of Why

Creative motives may be deceptive. We think we are creating a certain project with a certain intention, but we may later discover there are deeper and conflicting intentions. You may think you are writing a song for all humanity, but upon introspection, you realize the deeper motive is to impress a romantic interest. A writer may write a novel about robots thinking he is infatuated with them. On another level of his psyche, which he may not see clearly or admit, his eyes are on a film adaptation. Whether he is clear about his motives or not, the initial motive will have a decisive effect on the final product.

---

13 Giorgio Vasari, *The Lives of the Artists (Oxford World's Classics)*, Julia Conway Bondanella and Peter Bondanella, trans., Oxford: Oxford University Press, 1998, 177.

It's actually pretty simple. What's there upstream at the wellspring will make its way downstream to the sea. What's upstream is a question of motivation, which actually is a gauge of one's wisdom.

Shakespeare's Passions, Michelangelo's Contracts

The concept of the modern artist doing what he likes is actually relatively new. Before the nineteenth century, artists in general did not compose whatever they liked and then sell it to whoever wished to own it. Michelangelo did most of his work on commission, meaning that the motive or passion behind his work was first and foremost to fulfill a contract. Such a contract would at least keep food on his table (which he wasn't that interested in) and pay for the assistants in his studio. That the world now has such amazing works as the Medici Tombs or the ceiling of the Sistine Chapel is a greater testament to the genius of the artist, who within the confines of a work contract was able to achieve the heights of his art. Motivation: commission?

Shakespeare was driven to write his works by some great mysterious passion to create, right? The fact is, he was a partner in a business, working hard to sustain a commercial company and theater, with formidable competition from talented and often unscrupulous rival groups. Motivation: commercial success?

Shakespeare had pressure to deliver, time after time, on deadline, with a demanding production schedule and opening date. This is far different from a playwright who spends years working on what she sees to be the essential expression of her soul, with every care given to what she wishes to express, and minimal care to what a potential audience might want to see. Was the decision to write *As You Like It* a result of a production meeting at the Globe, where Shakespeare's business partners thought that a comedy would be a good idea to open the new theater they had built? Or did it come straight from some artistic passion in the playwright's soul? Did *King Lear* start from the primary motive to write a great play, or to create a box office hit? We can and should ask the same question to contemporary artists like Lin-Manuel Miranda or Spike Lee. Is it their passion to please the audience, or themselves? Can it lie somewhere in between? That Shakespeare was able to present his audiences with such astounding works of art, season after season, year after year, with continued commercial success, is a greater testament to his genius.

Michelangelo and Shakespeare are artists whose names we recognize. There are others who work anonymously, with no desire to be known. Have you ever seen a Tibetan thangka signed by its painter? The Chartres Cathedral was built with the initial motive to house part of Mother Mary's tunic. Did anyone who took part in building it over centuries of work sign their name on it? What was their motivation for contributing to this great work of art? If you weren't allowed to have your name listed in the program credits for a play you directed, would you still direct it?

Let's say Taylor Swift never gave concerts, never released recordings. She only performed by herself, or for friends. There would be no stadiums full of fans, no websites, no industry. Can we even imagine an artist of this caliber without the desire to be known? Could she possibly have risen to her level of artistry without the desire to perform publicly? Glenn Gould and the Beatles refused public performance in the latter parts of their careers, but they concentrated on creating music in the recording studio, where they felt they could do their best work, after which they released their works to an eager public.

The Swedish playwright August Strindberg admittedly wrote to "exorcise" his "inner demons,"[14] a phrase some artists have used to describe their journey. This may be a noble endeavor that requires tremendous courage and skill, but does it have to be done in public?

The first film or novel of many directors or novelists is often autobiographical in nature. Perhaps they feel the need to settle inner accounts, to perform such an "exorcism" on themselves. Though it could be a noble effort at self-discovery, it could also be a narcissistic exercise that doesn't necessarily need to be made public. After successful first novels or award-winning first films, some writers and directors have little left to say.

The American poet Emily Dickinson had little published in her lifetime and left hundreds of poems in a locked chest when she died. They are considered some of the finest of the modern epoch. But she didn't write them to be published, or even to be read!

We seem entitled to, even empowered by, our passions. But are we ever asked to examine whether they are good for us or not? The fact is, by examining our macro and micro motivations for undertaking creative work, if we are truthful to ourselves, we can identify and then change them. Changing your motivation changes your whole path and brings great insight into your creative endeavors. We spend most of our time working on the skills, craftsmanship, stylistic flair, thematic depth, and so on, that are built in during the process, but we rarely think deeply about the first cause, the overall motivation for the project. That initial

---

14 For instance see August Strindberg, *Inferno/From an Occult Diary*, ed. Torsten Eklund, trans. Mary Sandbach (London: Penguin Classics, 1979).

passion affects everything that comes after it. It is the cause of your final effect, and searching deeply to understand it is the greatest tool for self-discovery, and cultivating your personal wisdom.

This is perhaps the most overlooked aspect of creativity.

My Lesson in Motivation

I learned how to check my own motivation many decades ago, through a hard lesson. The first time I attended a Tibetan Buddhist teaching, the teacher entered the room, sat down, and said, "Before we begin, I would like all of you to check your motivation for coming to this teaching. Thank you." A long silence ensued, with everybody in thought except me. Then the teaching began.

I found this a bit unnerving. Check what? How could I be wrong in coming to a Buddhist teaching? Does anyone stop you at the entrance of Harvard to ask for your motivation?

The next time, at a different teaching, a different teacher entered, sat down, and said almost the exact same thing. I found every Vajrayana teaching starts this way, and the audience all closed their eyes for a moment to give the question some thought. I felt defiant. Who are you to question my motivation? I can walk into this room for any reason I want to, and you can't stop me. Then I quieted my ego and engaged with the question. The ensuing dialogue with myself revealed many things to me that I never thought of before. I found a crack I could squeeze into. The tool was to keep asking yourself "why?" If you are persistent and honest, there is always a deeper "why" to question the previous "why." The dialogue went something like this:

> Me: My motivation for coming to this teaching? I'm here to learn.
> A Voice from Inside: Why are you here to learn?
> Me: What's wrong with wanting to learn, to improve myself?
> A Voice from Inside: Improve? Oh. So something's wrong with you.
> Me: Uh ... well, certainly, I admit I am inadequate in many ways.
> A Voice from Inside: Why does admitting inadequacy bother you?
> Me: That's not what I said. Was it?"
> *Pause.*
> A Voice from Inside: So why Buddhism?
> Me: Well, I feel it can help me, but I don't understand it.

A Voice from Inside: Then why don't you go for Quantum Physics? It can also probably help you, and you don't understand it, either.

Me: Listen, it's none of your business. I am free to pursue whatever school of learning I want.

A Voice from Inside: Sure. After you explore Buddhism, go ahead and go for Hinduism, then Catholicism, then paragliding, then astrology …

It was a struggle that I could have called off at any moment. But I began to see how the continual honest questioning of your motivation brings you deeper and deeper into yourself. It can get brutal, but only if you are honest. After several rounds of introspection, I realized that something in me wanted a deeper understanding of the truth, of reality, of life. And I definitely would fail a course in Quantum Physics. The voice continued with the simple, persistent question, why?

A Voice from Inside: Why do you need to know the truth?

Me: Because as a human being living on this earth, I feel obliged to know what it's all about.

A Voice from Inside: So, you are searching for wisdom?

Me: I guess so. Yeah.

A Voice from Inside: For who?

Me: For me, of course. Who else?

The inner voice went silent. It was like, "Figure this one out, or we don't continue."

I assumed all along that learning was for yourself, wasn't it? Otherwise, for whom? I had unearthed the central question. The master's pre-lecture query started to make sense.

According to scripture, the proper attitude for listening to a Buddhist teaching is that everything you learn from this teaching should be used for the benefit of others. This is radical, indeed. Buddha truly was avant-garde. Not only did he proclaim, in the face of the powerful Indian caste system, that all beings are equal, but that one should learn and practice for the sake of others, not for yourself. In fact, if you attend the teachings expressly for your own gain, you will not be able to understand the true essence of that teaching. Therein is the paradox. If your motivation is not correct, the more you want to learn, the less you will learn, or you will misinterpret the teaching.

We need to study motivation in ourselves, in others around us. We do this by simply continually asking, "Why?" After answering the initial why, keep going, because there is a motive behind the motive, and so on. In my personal journey, my persistent questioning led me to understand that wisdom is an openness. The more closed we are, the narrower the spectrum for our wisdom and our creativity. The more open we are, the sky is no longer the limit, but a simple part of the openness and connectivity of everything. The greatest openness is to be a part of everything, and therefore there is no longer a you. Your motivation for doing the work is no longer about you. I began to understand that this is the road to wisdom.

Exercises and Further Thoughts

1. Do you believe that wisdom can be learned? How? Can you see the relationship between the "why" and wisdom? In life and in creativity?
2. The next time you go to any creative work, be it a film, an art exhibition, or a play, try to see and examine the motivation behind the work. This is necessarily subjective, but can you see how different motivations will influence the work in different ways?
3. Check your motivation for the current project you are doing. Can you see the alignment between motivation and result?
4. Have you noticed how criminal activity is often very creative? Warfare itself hinges on creativity. Make a note that creativity is a double-edged sword.
5. Should we consider the works of Fra Angelico, as well as the Balinese musician art, or religious props?
6. Create a dialogue with yourself. Start with the voice inside you asking the question: "Why do you want to be an artist?" See where it takes you. Try to be as honest as you can. Don't try to accomplish everything in one session. This examination can and should be spread out over time. Get to a point, stop, and remind yourself to pick it up sometime later.

CHAPTER EIGHT

HOW TO SEE

The real voyage of discovery consists not in seeking new landscapes, but in having new eyes.[1]

—Marcel Proust

Now that we have explored our why for creativity, and are aware that motivation is such an X factor, we can get down to generating the what and how. To accumulate wisdom in life and art, in tandem with exploring motivation, we need to recalibrate how we see life and the world.

The quote above, attributed to Proust, leads us to consider that the whole effort of the left side of our Creative Map is in learning how to see as a creative person. Our objective is to get out of the non-creative mode that most of us have been trapped in since childhood. How we see decides what we see. It's not enough to just temporarily think outside the box or brainstorm with colleagues. Those are just exercises that skirt the true mechanism we need to change, which is our minds. We need to learn, or relearn, how to see, in creative mode.

To do this, we first need to understand that the eye is only a sensory perception receptor. We figure out what we see with the brain. That is the simple reason why everyone sees the world differently, and though there are innumerable ways to see the world, we have been continually herded into seeing things in a certain way. There becomes a right way and a wrong way to see things, and we habitually rush to see things the so-called right way. This is the safe mode, the non-creative mode. People seldom consider there to be a problem with this, and so never consider there is anything to change, or how to change it. To learn how to see

---

1 Paraphrased from Marcel Proust, *Remembrances of Things Past*, Book 5, *The* Captive, trans. into English by C.K. Scott Moncrief (New York: Modern Library, 1929), gutenberg.net.au/ebooks03/0300501h.html

creatively is to expand our vision and enrich our lives by not deciding so quickly what is right and wrong. The work is on the mind, not the eye.

How do we work on our mind? What is there to fix, and where can we start fixing it? To begin, we need to see how our minds work. Just as we were able to slow down the process of inspiration, to see what actually happens when it happens, can we slow down the mind's process of seeing things, and see how it then swiftly passes judgment on those things?

Cleaning the Doors of Perception

> *If the doors of perception were cleansed, everything would appear to man as it is, infinite.*
> *For man has closed himself up, till he sees all things through narrow chinks of his cavern.*[2]
>
> —*William Blake*

The mystic English poet/painter Blake suggests that experience is infinite, but our perception of it is cluttered by dirty doors. If we find a way to clean our doors, we can see it all, and then anything and everything becomes possible.

That in itself explains creativity.

If Blake's doors are the doors of the box, then to think outside it is only a temporary venture outdoors, and soon enough we rush back into the comfort of the box, where everything is safe and defined. But for the true creative person, there is no box. It is as Blake proposes; the doors are crystal clear, and we can see through everything.

What Don't We See?

Seeing is the nexus of creativity. Seeing possibilities. Seeing connections. Seeing relationships. Seeing new ways of association. To gauge what we need to do to relearn how to see creatively, we should first understand what we don't see.

How often do we look at something and not even see it? Or not see it in all its depths and nuances? How many things did we miss today? How much of the

---

2 William Blake, *The Marriage of Heaven and Hell,* www.gutenberg.org/files/45315/45315-h/45315-h.htm

miss was intentional—you weren't interested? How much was just habitually not paying attention? You could have missed some everyday thing, like a sign posted about a delay in your train which was shut out through your headphones. Your eyes were open, but you saw nothing. Or you could have missed something crucial, not reading into an expression from your partner who is trying to tell you that your relationship is in grave danger. To put it simply, we have long been in a mode where we see only through our rational mind. There is another more expansive part of the mind that we have closed off, the intuitive mind. If we see through the intuitive mind, a new world unfolds, in touch with our feelings and sensibilities. One can walk through a forest and not see a single tree, but if you are seeing mindfully, if you have opened up your intuitive mind, you can see how amazing each and every single leaf is, and how each leaf is where it should be in relation to the trees and the forest.

To cleanse the doors of perception is to open your mind. As Anaïs Nin said, "We do not see things as they are, we see them as we are."[3] The artist Max Planck echoed, "When you change the way you look at things, the things you look at change."[4] The Snow Lion, a mythical creature in my play *Ago*, states the central problem by claiming people will not see her if she appears in person in a town: "People only believe what they believe."[5] To learn a new way of seeing, you don't need new eyes, but a retooled mind.

Retool what? It is not a question of changing the appearance of the things you see, but a systematic change in the way you look at the world. Our efforts should not be to enhance just the mind's critical faculties, but to change its flexibility, to work on toning down its critical bossiness. The creative mind always sees more connections and possibilities, without elaborating. Elaboration can stifle possibility. We need to start seeing things not as individual and separate from each other, but connected. Invisible lines connect things together, some in ways observable by science, others in more mysterious and less tangible ways. Connectivity induces creativity. The more you learn how to see, the more connected life and the universe appear to you. As the Vietnamese monk/poet Thich Nhat Hanh (1925–2022) put it:

---

3 Anaïs Nin, *Seduction of the Minotaur* (Chicago: Swallow Press, 1961), 124.
4 Quoted in www.goodreads.com/quotes/1246159-when-you-change-the-way-you-look-at-things-the
5 Stan Lai, *Selected Plays*, Vol 3, 280.

If you are a poet, you will see clearly that there is a cloud floating in this sheet of paper. Without a cloud, there will be no rain; without rain, the trees cannot grow; and without trees, we cannot make paper. If we look even more deeply, we can see the sunshine, the logger who cut the tree, the wheat that became his bread, and the logger's father and mother. Without all of these things, this sheet of paper cannot exist. In fact, we cannot point to one thing that is not here—time, space, earth, the rain, minerals in the soil, the sunshine, the cloud, the river, the heat, the mind. Everything co-exists within this sheet of paper.[6]

I often revisit this beautiful quote. The magic of life, and the source of creativity, lies in the interrelatedness of everything. A creative being is most creative when she sees and uses the interconnectedness of all things. To grow as an artist and as a person is to begin to realize how things relate to other things until everything seems to fit together in an interdependent co-existing whole. As John Lennon also put it in a more playful way: "I am he as you are he, and you are me, and we are all together."[7]

To be in a state of interconnectedness is a wonderful thing. It opens one up to a way of seeing without borders. Anything can connect to anything. Because everything is interconnected, creative connections are apparent in every moment. Creativity becomes easy.

Creativity Is a Process of Discovery

The moment of inspiration makes connections that lead to discoveries. Connections to the problem, connections to the solution. Connecting the problem to the solution. You need both. Then, the final product must make connections to the viewers, readers, and users.

Before all this can happen, the artist must first make a connection with the deeper and often unknown impulses in her own inner self. This means that sometimes we work on the answer without knowing the question. How do you solve, or even identify, an unclear question? This encapsulates the constant dilemma of the creative artist, and the reason why the artist who seems to be doing nothing is so busy. We knock our brains out to discover the problem, then exhaust ourselves

---

6 Thich Nhat Hanh, *The Heart of Understanding: Commentaries on the Prajnaparamita Heart Sutra* (Berkeley: Parallax Press, 1988), i.
7 Beatles, "I Am the Walrus," *Magical Mystery Tour*. EMI Records, 1967.

in figuring out its solution. Along the way, we start seeing connections that bring clarity and new understanding to our project. We rephrase the initial question to bring focus. Gradually the mist settles, and we arrive at, or you could say discover, or even uncover, our final product.

As Gaudi said, "Man does not create ... he discovers."[8] Creativity is a journey to discovery. The path challenges your way of seeing all the way. By seeing creatively, you discover.

The Magical Paradox

When I am working on a new play, I often have the feeling that it already exists in its perfect form, and all of my work is a labor to unveil it. It is as Michelangelo said: "Every block of stone has a statue inside it and it is the task of the sculptor to discover it."[9] He explained:

> The sculpture is already complete within the marble block, before I start my work. It is already there, I just have to chisel away the superfluous material.[10]

So, one way of putting it is that the journey of creativity is chiseling away all the static and garbage, ideas that aren't so great, to unleash the project into its external form. Without working on the stone, there is no way to discover the statue. This is the magical paradox of creativity: you need to work on your project, but you don't always know exactly what you are trying to do. But you can't know unless you work. The creative question cannot be defined unless you try to solve it; but how do you solve an undefined question? That is why creativity is often so maddening. It's like jumping onto some unknown shape and trying to find a handle. You don't even know if it has a handle, but if you believe in this unknown shape that is formulating in your mind, you have to jump. Often you slip off into the abyss, failing without even knowing why. But without trying, there is no hope. As sci-fi novelist Ray Bradbury said, "Jump, and you will find out how to unfold your wings as you fall."[11]

---

8 Antoni Gaudi, quoted in www.goodreads.com/quotes/8991736-the-creation-continues-incessantly-through-the-media-of-man-but
9 Michelangelo, quoted in *Michelangelo.org*, www.michelangelo.org/michelangelo-quotes
10 Michelangelo, quoted in *goodreads.com*, www.goodreads.com/quotes/1191114-the-sculpture-is-already-complete-within-the-marble-block-before
11 www.brainyquote.com/quotes/ray_bradbury_154628?src=t_hard_work

This is one reason why creativity is really hard. If anyone tells you it's easy, they may not have gotten this far on the path. As Samuel Beckett said: "If there is one question I dread, to which I have never been able to invent a satisfactory reply, it is the question what am I doing."[12] For those of us who grapple with the paradox every day, we wish we had Michelangelo's chisel in hand. It is a chisel that embodies both wisdom and method.

Creativity 101

Steve Jobs famously said, "Creativity is just connecting things."[13] Though this may seem a gross simplification, the process of combining inner files sometimes can be as simple as A+B. In fact, "A+B" is the basic equation the Creative App in our minds starts out with. Cloud + Dog = a dog in the sky. You are reading this book while having a cup of coffee. Combine the two and you either get a coffee mug disguised as a book, or a book that functions as a coffee mug. Any use? Probably not, unless you work for MI6 and need to have information encrypted into a mug.

We can take the book/mug exercise a step further and envision that a drink can be read, or a book can be drunk. We could aspire to invent a way to "drink" a book. Just as you can listen to an audiobook on a device, how about if you could drink a fluid that was *War and Peace*? Who knows? One day your Starbucks counter will be stocked with drip coffee bags labeled *Pride and Prejudice*, *Invisible Cities*, and a 10-pouch set of *Harry Potter*. This is a simple flexing of A+B.

All sorts of contraptions that we use are simply the combination of two objects or concepts. Bottled water. Skateboard. Cheeseburger. "Diet" + "Coke," "Self-driving" + "car." Hip-hop + musical theater = *Hamilton*—that one's not so simple, but you can find brilliant examples of this basic creativity, A+B, everywhere. For instance, the Coca Cola label on the bottle that, when pulled, became a gift ribbon.[14] To be honest, when "mobile phone" combined with "camera" (a Kyocera from 1999), I was skeptical. "Who on earth would want or need to snap a photo when they are talking on their phone?" I scoffed out loud. Shows you how much I know.

To practice A+B is to learn the basic way to see creatively. In the process, you learn to shed concepts and free objects to combine with one another. You become glue.

---

12 Samuel Beckett, *Molloy*, translated by Patrick Bowles in collaboration with the author, Grove Press, 1955, 183.
13 Steve Jobs, quoted from an interview in *Wired Magazine*, 1996.
14 See Ads OK Plz, "Ribbon Bottle (2016)," facebook.com/reel/1654289622191720.

A second exercise to understand creativity in its simplest form is what I call "Opposite Placement": Choose something in your sight, anything. What does it do? Now, make it do the opposite or something alternative. If you see your rug on the floor, put it on the ceiling. If you are looking at your dog, think that it meows. Invert the keys on your piano so that the highest note is on the left-hand side. Make your smartphone a charger, and the charger the phone. Any use? Again, it depends. Captain Marvel became a woman, and Nick Fury became an African American in popular culture through this simple inversion.

A+B and Opposite Placement should be standard brainstorming for any R&D department. A+B can automatically generate random concepts like Communist capitalism, Perrier-flavored Pellegrino, ice cream hotpot, Artificial Emotion—you name it. It can also easily extend to A + B + C... to eternity. Opposites can work on anything. The sun can become the moon, day night, summer winter, Arden Forest can be a barren desert. Romeo and Juliet can each or both change sexes, and Verona can become Mars. To those outside the creative professions, they may think that this is highly creative. But to us who work as artists, such thinking is just a normal thought process, almost an automatic approach to most everything.

Of course, it isn't guaranteed to work. Verona on Mars could become a grand disaster. I have seen terrible instances of A+B in real life, like Durian Pizza (sorry, I know some people love durian, not me). An iPad used as a plate to serve food. How creative, but how unappetizing. Beethoven's "Für Elise" has for decades been the sound of the garbage truck approaching your apartment on the streets of Taipei, harkening you to bring down your waste and dump it. Garbage truck + classical music. How creative! The smell of garbage is forever ingrained with classical music in the minds of Taiwanese children.

The sublime side by side with the ridiculous. It's what creativity can do.

These two exercises demonstrate creativity explained in its simplest terms. They are not worth much by themselves. Connecting A and B is easy. Connecting A and B for a purpose is slightly more difficult, but without purpose, such connections are meaningless exercises.

Exercises and Further Thoughts

1. Re-read Thich Nhat Hanh's quote on page 70. Does it make sense?
2. Start with anything in your sight, say a lamp in your room or the window on your wall. Try to do what Nhat Hanh did to this object: see how it connects to other things, and ultimately to all things.

3. Examine your own life in the same way. When looking at yourself, what do you see? Can you also start making connections and see how you are wondrously connected to everybody and everything?
4. Take notice of inventive things around you that are simply A+B.
5. Practice the "A+B" exercise in this chapter. Think randomly of any two things, and combine them. Interesting? Creative? Does it add up to anything worthwhile? Continue working on this exercise, combining two seemingly unrelated things.
6. Take the equation one step further and try "A+B+C." See how you can keep going.
7. Practice the "Opposite Placement" exercise in this chapter. Choose anything. It can even be a concept. Think of its opposite, or an alternative to it.

CHAPTER NINE

INSPIRATION'S WAREHOUSE

A Storage Space for Creative Files

Let us examine the file-storage function that is so crucial to creativity because what is stored in our minds is the raw material that we use for our creative inspirations and projects. In everyday life, our minds seem to automatically tag things as "important," which we keep, and "not important," which we disregard. Prominent events, which may be exciting or even traumatic, are naturally kept. But other things also stay: images, colors, random people and vague places, fragments of dialogue, words, dreams. These things are not necessarily important in the running of our everyday lives, but our mind has its own way of keeping what it wants and discarding what it deems unimportant.

Consider everything is stored in a "warehouse" somewhere in your mind. Then, during the moment of inspiration, your mysterious app activates and pulls from the warehouse, combining files that may have been stored years apart and have nothing to do with each other. The tree before you suddenly is linked to a love affair; a pickup truck drives by and the lyrics start coming for a song. This is what the mind of a creative person easily does. These connections may not take you far or deep, but then again, they may.

The key: our Creative App cannot pull files from thin air, or from other people's minds. It can only work with materials that are already in the warehouse. What seem like flashes of inspiration are actually moments of connection and assembly. Even conceptual breakthroughs by thinkers need to be based on concepts that are already there in the warehouse. Through what is already there, they can get to places that no one has gone to before. $E=mc^2$ did not magically appear in the air. It was the end of a long journey, where Einstein assimilated all the elements and tools that were either in his mind when he started or accumulated along the way.

What's in You?

The first key to creativity therefore is not your idea-generating abilities, but *what is stored inside you*. That is the raw material of creativity, without which you have nothing to generate ideas from. Inside you are the essential concerns at your core, your life experience, your storehouse of thoughts, emotions, images, concepts, love and hate, pity and fear. I can't help thinking that our warehouse must resemble the Brueghel painting referred to in Chapter Two in the account of my *Dream* inspiration, but it would be much more vast and complex, with emotional experiences floating around with other memories and concepts and subconscious images in an unbelievably expansive space.

And yet this space can be tightly focused. The beloved Japanese animator Hayao Miyazaki once said in an interview, "For my characters I take inspiration from people I know, who are around me."[1] I visualize the few blocks around the venerable Ghibli Studio in suburban Tokyo, an ordinary neighborhood with bland apartment buildings, convenience stores, and noodle shops. It is wondrous to imagine how the lady cooking noodles for the maestro's lunch perhaps became the old lady Yubaba in *Spirited Away*. Maybe a perennially expressionless errand boy in the office became "No Face." Note how the quaint-looking towns that are the backdrop to several Miyazaki films look like places he visited—Visby, Sweden, for *Kiki's Delivery Service*, or the narrow alleys of Jiufen, Taiwan, for *Spirited Away*. For Miyazaki, these people and places must have all been stored in his mind's file warehouse, dormant, waiting to be pulled and connected to different files.

Our consciousness is like a well. Deep underneath, the storehouse quietly grows.

Creativity Is Like Memory

Before there were digital archives of anything, ad agencies, architectural and design firms all had their own libraries of visual content. Designers could find references in the files for any project they were undertaking, or browse the library for inspiration. The file warehouse in our mind serves the same function, but for most of us, it is cluttered and messy. It has not been cleaned or organized for a long time, if ever. It includes many items that we are not even aware of, including subconscious dreams and desires that have found their way in over time. Much

---

[1] "Japan's Miyazaki Gets Golden Lion at Venice," www.abc.net.au/news/2005-09-10/japans-miyazaki-gets-golden-lion-at-venice

of it probably doesn't belong there. In fact, many of us aren't even aware that this warehouse exists.

If we examine the way our mind remembers something, creativity works in a similar way. Memories are files stored in the mind. Memory pulls from these files. So does our creative app in the act of creativity. A certain smell that reminds us of childhood can provide the inspiration for a feature film. Such a simple act of sense association happens all the time. The fact that we have voluminous inner files is why we don't need to go to encyclopedias of fantastic monsters to create fantastic monsters. We can find them in our office, or neighborhood, or just by combining some files.

At any moment, we are accumulating files, from conscious or subconscious sources. We are aware of this accumulation when we experience something particularly interesting or emotionally moving. Traumatic experiences may cause pain that is too much to go untreated or unexpressed. Much of the great work of art of the world comes through pain. This stores automatically.

What shapes our individuality is that each of us has a personal filtering system that works on everything that we experience. This filter strains and refines experience into personal meaning. It decides which experiences or images to keep and which to discard. Our mind is the operator of this filter. For most of us, it has been on default setting all of our lives, and we don't consider it as something pliable that can be manipulated. To be sure, it may be stubborn, and indeed it has made its own rules for years. But if you can see how it works, you can manipulate the mechanism and change it.

How does it work? Our inner filter works on the basis of prejudice, not necessarily political or cultural, but the simple bias of preferring one thing over another, of saying "this is good, that is bad," "this one is better than that one." Our filter jumps to make decisions. It immediately labels this experience pleasant, that experience not; this action good and that action bad; this person cool and that person geeky. Our filter is the first thing that touches our experience. It is a biased judge that proceeds to store files it likes, while discarding anything it doesn't like. We may think we are open-minded, but we must see that we are actually biased toward the most basic judgmental function: likes and dislikes. Even our concept of what is open-minded may be highly prejudiced.

The Pliable Tissue of Concern

To let every and all experience move freely into our warehouse is just not something the human mind does. That's why we forget things, purposely. On your bus trip to work, your sense receptors have captured all of the images that pass by the window, but the filter is only letting 1 percent go into your files, because none of it concerns you. If you happen to be writing a novel, and a key scene takes place on a crucial bus trip, then on a certain day, you may be paying closer attention to all the details of these images. On that particular bus ride, 100 percent goes into your files.

Or you may have stashed other images from your bus ride in your warehouse over the years: A stop light where you always wait 28 seconds, no more and no less. The quality of sunlight on the side of the building as the bus makes a turn. You can write about your bus ride scene easily based on what you have already stored in your mind.

What concerns you as an artist? As a human being? What concerns you contributes very much to how your habits are constructed. Concerns can be monumental or minimal. If you are concerned that AI will destroy the world, it goes without saying that you will take a particular notice of anything to do with AI. If you are concerned about how a burrito or a jiaozi tastes, sauces and dressings may more easily be registered into your files. If you are a painter, which company makes a better shade of blue in oils naturally will become part of your files. It's obvious.

What concerns you controls you.

So what concerns you? That is the pliable tissue we can work on. Understand what concerns you. Then analyze. After reflection, you may find, for instance, that all of your actions stem from a sense of insecurity dating from childhood, so all of your experience is being sorted with insecurity as the major principle. How does this help or hinder your creativity? How does this help or hinder your everyday life, your relationships, your happiness? It's all tied together, and the whole bundle can be changed together, by changing your concerns.

How Do We File Experience?

If you can see how your files are created through everyday experience, you can start exerting some degree of control over how they are stored. This starts by first understanding that they can be stored, or they can be discarded. Instead of letting it happen automatically, you can make a mental note of what you want to keep. Better yet, you can take notes in a physical notebook where you jot down things that strike you as interesting. This is standard for the creative person. Many wonderful creative projects grow from bits and pieces of a personal sketchbook. This notebook becomes a running commentary on your life, like a journal, through words and images and mementos. Any rationale can be used to start filing. Your physical notebook will no doubt leave imprints in your mind, where file storage will start to happen automatically.

Once settled in the mind, a file can ferment into other types of files. A purely physical image like sunset over war-torn Gaza is stored in your files. It can sit and ferment into a concept, about nature and the workings of humankind. When the Creative App pulls from your file warehouse, it is not just pulling images or stories or characters, but more importantly, thoughts and spiritual connections that have fermented over time between different files.

The Equality of Things

What concerns you shapes your attitude toward life. Your attitude decides what takes priority, what is secondary, what doesn't need to be registered in your files. The more we open up the settings on our filter, the more experience we let in. This brings us a greater variety of materials stocked in our file warehouse. Abusive relationships, a forbidden love affair, a long illness, a sudden accident—these painful events often dominate the space in your warehouse, the same as experiences of ecstatic joy. But you can also allow simple acts, such as having a cup of tea while watching the sunlight stream in the window, or the color of a lake, or a pair of lovers crossing the street, or the tattoo on the waiter's wrist, or the trees undulating in the breeze pass through your filter. The other day my therapist who has worked on my lower back for years told me that she went to the coastal city of Shenzhen to see her best friend from high school. They took a walk by the ocean. It was the first time she had ever seen the sea. Somehow this image is brewing in my mind. Two women, who grew up together in the rural midlands of China, each on their own path to make a living and raise a family, standing now at mid-age, together, by the sea.

Who knows where this file will go? It's been stored, though, in my warehouse, where someday it might ferment and connect to a completely different file stored in a completely different room to create a new play. Creativity is a sophisticated process of connectivity—emotions to words, smells to images, thoughts to colors, a gesture into a scene, a scene into a story. Any file, as long as it exists in your warehouse, can be pulled and assimilated with another file, and in this interaction transform into something unique.

What are useful files for creativity? This is a tough and very personal question. Everyone is interested in different things. But I believe deeply that all phenomena are equal in terms of their "worthiness" to be subject matter. All characters and stories are equal, long or short, happy or sad, complete or fragmented. Let's say we are inside Quentin Tarantino's warehouse. You might think that it would be stocked with all different aspects of violence. However, I would wager that there are an equal amount if not more files that deal with serenity, peace and love, and also files that deal with nothing in particular, like grass blowing in the wind, or smoke rising from a chimney. A Tarantino film is a kaleidoscope of files, as are most creative projects. That is why all files are in essence equal.

It is not that easy to see all experience as equal. We like and dislike things passionately, because we believe that they are not equal. But as creative beings, we have to believe deeply in the equality of all things. If we can do so, then our warehouse will be stocked full at every moment with files that can easily connect with others. Respect all experience, and all people. In time, experience will reveal its relevance. Inner files will easily be activated, because there is no bias, no hierarchy between them.

I often meet people who say to me, "I have a great story I would like to share with you." These stories are usually quite gripping and dramatic. But what I tell them is, a great story doesn't necessarily make a great play. In fact, incredibly dramatic stories often make for boringly predictable melodramatic works on stage. It's like my friend, the playwright Joyce Hsu said, "Great stories make terrible plays."[2] In the realm of content matter, there is no one subject that is greater than the other. Everything has equal potential. Therefore Aeschylus can use the Trojan War with its kings and princesses and warriors as the content for his trilogies, but Ozu can set up a domestic family situation in an ordinary Tokyo home and create as much epic beauty in one of his films. For many centuries, it was only the stories of kings and princesses and warriors and monsters that were deemed worthy of being included in creative works. But in recent centuries that has changed. Not only the social status of characters, even objects and materials used in painting and sculpture have been brought down to earth. You don't need to go to an art store to buy the best oils and acrylics. You can use any medium, or things that you find in your neighborhood or in your yard. Anything can be used to create a potential work of art, which can look like anything.

A person can travel the world, but the experiences he has may not meld into any significance. Another can lead a life full of rich experiences without venturing away from her neighborhood. Once you believe in the equality of all beings, and all things, you can see how creativity draws from everything, without discrimination. A billionaire's life can be worthless as subject matter; a beggar's life can become epic. A flower wilting in the window can lead to a major novel. The

---

2 Private conversation with Joyce Hsu, August 2024.

creative person naturally has strong and passionate views about almost anything, but sees the potential of all experience without prejudice. I may have lunch with Warren Buffet and then go home in time to make sure the plumber gets in to fix the sink. Neither appointment is greater than the other.

To see the equality of all phenomena is to be on another freeway to creativity.

Seeing Is a Habit

"You are what you eat." More so, you are what you accumulate, physically and mentally. Persistent accumulation over time has transformed the way we look and think. By acknowledging this simple fact, we can begin to take ownership for what we accumulate. Habit is the gatekeeper of accumulation. As Samuel Beckett says, "Life is habit. Or rather life is a succession of habits."[3] This succession of habits solidifies the original habits and we live life locked into habitual patterns.

Your habits represent your tastes, your likes and dislikes, your moral compass. You may think that habits are defined by your distinct personality and never change. But personality influences the building of habits, and habits in turn influence personality, in a cycle. If you examine carefully, while some habits are traceable to genes, most are acquired through life, and can be broken, like smoking or gambling. Others, you may not even consider changeable, like your habit of thinking, itself, and your basic likes and dislikes.

On pages 84–85 is the Expanded Map of Creativity, where many of the items we are dealing with are listed in relation to each other. As you can see, habits are formed on both sides of the map through experience, and directly influence how we see. In childhood, habit is like a sponge that soaks in prejudices. Good and bad, beautiful and ugly, evil and angelic. Our definitions of these are product of our habits, which we picked up somewhere along the line. We tend to consider them solid and immutable. But the fact that they were acquired means they are fluid and mutable. This gives us hope as it relates to creativity. If our habits are not conducive to creativity, we can reprogram them.

Try to see a habit arise when you see something and decide you like or dislike it, then grab your inner steering wheel. Can you see that it was a habitual judgment? Where did it come from? How have simple likes and dislikes morphed into opinions and bias? How stubborn are they? Consider your reaction to something, anything. Let's say we are on the streets of Taipei. I bring you to the most renowned street vendor, who makes the most delicious pig intestines in the world.

---

3 Samuel Beckett, *Proust*, (New York: Grove Press, 1957), 8.

How did your mind react to the fact that I am going to treat you to this delicacy? I am not asking you to judge your opinion. I am only requesting that you observe your mind and see how fast it makes up its mind. Can you see how jumping to conclusions is not really conducive for creativity? And if you sour toward pig intestines, you are missing out on something special!

A Sharp Blur

We now understand that seeing happens in two parts: the actual sense receptor sees the object, then the mind interprets the object. In the process of interpreting, judgment and bias barge in. Once we judge something, we are not seeing it for what it really is, but through the filter of our prejudice, which is our likes and dislikes. We spend most of our lives looking at the world in this way, not really seeing it for what it is. Once we see something, a value judgment is immediately stamped on it. If we are mired in predictable and long-standing habits that bring us to quick judgments that conform to standard thinking, how can we see original possibilities?

A big step toward creativity is to leap beyond strong personal likes and dislikes. This is not to let go of your individuality, what makes you you. That can express itself extensively when you get down to the work of shaping your ideas, but when you are searching for ideas, your strong likes and dislikes can be shackles that bind your creativity. To be original, you need to see the original face of things. Only then, can you shape and mold these things into something else.

Creative seeing has a razor-sharp focus, but the widest of wide-angle lenses. This goes for seeing in life as well as during creative work. Creative wisdom depends on seeing as many possibilities as we can. You can't see many possibilities if you are looking too hard. Creative seeing is the art of being in a seriously relaxed mode. Relaxed *and* serious. Only when you are relaxed can you take in more. Only when you are serious can you focus in on what you need.

This is the basic way to see creatively.

Exercises and Further Thoughts

1. Find where your creative warehouse is in your mind. It's where things have leapt out to you to combine with other things in a creative way. Examine what is in there. Can you see where these things came from, and why they have stuck in your mind?
2. Examine all of your concerns in life, starting from the most serious. During this examination, do you find concerns that take too much of your energy?

Do you find that you have too little concern for other things that you would like to start emphasizing? Can you see how adjusting your concerns in turn changes your habit?
3. Revisit your day. What did you miss? Why?
4. Start a notebook and physically write down these day-to-day things that interest you. Find your own way to organize them into different categories.
5. From time to time, compare your physical notebook to things that have automatically made their way into your mind's storage.
6. Examine your natural attractions to art or people or things. Can you look deeper, and see where these tendencies come from?

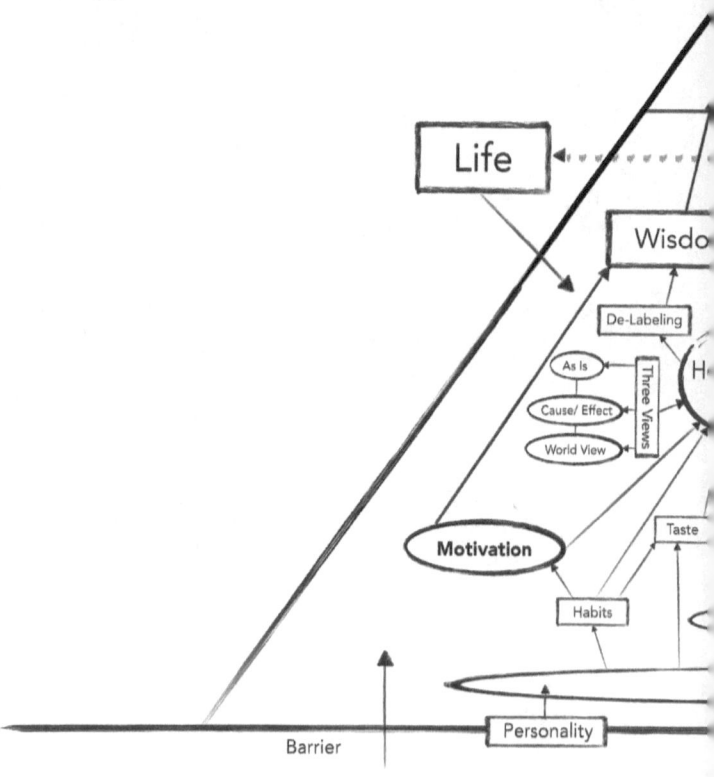

FIGURE 10.1 Expanded Map of Creativity. This is an expanded map of the creative path, with added items that are dealt with in the book.

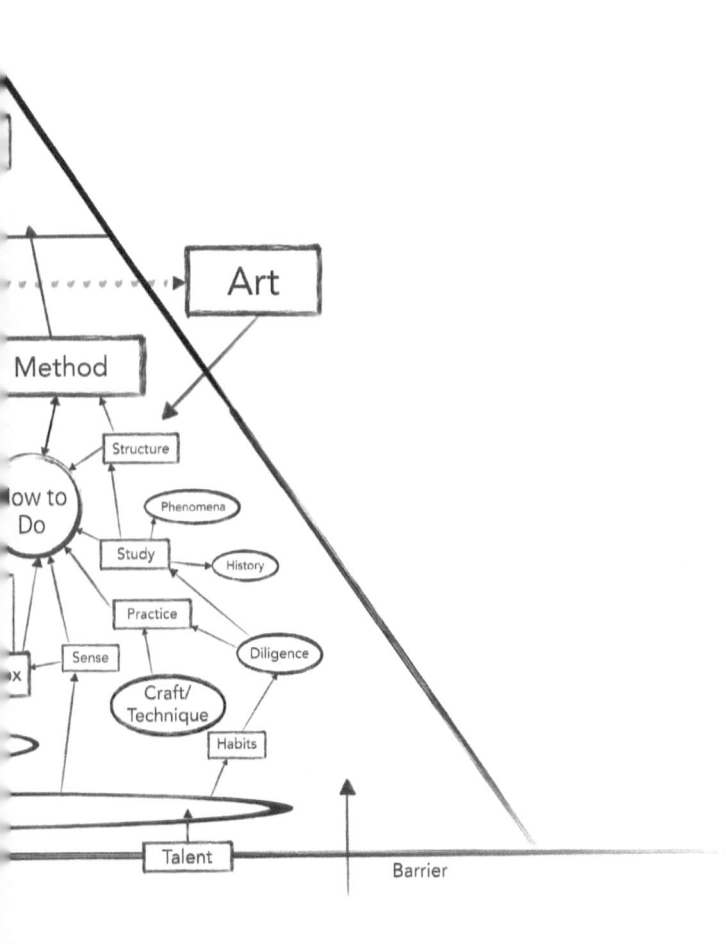

CHAPTER TEN

DE-LABELING

The Liberation of Objects

Before anything is recognized as anything, it is itself, pure and simple. But as people, we need things to have names. Our minds have the strong habit of attaching labels immediately to sensory inputs. We need names. They guarantee safety. They bring order. By putting names and labels on things, we are able to categorize them. But to put a label on something also limits the definition of that thing. This is a definite block to creativity.

Labels present a means to solidify reality, but creativity thrives in liquid or gaseous ecologies. Our habit is to immediately add a sticker to anything we see. This label describes what a thing is and how we should respond to it. Can we suspend this process of labeling? Just for a moment, can we just sit and watch a sunset without immediately jumping to conclusions about how beautiful it is? Can we just look at it, freely, without association? Before it was "beautiful," it was a "sunset." Before it was a "sunset," it was a round glowing object in the sky going down.

"De-labeling" funnels directly out of "How to See" on the Expanded Map (Figure 10.1, p. 84) and is an essential ability to develop on the path to creativity. For the brief moment we are able to see this pure face of something, that something is beyond labels and concepts. It is liberated because it doesn't have to conform to the expectations of the concepts that labels have attached to it. This liberation liberates your creativity.

An Ancient Theory of Relativity

As opposed to Confucius, his contemporary Laozi was, in my opinion, one of the wisest persons in human history. Pity he is not often read, even in Asia, and he is not well known in the West. I believe that his *Taoteching* (or *The Book of the Way*, one way of translating it) is one of the most creative books ever written. In Chapter Two, Laozi offers:

When the world knows beauty as beauty, ugliness arises
When it knows good as good, evil arises
Thus being and non-being produce each other
Difficult and easy bring about each other.[1]

Laozi's ancient "Theory of Relativity" illustrates our world of duality, in which we can only define ugly by referring to what we define as beautiful, evil through good. It's what Hamlet said roughly 2,000 years later:

There is nothing either good or bad, but thinking makes it so.[2]

Isn't it obvious? Everything is a concept of the mind. The values that we assign to things are exactly just that, assigned values. Nothing is beautiful unless you say so. Your Chinese is not standard only because one of all the dialects of China has been designated to be "standard."

Mind the Gap!

Creativity is the ability to see relationships where none exist.[3]
—*Thomas Disch*

In the creative mode, we understand how to take labels off things, or to refrain from sticking them on. Without names, things are what they are, not what you label them to be. By de-labeling what we see, we bring back the creative potential of every thing. Things or events are no longer limited to set conceptual expectations. A kite can become a plate, a plate can become a shoe, a solitary shoe set on a stage can become the opening of an evocative play. All sorts of creative possibilities arise because once we see something in its original purity and essence, it becomes free to connect with anything.

Laozi starts his classic *Taoteching* by de-labeling the whole work!

The Tao that can be spoken is not the eternal Tao

---

1 Lao Tzu, *Tao Te Ching Online Translation*, translation by Derek Lin, Chapter 2. taoism.net/tao-te-ching-online-translation/
2 William Shakespeare, *Hamlet*, Act II, Scene 2, Lines 268-70.
3 http://www.notable-quotes.com/c/creativity_quotes_v.html

The name that can be named is not the eternal name. [4]

This is enigmatic. Laozi is writing a book about an all-encompassing thing called the "Tao" and tells us up-front that anything that describes it is not it! Then what is the book for? The author has set up a challenging paradox where he uses a whole book of words to describe something that is beyond words, therefore beyond labels.

Though modern psychology and neuroscience have conducted extensive research on how the mind works, a detailed explanation of how human consciousness works has been present in Buddhist doctrine for over two millennia and may be useful to us. Not at all pretending to be an expert, I would like to explain the Buddhist concept for the purpose of introducing methods to de-label things in your life, for use in creativity.

In different schools of Buddhism, mental activity is described using six, seven, or eight consciousnesses. I would like to focus on the eight consciousnesses developed in the tradition of the Yogācāra school of Mahayana Buddhism.[5] In an oversimplified explanation, the first five are our sense perceptors: eye, ear, nose, mouth, and touch. The sixth, the mental consciousness, is the moment the mind attaches itself to the object. What happens next, the seventh consciousness, in my understanding, is the moment after the sixth consciousness has engaged the object. This is where labels and judgments are tagged onto the object, including opinions and emotions. Likes and dislikes take shape here, and whatever has been sensed now takes on "meaning."

In the instantaneous moment between the sixth and seventh consciousnesses, there is a fleeting gap, an undefined space therein.

If we are able to identify this gap and extend it, we have created an expansive space for creative things to happen. Another way of explaining it is to be able to rest in the pure perception of the object, the sixth consciousness, and not proceed into the seventh. It is like putting a stop sign there: Do not proceed to the next step in the normal thought process.

This is an advanced switch that immediately turns on the creative mode.

---

4 Lao Tzu, Chapter 1.
5 The Wikipedia page for "Vijñāna" is a good place to start exploration of the topic: https://en.wikipedia.org/wiki/Vijñāna. Matthieu Ricard also has a short but clear explanation in "On Consciousness," https://medium.com/@matthieu_ricard/on-consciousness-38d7e6a84ed

The gap connects to everything. The moment reveals all possibilities. Learning to be aware of this gap does not happen in the domain of art; it is mind training. Such mind training is usually undertaken not for the sake of art, but for the sake of living a more mindful life, but it has its definite advantages when applied to creativity. In mind training, the practitioner trains in a specific way to see how thoughts attach themselves to perception, then learns how to retard the process of attachment so that thoughts can be held back for a split moment. This moment can then be lengthened through further practice. To begin, you need to develop the ability to see your own thoughts. Then you can start reining in the wild randomness of your thoughts, and through mindful awareness begin to take control of your own mind.

If you can leave things as they are in the moment of perception, you will find yourself in a state of consciousness where you are not attached to anything. Your mind has not glued itself to what your sensory receptors have sent to it. Everything is just—there. In this state, you have turned off your mind's elaboration function, and so everything before you is equal. You have not added any conceptual value or meaning to anything you see, hear, or feel. Anything can relate to anything, and new meanings can arise from these new relationships. This is creativity in its most abstract sense, yet it is very palpable.

To be able to access this gap means that you acquire a great openness in your life. You can move through every day without labeling things, thoughts, or people, and in your unattached state, anything can attach to anything. To have this ability is like having a secret tool for creativity. A+B happens automatically and continually.

Without this practice, we are at the mercy of our likes and dislikes. With labels stuck on everything, we erect an obstacle course of meanings based on our prejudices. With practice, we learn how to see without sticking labels on things, and any thing can be anything.

How can we stop the interpretation, and just leave the sense perception as is? This seemingly simple mental trick is not so easy to put into practice. There is a whole school of Tibetan Buddhism where this kind of meditation forms the foundation for the practice called Dzogchen, or the Great Perfection. I borrow these concepts here to explain creativity. What I offer is incalculably shallow in comparison to the Vajrayana teachings, which you should refer to if you seek authentic guidance.[6]

---

[6] A good place to start would be Tulku Orgyen, *As It Is*, Vols. 1-2, trans. and ed. Erik Pema Kunsang and Marcia Binder Schmidt (Rangjung Yeshe Publications, 1999).

This is a way to see things as they are and not as they have been defined. It is a wonderful tool to have.

Wisdom Is Space

Why is the gap between the sense perceptor's perception of an object and the labeling of the object filled with creativity? Because it is the space where things have not yet been defined. In a space where there are no definitions, all definitions can arise. In a space where everything is as is, anything goes.

Frank Lloyd Wright said, "Space is the breath of art."[7] Creativity needs space to happen. Space is needed to connect things. Just like you need earth to plant trees, the seeds need space to sprout and grow. A wheel cannot turn and move without space. A cup cannot hold tea without space. You cannot read a book without the space to turn the page. It is the same with concepts in the mind. Our minds are filled with all sorts of clutter. Thoughts tear through like a torrential river that cannot be stopped. Thoughts flood the mind. To create the space for creativity to work, we must *unblock* cluttered space, clean up the junk, stop the flooding, and slow down the river.

Our new way of seeing is an open way of seeing, a seeing that creates space. The more expansive the space, the more conducive it is to creativity.

Wisdom is space. Creativity is about finding new ways of seeing. At the heart of learning How to See is the ability to see things as they are, and refrain for as long as possible from labeling. If we can do this with everyday objects, we will be able to do this with larger and more complex things such as emotions, concepts, and relationships. Life itself will be open for us to look at without bias. Without bias, all possibilities are pregnant within.

Creativity As Is

When you are conceptualizing your project, thinking rationally is of course the normal way to go. But during rational thought, labels keep blocking your view, and you tend to overthink and over-plan everything. If you can train your mind to stop conceptualizing when needed, it can suddenly free things from concepts, from labels. We are closer to the truth of reality, the pure flowing phenomena of the world. By not attaching labels, by not seeking direction, direction may come.

---

7 www.brainyquote.com/quotes/frank_lloyd_wright_127728

This ability is of most use during the conceptual phase of your creative project. Once you get down to the actual work, you need to revert back to your rational and conceptual way of thinking in order to get things done.

If you are in my field, theater, though, the ability to see without attachment may also prove valuable when you are in rehearsals. If I can put myself in this state while rehearsing, I find that my sight is actually more expansive. I can intuitively see which actors are in their roles and which are struggling to get in. I also see the truthfulness of the scene I have written and what parts are superfluous, making revisions easy. It may sound odd, but I trust my judgment when I am not thinking, but just seeing. I see more when I let go of my critical faculties than if I actually employ them.

It is the same if you are a painter or musician. If you are a conductor, stop looking at your score. Concentrate on what's happening before you and just let go. By letting go, you suddenly have access to the natural state of the moment. What comes into your sensory perception at this time are not the details of the viola or flute parts, or tempo or structure, but the whole thing, all at once. You are hearing the whole symphony but not elaborating on it. Elaboration often gets us into trouble, leading to judgments which may or may not be correct. Non-thinking is a method of emptying ourselves of concepts. Does this deprive us of critical thinking? As I said, in my experience there is no need for critical thinking in these moments, because you easily and naturally perceive what is going on. You see and hear everything that is going right, naturally, and likewise any little thing that is going wrong. It is a natural and organic streaming of your critical facilities.

There is no second-guessing what you see in this non-attached state because there is nothing to second-guess. You are not asking for anything, but it shows you everything. It's all just there. You see the truth of the moment without elaboration. You are in that moment where everything flows, and it is easy to just know what's going on. As Thich Nhat Hanh says, "When we look deeply into the heart of anything, it will reveal itself."[8] The deepest way of seeing is without critical thought or prejudice.

Listen to John Coltrane's famous solo on *Giant Steps*. My god, what was he thinking when he was playing this solo? Or should we correctly ask, what was he *not* thinking? It is precisely this non-thinking that we need to learn. Some people are better at it, but with dedicated practice, we all are capable of it. The key is in

---

8 Thich Nhat Hanh, *Old Path, White Clouds* (Berkeley: Parallax Press, 1991), 120.

learning to calm the mind first, so that we begin our seeing without a cluttered mind full of labels and concepts.

A Crack in the Ground

When I was starting out as a young professor in Taipei, I translated for the composer John Cage and choreographer Merce Cunningham when they performed together in Taiwan in 1983. I guided them on a tour of the National Palace Museum, which, through a quirk of history and the efforts of many courageous individuals, holds countless treasures from Imperial China that may not have survived had they not been brought out of mainland China after the Chinese Civil War.

We went through the main exhibits. Mr. Cage gazed intently at the priceless art treasures, marveling at the exquisite landscape paintings and ceramics, and the carved jade cabbage and piece of fatty pork, which were signatures of the museum.

The tour ended. As we exited the museum, on the plaza in front, he suddenly stopped and looked at the cement ground. I didn't know what he was looking at. He beckoned to me. "Stan," he said, "Look. How amazing." I took a look, flustered. It was a crack in the concrete. Like any crack in any concrete. He was immersed in the sight for a moment, then he smiled, and we proceeded down the long, wide stone stairs.

Decades later, I still think back to that moment. Was that a critique of the museum? Or perhaps a comment on over-interpretation? Was he trying to teach me something? Or was that just him being him, John Cage, the composer of *4'33"* appreciating the beauty of a crack in the ground? During the tour of the museum, we had been putting so many labels on everything—what dynasty, what style, what level of artistry, and so on. This certainly was a master class in de-labeling.

It didn't end there. We hopped into a taxi. If you were ever in a Taipei taxi in the 1980s, you would cower at the absolute chaos. All sorts of vehicles, cutting in and out at different rhythms and high speeds. I looked at Mr. Cage. Whereas I was searching for a seat belt that didn't exist, he was smiling benevolently, taking in all of the cacophonic rhythms that were Taipei traffic. He said to me, "Isn't this nice?" It was literally music to his ears. For him, there seemed no borders between sound and music, art and life.

Later, at a lecture event, the music scholar scheduled to translate didn't show, and I was forced onstage to do simultaneous interpretation for the live audience. There I was, at the mercy of John Cage. With his humble smile, he began: "I don't want this to be a lecture, so I will recite a recent poem of mine." That was easy. Then he started: "My memory of what happened was not what happened." I felt like I was going through a translator's exam. After I translated, he turned to me and smiled, nodding in approval. I thought, in approval of what? I wasn't aware that John Cage spoke Chinese! But his nodding was more than approval. It was an affirmation that I should just let go, go with him, wherever he took me. And that's what I did, because that first line of poetry was the easiest. What followed was very stream-of-consciousness. If you took one second to think about any single word, the whole stream would be gone. You had to just go blank, let the words come in, in English, and go out, in Chinese.

It was an important lesson for me. No judgment. No rational thoughts. Let yourself go, and the translation will flow through you. I made it through the session. Friends said I did a great job. Great job or not, I doubt that any of it was intelligible.

Their performance in the theater was on another level of de-labeling.[9] Mr. Cage brought three musicians with him. They collected dry fallen branches from the elementary school next to the theater, where they proceeded to mic up large cardboard boxes used to transport their equipment. During the performance, Cage used the branches to scratch the boxes at differing speeds and intensities, creating excruciatingly loud sounds that can only be called noise. The Cunningham dancers danced according to their own choreography. Sitting before the stage, Mr. Cage would watch keenly, then carefully choose a branch from the many that were lined up beside him, like a samurai choosing his sword. I think I could discern the slight difference in the scratching sounds when he used a different branch, but it wasn't much.

This was not a dance recital, nor was it a musical concert, nor was it a combination of the two. It was a virtuoso lesson in de-labeling, which brought us all into a new space, if you knew how to let go.

Exercises and Further Thoughts

1. Try to see your thoughts appear when you first look at something or someone you know. Try to identify the moment you put the label on. Consider how labels hinder creativity.

---

9 Merce Cunningham Dance Company with John Cage, performances at Sun Yat-sen Memorial Hall, Taipei, Taiwan, January 24, 26-27, 1984.

2. Read Laozi's *Tao Te Ching*. There are very many versions online in English, which differ widely in translation and interpretation, because the original text itself holds such cryptic qualities. I have even used different versions for quotes in this book. I would suggest the version of Stefan Senudd to start with,[10] and you can explore other versions based on your reaction to this version.
3. Look at the sky. What kind of space is it? What is it confined by? What can occur within it? Compare your mind to this space.
4. How quickly do you judge something or someone? Can you see how this judgment is just the mind attaching itself to a concept?
5. When you judge, stop for a moment and ask yourself to hold on for a second. Why am I jumping to this judgment? Are there any other possibilities?
6. Look at the view before you, whatever it is. In your mind, create a "negative" of it, swapping the foreground with the background, so that space becomes the prominent element in your view. Practice this in different situations. Can you see how much space is available for you in your mind to create?
7. Basic meditation exercise: Sit in a comfortable position and calm your mind. Concentrate on your breath. Simply be aware of your breath coming in and out. Thoughts will come, but let them go. Do this for two minutes. If for nothing else, let this exercise show you how cluttered your mind is.

---

10 Stefan Senudd, *Tao Te Ching, The Taoism of Lao Tzu*, www.taoistic.com/taoteching-laotzu/. It is also available in print at online booksellers.

CHAPTER ELEVEN

THREE VIEWS

Your view is what you see from where you are. It is not just physical sight, but your take, what you observe entwined with your opinion. The external mingles with the internal to create the view. Your view is a display of your wisdom, which reflects directly on your creativity. Cultivation of your view is direct cultivation of your creative potential. On the Expanded Map, next to "How to See" on the Wisdom side, are listed "Three Views": World view, Cause-and-effect View, and As-Is View. They are to be developed in the domain of life. Working on these three views will reshape how you see, toward the cultivation of your personal wisdom, which directly enhances your creativity.

World View

> Having traveled the world, has the world become bigger or smaller to you?[1]
> —*Chen Ke, the tour guide in* Crosstalk Travelers

How you see has everything to do with your vantage point, where you are physically, intellectually, and spiritually. If you are on the top of a mountain, you can swivel around and see far in all directions. If you are at the bottom of a well, you are the proverbial Chinese frog, who can only see the well's walls.

Your world view is simply what you see from where you stand. Where you stand determines your vision, how far and deep you can see. It is also what you believe in, what the world and your life mean to you, what your values are. Your world view does not make you creative in itself. It is the foundation for your

---

[1] Stan Lai (Lai Shengchuan), *Crosstalk Travelers (Nayiye zai Lvtuzhong Shuoxiangsheng)* (Beijing: CITIC, 2020), Scene 6.

creativity, and your creativity works off of it. If mature, it brings purpose, depth, and conviction to your work.

If you maintain a shallow and biased world view, no matter how far you travel, new landscapes will bring you little but photographs and passport stamps. If your world view is broad and open, you can sit in your room, and the cosmos will spread out before you. You will see new landscapes in the convenience store across the street, or on the street itself. You will see invisible lines connecting incongruous objects. You will find analogies between things everywhere. And then, when you do travel, you find intercrossing lines among the new things you see, new experiences you have, connecting everywhere you go.

The great works of humankind all display deep insight that comes from the world view of the author. The great artists share their view through their work. If your view is from a figurative mountaintop, it certainly is broad, but it may also be lacking in details. If your view is from ground level, in the marketplace, for instance, your eye may not see far, but your soul may be deep, and details jump out at you in vivid shapes and colors. If creative work is not supported by the foundation of a world view with depth, you may at best be someone who makes interesting things.

World view encompasses the big topics. Time. Space. Good and evil. Your view of the world is inevitably tied to your view of what is unseen, beyond. How you understand life goes through your understanding of death. What is the meaning of suffering? The big topics influence all the subtopics of our lives: How should wealth be distributed? What is a fair justice system? Down to: What profession should I aspire to? How best to educate our children? Who shall I vote for? Should I become vegan? And then even the smaller topics: What book will I read next? What's for dinner?

This is all very obvious, but it is a reminder of how broadly our lives and our creativity are influenced by our world view. Oddly enough, many of us grow up without having one, or at least without having a personalized world view that has developed through reflection, not just a copy of what is socially or politically correct or in vogue. This may have something to do with the absence of wisdom, which we have discussed in Chapter Four. This is unfortunate, for those without personal world views have little choice but to follow what others tell them to believe in. Their creativity has little foundation to build on.

Accompanying your world view is your view of art. What do you consider the purpose of art? What do you consider the purpose of your art? The great art of history has been made for different purposes. Much of it is functional, like buildings or jewelry. Some of it is for the healing of a personal soul. Some of it is an expression of the mystery of life, or perhaps the incomprehension of the mystery.

I do not propose any standard answers to the questions posed above. But you must make an effort to answer them. Formulating one's world view is essential personal business that must be tended to, much more important than tending to personal finances. Without a mature worldview, there can be no mature creative work, and you won't even have good ideas to spend the finances you have accumulated. Your world view is the mothership of all your creative ideas and concepts. There is no cheating on it. How high your highest thoughts are, how radical your radicalism is, how compassionate your compassion is; they are all under your world view.

The Floating World

Many people with artistic sensibilities are reluctant to settle into a world view, preferring a "floating around" mentality, checking out this and that, studying different ideologies, moving in and out of different artistic styles, choosing not to commit when possible. This is rather common. Many creative people tend to be critical of those with set views. They instead like to keep things open, and indeed, openness is important. For some, it is more exciting to just fly, with nothing to tether oneself. Indeed, this seems enticing, but from my point of view, flying is not interesting unless it starts from the ground. Getting into all sorts of styles and ideologies without a grounded world view is like shooting confetti into the sky. If you are chasing kites, but you are a kite yourself, you will have a problem. Chasing kites from the air is not easy because everything is in motion and can become disorienting. If you are grounded, your viewpoint is set, and you can see how and where all the kites are flying.

Your world view is your ground, but it is also your height and your depth. It comes through years of reflection on your own experience and thoughts on the human condition. It is what you believe in. It defines the parameters of your creativity. Live conscientiously. Try to find the humanity in everything you see, no matter where your vantage point is. Try to always see the viewpoint of others, particularly those you do not agree with. These are what nurture depth in your world view, and it passes on into your work.

Cause-and-Effect View

What I call the "Cause-and-effect View" is developing the observation of how things become things. To be able to see cause-and-effect is to be able to see how nature and humans work, how things evolve, why people become the way they are, why relationships are formed and broken, everything. To understand the cause of anything is always more powerful than to study the effect. By understanding cause-and-effect, you know how to structure a story, you know how to depict a character, you know how to write a dialogue, you know what should happen first and what should happen next.

A few years ago, I was on a difficult trek in Bhutan to a remote place in the Himalayas called Singye Dzong. On the way, chatting with one of my fellow travelers from the United Kingdom, I learned that he was developing, with other teachers, a new education system that they hoped to implement in Bhutan. The whole educational philosophy was based on the simple idea that the students had to know where everything they used in class came from and where everything was going to. The blackboard, a fork or spoon for lunch, a plastic bag, whatever it was, they needed to know its origins and what would happen to it after it left their hands. Through this, they would learn how things were made and how they would impact the environment. Same with activities, like soccer. Where did this game come from? Who invented it? What kind of person was he? Where did the ball come from? What is it made of? Where did the field come from? And where was it going after it was used? The equation became more complex with emotions. If a student got angry, you would ask her to trace where the anger came from. If they laughed, trace where the laughter came from. Then, where does it go after you finish using it?

I thought this was brilliant in its simplicity, and a rather radical rethinking of what is most essential for children to learn. Indeed, to know cause-and-effect, or as it is sometimes called in an easily misunderstood word, "karma," is to know much indeed. If there was one principle to choose to build an education system on, to teach children about life and the world, and art, this might be it.

Causes do create effects. It's simple science. All effects become causes for future effects, and so on and so forth. To study cause-and-effect is to understand how things work in this world, from nature to human nature, to yourself, your family, loved ones, and friends, to your society, its economy, political system, culture, and so on. To stop the bully in the schoolyard, it may be more effective to understand how the bully came to be, and what are the effects of the bully's actions. This may lead to long-term solutions beyond simple confrontation.

Karma is often very understandable. A seedling drops from a tree. If given the right circumstances, it will proceed to grow into a tree. That's simple biology, but that's also karma. Atmospheric conditions may in a hundred years create a thunderstorm, and the lightning may strike the now very tall tree, splitting it in half. We are left to ponder the karma between the lightning and the tree, the answer to which could come from a scientist as well as from a soothsayer.

Nothing can happen without a cause. For the observable universe, this is how it is. Sometimes in life, things just don't make sense. But that doesn't mean that there is no cause-and-effect. It may be that we are not developed enough to see how it is all unfolding. For unobservable things like beginnings, different religions have different interpretations, as do scientists.

For those who believe in cause-and-effect, for it all to make sense, there can be no exception, so there must be a cause to any beginning.

To understand the interplay of cause-and-effect is to know how things work in life and in art. It is wisdom, and it is method. It can be applied to anything, any event, any personal relationship, a life, the life cycle of a company, a country, anything.

We can also decide that everything is random and there is no cause-and-effect. If that is in fact your belief, I would ask you to continue to observe and reflect. To not see cause-and-effect in a relationship, for instance, does not necessarily mean that there is no cause-and-effect. It may mean that the causes and effects are too complex for us to comprehend completely.

As a playwright, the simple fact is that you need to write a play that has logical causes and effects, without which you could not put a story together. To write a story that makes sense from beginning to end means that all the causes and effects are working in tandem. To write a character who is believable, and hopefully engaging, we need to know the causes that have shaped them, and what effects those causes will bring. Even if you are working with a deconstructed narrative, you still need the logic of cause-and-effect to put the fragments together.

The world is your playground for examining cause-and-effect. Not just physical events, but all human emotions as well. To see these forces at work is important for any creative artist, not just psychologists and detectives. Understanding cause and effect in life greatly enhances our understanding of people and increases our empathy toward things that people say or do in various situations. When Putin declared war on Ukraine, my immediate thoughts were not political. I wondered about the deeper personal causes that could have led him to that cold-blooded moment. Of course, I could never know. Maybe even he doesn't know. But my first thought was bordering on the absurd: Something must have happened to him, I mused, "His girlfriend dumped him." Or maybe he has cancer. Sorry if I may sound flippant in the face of the violent horrors of war and aggression, but absurd causes are the only logical ones I could find for anyone to do something so abominable.

A Kettle Boils

If you can see cause-and-effect in simple things like how a kettle of water boils, you can see complex things like the rise and fall of a monarchy or the success and failure of a business. If there were no cause-and-effect, there would be no reason to study history. Nothing would be connected to anything. The universe would be totally random. Gravity could fail us at any moment, and we all could fly into the sky.

As a sports fan, when I watch a game, I am not so enamored by the highlights, the slam dunks, the home runs, or the touchdowns. My playwright's instinct is to seek out the causes and effects that make the game turn and create victory or failure. Sometimes from my point of view, games are won and lost not on a buzzer-beating 3-pointer, but at simple, mundane moments, like a coach calling a timeout at the wrong time, or a player passing away an open shot, stunting momentum. This could be the single cause that leads to the effect of loss. Maybe I don't get as much enjoyment out of sports, watching the way I do, but I do seek the causes that turn the tides. They are often very undramatic or have already happened behind the scenes, a few days before. This at least proves that Chekhov was right: We don't fall in love every day or want to kill someone every day. Let the events on stage be like those in life. To really understand what's happening, don't always follow what is glittering the brightest. Often the most sensational events are the effect, not the cause. But stories are only compelling when the causes are compelling.

Mind Reading

As a playwright, I must be inside the minds of my characters. One way to get in is through studying the causes and effects influencing the character. This works in life as well. If you look, you can see it around you. Causes lead to hatred in one person toward another. Hatred leads to anger. Anger leads to violence, which leads to more violence. And so on and so forth.

Sometimes we see very obvious causes that should lead to disastrous effects, but those effects do not come. Does this prove the laws of cause-and-effect are invalid? The Chinese say, "It's not that there is no payback, it's that the time has not ripened." For most Asians, time is a longer concept than in the West, stretching past a single lifetime. Cause-and-effect is not justice in the legal sense, for it does not have any sense of right or wrong. It is simply physics, or the physics of emotions, or the physics of life.

Understanding cause-and-effect also links us back to nature. Models of cause-and-effect are around us everywhere: in the wilderness, in the sky, in the weather, which is perhaps the purest manifestation of cause-and-effect. Weather forecasting is simply saying out loud what the data shows you: the causes that will create the effects of the next weather system.

Not-So-Instant Karma

Start with anything. Let's go back to the coffee mug you are drinking from. Why is it in your hand? Because a friend of mine gave it to me. Why? Because I did something for her. Why do you know this person? We met at my cousin's wedding. You can go on, analyze how your cousin knew your friend through another friend, and how they became friends, and so on and so forth, until you might trace the coffee mug to your ancestors and how their migration trails led to living in the same city and so on. And this only explains how you came to know your friend, not why she chose this mug, where she bought it, and how it was designed and manufactured, probably in some town in China. From a humble coffee mug, we can connect with a complex web of interconnected lives and objects that goes far beyond your personal sphere.

Such is the power of being able to read cause-and-effect.

When teaching students directing, I always tell them, "Direct cause, not effect." This means if a stage direction in a script demands that an actor cry, don't tell the actor to cry, but explore the causes for the actor to experience sorrow. Then maybe she will cry, maybe not. Maybe she will react in a totally different way that is even more powerful. Sans tears. If the causes are read correctly, the effects will never be wrong, no matter if they differ from expectation.

Effect without Cause

I empathize with my friend Lin Ching-hsia, the superstar of the heyday of the Mandarin film industry starting in the late 1970s, who played the lead role in my film *The Peach Blossom Land* (1992). She told me she was often in such demand that she would be under contract for four different films at the same time, all shot simultaneously! In the same day, she would be chauffeured from one location to another, where her male lead might be the same guy as on the previous set. There would be little time to review the thin script. She would change clothes (similar), have her hair redone (slightly), then, as the camera rolled, she was asked to cry, throw temper tantrums, and look moody, with no clue why! She was a master at creating effect without cause. This period, when she vaulted to superstardom, certainly laid the future foundation for her captivating on-screen artistry.

In a play, as in a film or novel, it is the same. Know the causes behind your characters' actions, and you will know how to write your play. Without this knowledge, your work can easily ramble without a core, presenting effects without causes. To put it simply, it is not believable. Though effects may be flashy or interesting, they certainly cannot in themselves create compelling fiction or theater. It takes the interplay of cause-and-effect to really capture an audience's attention and hook them into a play or film.

Life, moment to moment, is the most amazing creation, each moment funneling out of the previous, in a never-ending display of creativity. Spend time observing this, just soaking in how incredible each moment is, having come from the previous moment. When you observe in this way, you may find that nothing is random. It all unfolds logically, the last moment to this, this moment to the next. The clouds roll in, then roll away. It looks so beautifully random, but every second can be explained by complex meteorological instruments. This is the greatest example of cause and effect, and the greatest teacher for our creativity.

As It Is

The third view we need to develop has been discussed in the previous chapter. It is the simplest, yet the most difficult. It is the ability to see things "as is," as they are.

Don't we? Actually, not usually.

The "As is View" is a view that sees the world without labels. We understand now how labels get in the way of creativity. The remedy is to learn how to de-label things. The "as is" view is your greatest tool for de-labelization, after which your mind is free to become a super receptor. When you are in the "as-is view" mode, you see objects and people in full, not partial view, without disguise or pretense. This is not easy to master. It is like being in a state of meditation while you are actually working. The results are best kept private, to be used in creative work.

Flowing

In recent decades, much has been much written about what is known as the "flow" state. Flow has been defined as an "optimal state of consciousness where we feel our best and perform our best."[2] When in the state of flow, one is highly

---

[2] Quoted in Steven Kotler, "Flow States and Creativity: Can you Train People to be more Creative?" www.psychologytoday.com/us/blog/the-playing-field/201402/flow-states-and-creativity

and intently focused, totally immersed in whatever one is doing, exceedingly productive and creative. There is a loss of awareness of time and self. The term "flow" was first coined by Mihaly Csikszentmihalyi, who pioneered positive psychology.[3] I am not qualified to say whether Csikszentmihalyi's flow state is the same as what I call the "as is" state, or the "non-attached" mode, but it seems related. If there are two parts to the equation, focus and letting go, I would say that the flow state puts more emphasis on focus, and the "as is" state puts equal emphasis on both.

Flow is also informally called "being in the zone," a special state where time does not seem to exist. Everything happens naturally and easily. As an artist, the flow state is a place I am familiar with and a place where you would want to be. When I am there, there is great focus, clarity, and energy. Everything is sharp and clear. There is no question of confidence in decision-making. You just work, and everything is right.

I recall writing Act 4 of my play *Ago* at the Musical Offering, my favorite Berkeley coffee shop in 2019, in one sitting. I certainly was in the flow state. The dialogue flowed from my fingers onto my laptop computer screen. As I typed a line of dialogue, I swear the next line appeared on the screen, waiting for me to fill it in. And so on and so forth. The lines kept coming faster than I could type. When I was finished, the on-screen prompt vanished, and I knew I was done. I had lost track of time. I found tears on my face. This may sound out of the ordinary, but for writers, artists, and scientists, I am sure many have experienced this state. When you are in the flow, you are actually in the flow of your project itself. Your project is flowing into existence, and you are flowing with it. Of course, this is the fast track to composition.

How to get there? As I said, there has been much written about this. For flow, it seems you need an inordinate amount of focus. For me, it is a simple state of meditation. To let go of thoughts, to just be in the moment. Maybe you think that to do this, you need a meditation mat, bells, and whatever props, which would seem out of place in a rehearsal room, a board meeting room, or a coffee shop. But it's nothing like that. With practice, you can just go there.

To be in the flow state is simply to flow, which infers that we usually are not flowing. We are impeded by so many things, mostly thoughts. To flow, you must let go of rational thought and surrender yourself to the moment of creativity, letting it take you into the flow of your project. But most of us have a stubborn

---

3 See Mihaly Csikszentmihalyi, *Flow: The Psychology of Optimal Experience* (New York: Harper Perennial Modern Classics, 2008).

defense system that protects our rational judgments and decision-making, so that it is highly difficult to disable our rational faculties and "surrender" to the flow.

The Tibetan word for "wisdom" is *yeshe*. It means "knowing right from the beginning," or a knowing that is pristine, primordial, untouched, "and has been there all the time. It is the way it always was."[4] Ringu Tulku Rinpoche says that "*yeshe* is the most natural state of our awareness or consciousness, which is unstained, uncontrived and completely ordinary. It is there all the time, but we don't recognize it."[5] This is the most profound definition of wisdom we have encountered so far. "Flow" or "as is," both are touching this state of knowing.

It might be helpful to know that there are many options for meditation training to gain the "as is" state. There is a devilishly simple exercise at the end of this chapter that you can start with. I urge you to find a qualified teacher for further practice.[6]

Your Personal Lie Detector

One day during my apprenticeship, I observed my mentor Shireen Strooker challenging an actor for not being truthful on stage. "You're lying to your audience," she told the actor. "That's a terrible thing to do on stage." The actor was flabbergasted at the accusation. "I'm being truthful to the character," he objected. "No. You are a liar." The actor then admitted it, and asked how Shireen could know that, actually, there was a psychological obstacle inside him that hindered him from getting at the truth of the character. Shireen said, "I have a built-in lie detector. Don't try to fool me. I will always catch you."

I studied her during the ensuing rehearsal. I saw that she was simply "seeing" with great concentration while letting go of her preconceptions. This is "as is" in action. It is a concentrated focusing on something or someone, while simultaneously letting go. It is a letting go of oneself in the moment of focused seeing.

That is how I understood it, and that is how I practiced doing it. It wasn't really that hard. I would focus on any random thing, for instance, a singer I saw on television. I would focus on her expression, then let go. Suddenly I was seeing that, though she looked like she was totally into the song she was singing, behind the costume and makeup, she was actually distracted, preoccupied, and therefore

---

4 "Wisdom," in *WikiRigpa*, www.rigpawiki.org/index.php?title=Wisdom
5 Ibid.
6 A wonderful book that is both advanced and also for beginners is Matthieu Ricard, *Why Meditate?*, trans. Sherab Chödzin Kohn (Hay House, 2010).

holding something back. Over time, I have gotten to trust this instinct, but since it is so subjective, I can never be too confident, and I never use it outside of my own work.

Let Go and Hold Everything

By letting go of ourselves in the moment, we create a space where subject and object are on equal ground. Without anything added, we can truly see the object for what it is. We can observe Beyonce without the concept "she's Beyonce" and all that label connects to, and see a person, very plainly, in all her qualities. You may wonder what use there is in this, because you may argue that the whole purpose of seeing Beyonce is seeing all of labels and packaging that have been built up so painstakingly around her. This is a way to cut through all of that, if you wish to.

Let go of what? If you are truly focused on something or someone, when you are really "seeing," you naturally discard yourself. You need to ask your self to stand aside for a moment so you can really see. This is very different from using our mind in its normal bossy way to arrive at opinionated decisions.

Practice looking at things, or at people, or at situations. Then just let go, try to forget yourself as you are looking. This is a highly concentrated form of gazing. It's not easy, for our minds are very control-oriented. It may also look very rude. When thoughts arise, as they inevitably will, examine them. Am I putting labels on the thing I am looking at? Am I enforcing *my* views on it, or am I really seeing it as it is?

Don't practice when you are driving or biking or operating any machinery!

We let go as a way of getting back in. In this way, we can see things with pure awareness. By letting go, we let go of extraneous things and connect with the essential. You could also say we reestablish connections that were already there, connections we have lost through the busy-ness of life, and the ultra busy-ness of our minds. This is a rather chilling statement. The world is as it is, but we are seldom there. Where we are is within a construct of labels and concepts which are not the actual things in themselves. What we see and feel is such a minuscule percentage of what is really happening around us. How can we aspire to creativity if we can't even see the world faithfully?

Q&A sans Q

I have had the great fortune to learn from and spend time with many great spiritual practitioners, and I know from personal experience that they can *see* so much more than I can. To share one small example, I recall a time when my first Tibetan teacher, Venerable Gyatrul Rinpoche (1925–2023), was staying in our Taipei house, where he was giving Buddhist teachings every evening for an extended period of time. Every morning, we would have breakfast together, and I would have the chance to ask him questions. Though I greatly cherished these breakfasts, I often found myself checking my watch to see if I still had time to chat. When time was up and I had to go to work, I would politely excuse myself, leave quietly, then rush to my car and speed away.

As time went on, Rinpoche started doing an amazing thing: at breakfast, he would start answering my questions without my asking them! At first, I was startled, but as the days went on, this became standard. I knew that he could absolutely *see* my mind, the questions I wanted to ask, and my anxiety about time. He decided not to waste time with questions but go straight to the answers. Quite cool. This wasn't even an issue that we discussed because it happened so naturally.

Over the years, I can say that I have developed a "lie detector" of my own, which I use with confidence when I work, and which my actors respect. To an extent, when I am teaching, I can see what question a student is going to ask beforehand. I can also see people's minds, to an extent, at times. This isn't some special clairvoyance or superpower, but an ability that all good playwrights, screenwriters, and novelists, as well as directors should have. How could I direct actors if I couldn't see their true emotions or thoughts while they were acting? It is a heightened way of seeing that anyone can develop, and many have, and has everything to do with the ability to see "as is."

By exploring the laws of cause-and-effect, we begin to understand how things work, both in the short term and on long-term basis. By seeing things as they are, we can also understand their original face. Experience and reflection bring us to a deeper understanding of the world, shaping our mature world view. We see life and death, day and night, the cycles of years and eras, and we understand these things on a personal level, on our own terms.

This is how the Three Views work together. With cultivation of and maturity in these views, you will definitely obtain new eyes, advanced eyes of wisdom to see the world, to see experience, to be creative.

Exercises and Further Thoughts

1. Examine your world view. How has it evolved? Take some time and discuss it with someone close to you.

2. See how, under your world view, you have developed many smaller views toward other things, and how all the little views trickle back to your big views.
3. Pick anything in your sight. Analyze the causes that brought it into your sight, and what the effects of those causes may do to bring it to its future.
4. Pick any person in your life. Do the same thing. Analyze the causes that brought this person into your life, and what the effects of those causes may do to bring him or her to their future.
5. Do the same for yourself. Examine the causes and effects that have brought you to where you are and will bring you to where you will be.
6. Think back to any moment you have been "spaced out." What was it like? Can you replicate that state of mind? Can you see that, though it seems blank, it is the blankness that gives it potential to be filled?
7. Meditation exercise for Flow and As Is: Sit comfortably and be at ease. Then, think of nothing. Do nothing. Can you keep this state for one minute? Observe your mind when you are trying to do nothing with it. This is perhaps the most direct exercise to experience the gap and gain the flow state, but it is also the most difficult.

CHAPTER TWELVE

MOTIVATION RE-EXAMINED

Is Creativity a Chronic Illness?

We have approached this elusive thing called wisdom through asking the fundamental question "why" we do what we do, and recalibrating how we see the world, toward the goal of understanding who we truly are, and how we see life from where we stand. Without such questioning and restructuring, we are at a decided disadvantage, in life as well as creativity. By beginning our inquiry, we run into difficult questions.

Why is it such a big deal to express? Granted, the genuine artist understands the sanctity of the process of creating. Somehow, if his project can reach fruition, it is assumed that this final product will be of benefit. For whom? The audience or the artist? Could it all be one big ego trip? Is one more noble, or more unique, if one has the urgent desire to express? In fact, could it be possible that one is nobler *without* such desire? Using these criteria, how would, say, Kanye West match up versus Emily Dickinson?

Toward the egoistic pole in the spectrum of motivation, we have found those who use art and creativity for material gain. Using motivation as criteria for categorizing, you might want to call them businessmen and not artists. There are also those who use creativity as a means toward self-revelation, exorcism, or therapy, and you could call them patients. Though this may sound normal, an artist seeking himself in art is like an athlete seeking herself in sports, or an entrepreneur seeking the meaning of his life through his enterprise. This sounds reasonable. We see it all around us—to find the meaning of one's life through one's work. But wouldn't it make more sense to seek the meaning of life through life?

In this flawed quest, we might identify a certain confusion of modern humanity.

A few of us really believe that we can change the world through our works. Some of us believe that we can transform ourselves through the work. But for too many of us, it is something that we just do because we need to, and this doing pleases us. Creativity can become a habit, a way of life, and very appealing at that. For many artists, creativity gives them a sense of purpose, a reason to get up and work.

I admit my own desire to express, the desire to create, and the satisfaction that comes from doing so. In my earlier career, I was not bothered by this. In fact, I felt empowered. But in more probing moments, I would ask myself whether this desire was healthy or not. Many things we do in life make us feel good. But is that sufficient justification for the deed, and are there side effects? My work as a playwright-director is seen in public, and for that I feel obligated to check my motivation as often as I can, as well as, it goes without saying, the quality of my work. People invest time and money to see my works. What am I giving them in return?

I have been blessed with a long career where audiences are generally receptive to my work. This brings forth an even more urgent need for introspection on several levels. When in demand, most directors rush from one project to the next, their lives full with their work, and this seems an ideal situation for an artist. But I ask myself: Is my continued success a drug that keeps me moving on to the next project, the next high? Why are new ideas always brewing in my brain? Is this genius, or illness? Can the need to create be a disease?

People ask me what makes a good actor. I tell them, to start, you need the basic urge to be looked at by others. I don't have that, so I have never aspired to be an actor. But I admit I have the urge to be looked at from a different angle, as a writer and director. Not only do we want to be seen, our words to be heard, we desire that our words be influential. Isn't this at least a type of arrogance, a belief that your thoughts and feelings can have relevance for others? And to have this desire day after day, year after year, isn't this chronic arrogance? Does this arrogance propel the making of great art?

If sickness is too strong a word, I am willing to call it an imbalance. The creative desire is a kind of imbalance in me. It leads to many types of obsessive behavior and ultimately to creative works. If I cannot stop, if creativity is some sort of sickness that is continually prodding me to work, is there any way I can let it be used in a beneficial way, not just for myself, but more importantly, for my audiences? Here is the crux of the debate. Here is where I must question my motivation every time I start a project and at every moment I am working on it. Is it a gift to an audience, or am I throwing out my garbage at them? Or worse, am I unaware that the most important function of my work is to satisfy my hungry ego?

These are painful but necessary questions.

Awards Rehearsal

A student of mine was acting in a film. She told me that the director had asked her to take drugs to better understand her role as a drug addict. "So," I said, "if your character murders someone in the film, that means you have to go out and make a few killings, right?" I told her she should tell this incompetent and selfish director to shove it.

My student revealed to me that this director spent his time between shots on set refining some mysterious document. It turns out he was drafting his thank-you speech for future awards ceremonies. What? So the motivation for the director to make this film was to win the Palme d'Or at Cannes? OK. So what do we read from this? If that is his main motivation, he may luck out and make a great film, but I doubt it. He didn't. The lesson remains the same: motivation is what you sow, which is in direct relationship to what you reap. If you desire an Oscar, then what you reap is either an Oscar or no Oscar. If you desire to make an art film, but it turns out to be a commercial hit, you may be considered a success in the film industry, but personally, you feel failure. On the other hand, if your goal for making a certain film is to gross 200 million and you do, you consider this film a success, no matter how terrible the reviews are.

In the back of all directors' minds is the Palme d'Or or Oscar or Golden Bear, but grounded directors know that this is some insignificant concern that they keep way in the back of their minds. If it comes to the forefront, they are in trouble, because the desire for winning a prize is not something you want to be occupying brain space when you are in the complex process of making a film.

Wisdom without Method

With great method but little wisdom, we can create works that may be dazzling to behold, but carry little deeper interest. What about works with little method, but lots of wisdom? Are there works that rely on wisdom alone? Konchog Lhadrepa, a master of Tibetan painting, said:

> If one is very skillful, and draws a very beautiful Buddha without any respect or altruistic attitude, someone with just a good hand, even if the product is aesthetic, there is not much benefit from it. On the other hand if someone is filled with Bodhicitta [compassion], even if he is not so skillful, the product is worthy of putting on an altar. This doesn't mean we can draw a strange

looking Buddha. We must respect the canonical proportions of the Buddha. But we don't need to be an astonishing artist. Even without proportions, with full faith, we can produce something valuable [...] our state of mind and attitude is what makes the difference.[1]

In Konchog's mind, for sacred art, passion trumps skill. Here, the passion is compassion, the altruistic wish to benefit all beings. Though we would not be so presumptuous as to think that we are creating "sacred" art in our mundane world, with compassion as motivation, even a work with lesser skills would be worth more.

In contemporary arts, there are many works that cannot be judged on the merits of technique because there is little technique involved in the work. In such works, motivation becomes almost the only criterion to judge with. The seminal example I think of is Marcel Duchamp's *Bicycle Wheel*, which is what it says it is, a bicycle wheel. Not a painting or sculpture of a bicycle wheel, but a bicycle wheel. As to its motivation, the artist said, "I had the happy idea to fasten a bicycle wheel to a kitchen stool and watch it turn."[2] This may explain his urge at the time to simply combine A+B but does not explain his motivation to later champion so-called ready-made objects, which art historians affirm is the purpose of the piece. If you thought that the value of art is in technique, Duchamp forces you to think again.

Similar works abound. Pietro Manzoni's *Merda d'artista* is just that: canned shit of the artist, which has been exhibited at prominent museums and in recent years, sold for €275,000 a can at Sotheby's. I do not believe that this artist was so narcissistic as to expect us to marvel at the texture or smell of his excrement. His motivation obviously was to shift our conceptual habits, how we see, excrement as well as canned food. In these examples, the motivation for making the work becomes the most prominent feature of the work itself.

Relax!

Though we have spent a lot of time emphasizing motivation, I admit that it should be a burden to be always thinking about it. On re-examination, we can, and

---

[1] Konchog Lhadrepa, lecture on "Sacred Art," Shechen Institute, Bodh Gaya, India, December 10, 2003, translated from the Tibetan by Matthieu Ricard, transcribed by Stan Lai.
[2] Quoted in Alexander Wolf, "Duchamp's Bicycle Wheel," *Gagosian*, gagosian.com/quarterly/2014/08/15/duchamps-bicycle-wheel-timeline/.

sometimes should, be totally free of it and just be creative. Doesn't that sound good? Examining motivation is a wonderful tool if you encounter problems during the process or want to make a deeper evaluation of a finished work. During the actual creative process, you might not want or need to bear down too hard on yourself. Without thinking about all these things, we can work freely and purely.

There is a time for everything. Introspection does not mix well with actual creative work. You can't be analyzing while you are making. For a dancer, if you think while dancing, you fall. Creativity must be fun. There must be an aspect of play in your work. Some of the greatest works in history have this joyful, playful purity, which could easily be hampered by constant self-reflection. That is not what I want you to do. I do want you to have the tool of motive examination at your disposal, because it is one of the sharpest and most powerful tools you can hold, but not while you are in the actual dance of creativity.

It is so important, and not at all easy to learn, to inspect your motivation for doing any creative work. It is also essential to understand that this inspection should not intrude into every moment of the actual creative work.

Exercises and Further Thoughts

1. Would you consider creativity an illness? Is obsession with anything an illness? Does one need to be obsessed with creativity in order to be good at it?
2. Have you seen works brimming with sincerity and purity of expression but lacking craft? What is your assessment of such work?
3. Have you seen art made with ready-made objects? Do you consider it art?

PART FIVE
The Source

If you don't realize the source
You stumble in confusion and sorrow.[1]

—*Lao Tzu*

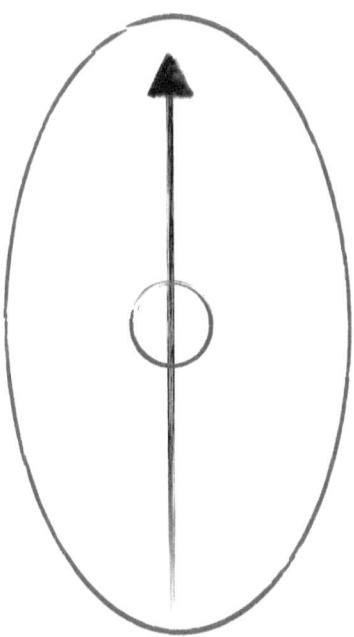

---

1 Lao Tzu, *Tao Te Ching*, a new English version by Stephen Mitchell (New York: Harper Perennial, 1988), Chapter 16.

CHAPTER THIRTEEN

THE TAO IS A WELL

Connecting the Personal to the Collective

So far, we have explored creativity through the interplay of Wisdom and Method. Another way of approaching it is through the Source and Barrier.

At the bottom of the Creative Map is the Barrier, under which is the Source. This is the source of primordial creative energy. It is where you connect with the primal energy of life, which is connected to everything. It is a collective life force that is super-fluid and thus brimming with connectivity and creative possibilities. You can consider it like nature in all of its creative forms. One of Laozi's explanations of the unexplainable "Tao" is:

The Tao is like a well:
Used but never used up.
It is like an eternal void:
Filled with infinite possibilities.[1]

This definition of Lao Tzu's Tao works for our source: a well that holds limitless things, and is itself limitless. It is primordial space. Inside this space, there is no duality, just a simple oneness. There is no you or me, past or future, this or that. It is a primordial oneness that we can all experience if we can breach the barrier. It is a power both beyond and within us. Our relationship to this source varies depending on how thick and solid our barrier is. For creativity, the thinner and more porous the better.

Sadly, few of us are fully connected to this source. Just like the boy whose mother negated the dog he saw in the sky, strong barriers have been erected in our

---

1 Ibid., Chapter 4.

minds to ward off the source. You can think of this source as everything outside the box we are asked to think outside of, and the barrier is the box that we have erected. To take down the barrier is to take down the walls of the box, which were artificial to start with, created by our individual and collective minds. Without the box, creativity permeates your life, with no need to think, and no need for a box to think inside or outside of. Your personal creativity is connected to a vast, greater collective creativity, and simply flows.

This is one entry portal. Another is simply through our sense of mystery. As Einstein said,

> The most beautiful thing we can experience is the mysterious. It is the source of all true art and science [...]. To know what is impenetrable to us really exists, manifesting itself as the highest wisdom and the most radiant beauty, which our dull faculties can comprehend only in their most primitive forms—this knowledge, this feeling is at the center of true religiousness.[2]

Mystery connects us to possibilities. The etymology of the word "religion" is the Latin *religere*, which literally means "to connect." The Source as I frame it thus may be the source of your own personal religion or cosmology, understanding that the true meaning of religiousness is to connect to something greater than ourselves, to connect to all beings and everything. In fact, to be connected to the Source is to be connected to your innermost being. Internal and external merge in this wonderful place. To be cordoned off from it, you are deprived of natural creativity.

The Source is Chaos

Another way to understand this source is to see it as chaos. Though it retains all things, the source cannot possibly keep and present everything to us in an orderly fashion. Everything is floating around at different velocities in this all-encompassing source. To consider it chaos is necessary and helpful to how we work with it.

Though, by nature and definition, chaos is disorder and confusion, within it arises infinite possibilities. Anaïs Nin noted, "In chaos, there is fertility."[3] The composer Stephen Sondheim said, "Art, in itself, is an attempt to bring order

---

[2] Albert Einstein, *Living Philosophies*, quoted in *Goodreads*, www.goodreads.com/quotes/tag/curiosity
[3] Anaïs Nin, quoted in *Goodreads*, www.goodreads.com/quotes/tag/chaos?page=1

out of chaos."⁴ This is key. When navigating the chaotic waters of the Source, we are able to perceive that order is something that can be constructed through the chaos. In fact, order and disorder are not so different, but two sides of the same coin, like a photograph and its negative image. As Jung said, "In all chaos there is a cosmos, in all disorder a secret order."⁵ Our first task is to be able to access the source, the chaos, after which we must become adept at navigating the waters, to find the order within the disorder. Then we attain the ability to extract the elements that are freely flowing within, to be able to see the secret order of things, like John Cage in Taipei traffic (Chapter Ten).

To be able to view and get into a painting by Jackson Pollock, for instance, whom we will speak more of in Chapter Twenty, is to be able to directly experience what Jung is talking about. We can even consider that Pollock is painting the source as he experiences it, or chaos, which may be the same thing. But in this chaos is a cosmos wherein lies its own sense of order. What I call the Source may or may not be the same as Jung's concept of the Collective Unconscious, or the Eighth Consciousness in Buddhist Psychology, which we did not get into when dealing with the sixth and seventh consciousnesses in Chapter Ten.⁶ I will leave it at that, understanding that there is an intersection of all these concepts, in a place where language has little explanatory use.

What is Blocking Us?

Training in creativity can be understood not so much as training to accumulate creativity but training to clear the obstacles that are in the way of what has always been there. Thus, we do not attain creativity in so much as we enable our primal creativity.

The Source contains our primal creativity. The barrier in the map is the fuzzy line at the bottom. Depending on its thickness and solidity according to the individual. It is like a prison wall that holds the source outside. The problem is, the prison is inside. The barrier has imprisoned us in our own minds.

---

4 Stephen Sondheim, in *Brainy Quote*, www.brainyquote.com/quotes/stephen_sondheim_331419?src=t_chaos
5 C.G. Jung, *Collected Works*, Vol. 9, Part I, "The Archetypes of the Collective Unconscious," Ed. and translated by Gerhard Adler and R.F.C. Hull, Princeton University Press, 1954, p. 66.
6 *Wikipedia* provides a solid start to researching this broad topic: https://en.wikipedia.org/wiki/Eight_Consciousnesses

For those who have a very solid barrier, everything in life is rigid. Rules and regulations are important and must be followed. For lawyers or accountants, the barrier may actually be helpful as a restraining element. For artists and designers, a fine balance must be struck. To breach the barrier can be inspiration for some, trouble for others. Once the source is accessed, one's mind becomes naturally open to different possibilities that were closed when the barrier was solid. If the barrier is totally broken down, like the Berlin Wall when it fell in 1989, East and West become one. Everything is free to flow everywhere, including chaos.

I continually emphasize how creativity needs space to function, something the barrier tries to keep out. All the practices of de-labeling and learning how to see things as they are build space in our minds, providing the space for ideas to connect to other ideas, subject matter to other subject matter. Releasing the energy of the source is like filling this space with limitless fresh new space. We become more open, more—spacious. In mind, in action, in creativity.

The barrier runs through the bottom of both sides of the map, so it also needs to be breached by method as well as wisdom. If you possess top-level technique within the confines of the barrier, you can only go so far. Once the barrier is down, method can become magic. The source presents limitless space for you to utilize your skill sets.

Breaching the Barrier

How to breach the barrier? The first thing is to realize its existence and examine how it came to be. Barriers are usually erected for safety measures. Boundaries are necessary for social order. Some societies have higher and thicker barriers to control individual behavior or thoughts. Our inner barrier serves the same function. It is there and has grown since childhood to rein us in for safety purposes, but inadvertently it has reined in much, much more.

This barrier cannot be broken down through violent means. It can only be slowly eroded through self-reflection and contemplation. The gap, referred to in Chapter Ten, is perhaps the most viable inroad into the source. By being in that gap, the walls of the barrier start to erode. The openness afforded by the gap connects directly with the primal energy of the source, and you have already accessed it while building a stronger and stronger connection to it.

The habitual view of the world is that of duality—ourselves in opposition to the external world. Without training of the mind, we are stuck in this duality mode, the only mode we understand. The gap affords us with a temporary respite from duality. There is no duality in the source. It is a place of oneness. There is no me, no ego. There is just being. The gap creates space in our minds and erodes the barrier. Once the barrier is broken down, space is everywhere.

To break down the barrier and let the source immerse the whole map is the most creative mode we can be in. The quickest way to break down the barrier is to see the world without duality, without subject and object, with just being. If we learn how to de-label our perception, we have already begun to breach the barrier. If we train our minds to be empty of thought, we can access this source at any time.

The Clutter

A sudden leap to non-duality is difficult indeed. It is such a radical shift from what we are habitually accustomed to. A more gradual way to approach the source is to see how cluttered our brains are. There is just no space in our minds to be creative because at any given moment, our minds are so full of so many random or structured thoughts, sensations, and emotions. The world is a much noisier place than it used to be. Distractions are everywhere, filling the mind with random materials that clutter up the space that normally can be available for creative connections. We need to free up the space in our minds to maximize our creativity.

The source is there, and it always will be. It's just covered up by all the clutter. Put your mobile phone aside. Quiet your mind and all the clutter will quiet down. The source will appear. It is naturally there, but it is as if we have wrapped it up in layers of thoughts.

Our thoughts are the barrier.

How to slowly unwrap everything actually goes opposite to the way our brain normally operates. We tend to think in order to unravel questions. Here, we need to un-think, to not think, for questions to answer themselves.

As you succeed in making breaches, the source enters your mind freely and expands the space of your mind. Where once the mind was small and cluttered, so crowded that it was almost solid, breaches in the barrier bring in space, like fresh air coming through cracks in a closed attic, breaking down the clusters of clutter, freeing them to float around in a more spacious mind. The more you access the source, the more space you command. Eventually, the barrier is broken down and the rich source of creativity expands out into all reaches of the map, left and right, up and down. The source then is not some special thing you have to tap into but available to you at all times.

Consider yourself a receptor, and you may take whatever you need from the source. Consider yourself a vessel, and the source may fill you to the brim with its energy.

Upgrading Experience

Experience is the basis for all the material you create with. But if the source is blocked by the barrier, your experience is informed by mundane life only, and its interpretation is reliant on the wisdom of mundane life. You are working within the self-contained logic of the mundane world, where everyone is trying to get ahead based on limited resources. In the following figure, the barrier is depicted as surrounding us on all sides, with the source outside, beyond. How can we see outside this circle? How can we bust through the circle? If there is no infusion from the source, where are we as a collective humanity going? It is as if we exist in

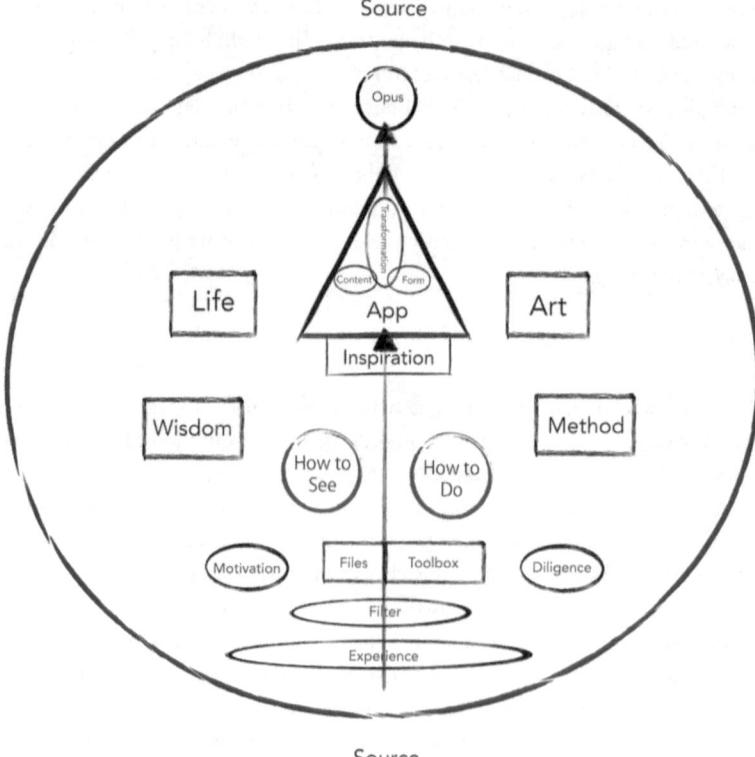

FIGURE 13.1 The Source with barrier surrounding.

a barren environment where information keeps piling up and getting transferred but cannot grow in meaningful creative ways.

Look at the arrow that goes from the Source at the bottom up to the creative product. If your source is compromised, then the arrow always starts from within the circle (see Figure 13.1).

If your barrier is removed, look what happens (see Figure 13.2). The source is open, permeating everything. You are now connected to something beyond, something greater, including chaos, which flows freely throughout your existence. This should not be considered a disadvantage at all. To be creative you need to have the courage to allow chaos to flow, and you should see chaos for what it is, without the label of positive or negative. It is complete disorder, through which order can arise. The "force" is now with you, and you have the resources to make amazing and transformative things:

With the barrier gone, everything becomes fluid. Much more *knowing* (not knowledge) is flowing in the chart. This is certainly a game changer. Not only are you connected, but you also have the ability to connect the viewer, through your journey, back to the source. Maybe we shouldn't say "back," but "forward," or, perhaps more accurately, "through" to the source.

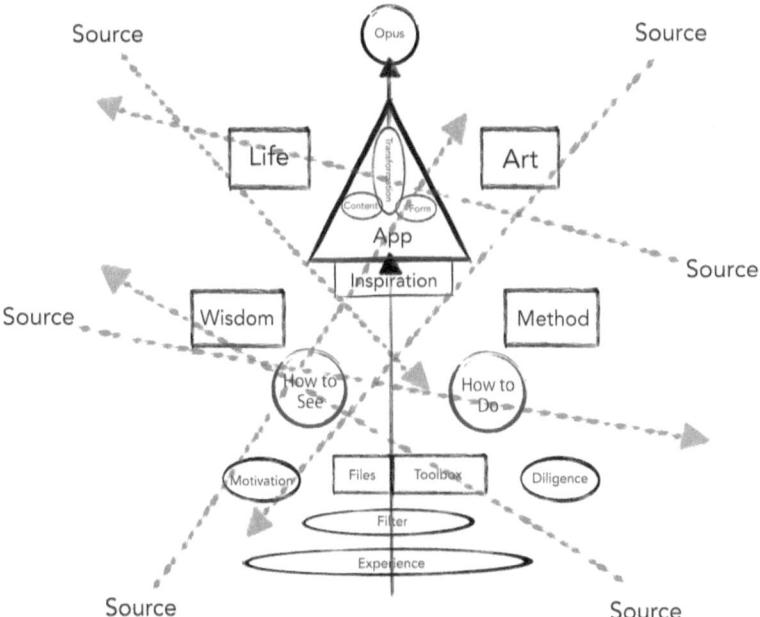

FIGURE 13.2 The Source with the barrier removed.

Without the barrier, the source permeates our life and art. It is a lubricant, an informant. It connects our views, our contradictions, our queries. The barrier has been built up through concepts and habits that have been with us for centuries. The barrier is what defines what is good or bad, right or wrong. Once it is down, these concepts are all softened and broken down into open-mindedness. When the barrier falls, where once was a dark wall now flows brilliance, bringing forth an illuminated understanding of life, a more tolerant existence, and a more compassionate way of being.

Once we gain access to the source, our creative works gain a greater openness, a vastness that comes with being in touch with the source, which connects everything. We live a grander existence and see things in a grander light, which actually is a humbler light. We recognize our smallness, which makes us big. We recognize our insignificance, which bestows extraordinary weight on us. We are poised, through our creative journey, to lead our viewers to break down their own barriers and access the source.

Exercises and Further Thoughts

1. Examine your inner barrier. Where are its limits? What does it protect? Is it worth it to consider bringing it down?
2. Have you ever experienced "oneness" as opposed to duality? Was this inspired through daydreaming, or substances, or nature, or meditation?
3. Have you ever experienced the Source as described in this chapter? If so, recollect what the experience was like. Do you think this is some place that you chance upon, or is it possible to access it on demand? What name would you give it?

PART SIX
Creative Method

"*To find a form that accommodates the mess, that is the task of the artist now.*"*
—Samuel Beckett

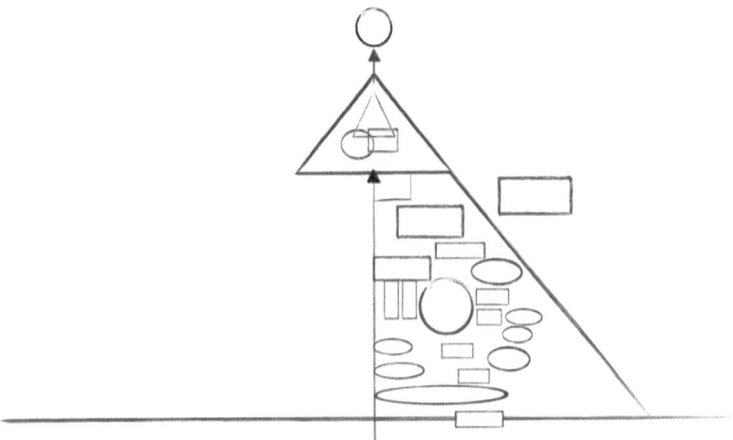

---

* *Samuel Beckett, quoted by Tom F. Driver in "Beckett by the Madeleine," Columbia University Forum 4 (Summer 1961), 23.*

CHAPTER FOURTEEN

DOING

The Wisdom of Method

Method is what people usually consider the normal thing to learn in art and creativity—How to do it. We now understand that it is only half of the equation, how to execute our creativity once the inspiration comes, how to find the form for our content. This is the domain of the right side of the Creative Map that includes all the things we normally learn in art school, or in business school, or as a woodworking or costume shop apprentice—the technique and craft of the field. It also includes knowledge of structure, and the crucial ability to organize and put content together into a viable form.

To do, we must first be. Without wisdom, method is just techniques and skills. If your wisdom is solid, method becomes the trustworthy maker of what emanates from that wisdom, the doer that manifests what wisdom has conceptualized. The creative idea that comes in a flash needs to be given a body. Most ideas appear too quickly or are too abstract to identify in the moment what method can be used to physicalize it. In rare cases, method comes with the flash, all-in-one. This is fortunate. Mozart, one of the most creative persons of all time, explained this "all-in-one" composing process:

> When I proceed to write down my ideas, I take out of the bag of my memory, if I may use that phrase, what has been previously collected into it in the way I have mentioned. For this reason the committing to paper is done quickly enough, for everything is as I said before already finished and rarely differs on paper from what it was in my imagination.[1]

---

1 Wolfgang Amadeus Mozart, quoted by Craig Duke in *VI Control: Musicians Helping Musicians*, vi-control.net/community/threads/mozart-easy-as-that.3264/

Mitsuko Uchida, one of his foremost interpreters, said: "In Mozart it seems as if there was no premeditation."[2] Inspiration and execution, content and form, wisdom and method all seemed to happen simultaneously. For genius-level artists like Mozart, composing all happens and is finished in the mind. The actual doing is the writing down of the music, not unlike the function of a printer attached to a computer. It was the same for Michael Jackson, who envisioned whole songs in his mind before entering the studio to record them, as noted by production team member Chris Senger:

> One of the most notable aspects of Michael's recording process was his ability to hear the final product in his head before even stepping into the studio. He had an uncanny sense for the complete arrangement of a song, from the melody to the instrumentation and even the smallest sound effects. This vision guided every recording session, ensuring that the final track matched the masterpiece he envisioned.[3]

Unfortunately, we are not all Mozarts or Michael Jacksons, and we live in times when forms are no longer prescribed by tradition. Figuring out a method is an excruciating process that absorbs most of our creative time. For the beginner, method is absolute madness. It is a chaotic scramble to put things together, not knowing what should go where. Gradually, over time, with practice, you will acquire the wisdom of method.

You cannot cut corners with either wisdom or method, but to understand that they must work together is the greatest shortcut.

What Works?

Learning how to do is learning how to put your creative project together in a way that works. What works? I recall my personal master class that motivated me to learn what works and what doesn't in the theater. When a creative work works, it can become a true thing of beauty, as well as a transformative experience. Beauty

---

2 Mitsuko Uchida, quoted in Fiona Maddocks, "Mitsuko Uchida: 'You Have to Risk Your Life on Stage,'" *The Guardian, August* 12, 2018. www.theguardian.com/music/2018/dec/04/mitsuko-uchida-pianist-schubert-mozart-70th-birthday-interview

3 Chris Senger, "Chris Senger's Post," Facebook, November 15, 2024, https://www.facebook.com/story.php?story_fbid=484478041273471&id=100091338585007

is not just experienced in outer appearances, but in how everything fits together to create that final form. When everything is working together, a creative work becomes a living organism that functions perfectly by the design and execution of the maker, weaving a spell that draws and keeps the viewer locked in for as long as designed. When a creative work doesn't work, it is like a poorly designed house that simply falls apart. As viewers, we are left outside, not being drawn in, because the artist is not able to create a spell.

In some disciplines, what works or doesn't is all part of tradition. How to make a stained-glass window, how to design a Japanese Zen rock garden, how to put together Miao folded-cloth piecework. For most of these things, you learn the traditional way, and then just keep doing it until you attain mastery. Somewhere along the way, you may make innovations to tradition, but that is not your goal. Your goal is to learn to do it right, the way those who perfected the craft did it.

For other fields, there is much more leeway in defining "what works," though there are standards that can serve as templates. In popular songwriting, the solid traditions of the Great American Songbook and the Beatles era are there to learn from. A song as short and simple as Gershwin's "But Not for Me" is like a swatch that has distilled the essence of the popular song, and can be used to pattern any number of songs. But where once they were models to look up to, now they are only references for our changing times. Many fields today have severed themselves from tradition, from the "right way" of doing things. My own field, theater, is now like this, and anything goes as long as you can make it work.

Playing Without Rules

If there are no longer any rules, that doesn't mean you can work without rules. Things will not work unless you have some principle behind them to give them cause to work. You have to make your own rules, and your audience must accept these rules. What worked well in other eras may be great starting points, clues to what works in any era, because though times change, the human heart faces the same existential questions, responds in similar fashion to the same primary emotions, and recognizes the same elemental shapes and structures.

In history, there have been artists who seemingly jump out of nowhere, unattached to any tradition, like the illiterate Taiwanese painter Hung Tung, who lived in a small fishing village in southern Taiwan and didn't start painting until he was 50, after which he forged a uniquely personal aesthetic. He didn't study the old masters, East or West; he just did what he wanted. This is a rare instance of individual genius succeeding in creating his own genre. It goes against the conventional wisdom of studying everything that has been done before us, as much as we can, so that we have a well-stocked toolbox that can be applied to any situation. If you can succeed in creating your own path without referencing anything done before, more power to you. It's just not very likely to be done. You would have to be living on a desert island or in a mountain cave to be able to escape all of the influences that bombard us.

Take the example of my own discipline, theater. If I'm directing a play by Brecht, for instance, I could just do it any way I want to, without referring to any past productions, just going by my feeling of the text. But I think the sounder way to go about it, which in my estimation actually yields more creative possibilities, is to research everything about the historical context, as well as the production history of what other directors have done before. Because I am confident in my own individual artistic style, I do not worry about being influenced by such references. Doing research lets me gain deep insight into the work itself. Then I feel prepared to go in whatever direction I want to.

You may think that knowing too much takes the mystery and spontaneity out of your work, but spontaneity can only happen meaningfully if you are working on solid ground. Without ground, you cannot run or jump. You can try to fly, but there will be no ground to land on. If you go to work knowing as little as possible, you might make something brilliant, but more often you probably will stumble. I cannot imagine any director taking on Brecht without knowing Marxist theory and German politics of the 1930s. If you understand all the parameters, there is so much brilliance to be explored freely within.

When other directors direct my plays, I sometimes feel they are put into a difficult predicament. These works, from a living author, have been known to work, very successfully, under my own direction. There is a director's code embedded in each piece. If you have solved and follow the code, you are guaranteed to succeed. But today's director does not easily submit to what is proven to work. She needs to make her own mark on the work, which is totally understandable. This is a dilemma not easily resolved. Is your motivation to render an authentic version of a Stan Lai play, or to take it in a different direction and make it more yours than mine? We can see that this is not a question of method, but more of motivation.

A Russian *Three Sisters*[4] at the Wuzhen Festival used rock and roll extensively in a deconstructed text that lasted four and a half hours. To those who did not know Chekhov, and that was most of the Chinese audience, nothing much made

---

4 Antov Chekhov, *The Three Sisters*, production by St. Petersburg Lensoviet Academic Theatre, directed by Yury Butusov, Wuzhen Grand Theatre, October 25-27, 2019.

sense, though. But to those who know the play as the Russians do, it was a brilliant interpretation that took the original far away to a place where much more might be revealed to a contemporary audience.

In my version of Chekhov's *The Seagull* (1990, 2014),[5] I made it my task from the beginning to let the Chinese-speaking audience, the great majority of whom had never seen a Chekhov play (I would venture to say at least 99%) truly experience the play the way Chekhov wanted them to. This in itself is problematic and assumes that I know what Chekhov wanted. In my own translation, I made a point to change absolutely nothing, *except* the location and time. I set the play in 1930s China, in an estate in the south (in which case I had to change all the names and the place names). Everything fit. The prima donna actress, her avant-garde writer son, her popular fiction writer boyfriend, and the aspiring young actress, and resonated more, I believe, because the audience was able to easily follow the characters and story and not have to worry about cultural nuances, not to mention the excruciatingly long Russian names that had now become simple Chinese names. This way I could concentrate on presenting the highly difficult Chekhovian aesthetic, where the story resembles life more than story, and climaxes come at odd places.

What works? If your audience knows Shakespeare, you can put *Hamlet* on Wall Street. Otherwise, you might have to check your motivation for why you want to create something that your audience will *not* understand.

How Your Work Works

A novel has to work. An invention has to work. An ad campaign for a political candidate has to work. We need to find what Beckett referred to as "a form that accommodates the mess."[6] The way creative things work is the same way that anything works. They must be constructed well, with proper method, so they are sturdy and don't fall apart, and they must combust in time correctly. They must have a certain rhyme and rhythm that the viewer relates to. Understanding how things work comes from careful observation of natural physical occurrences like rain, or autumn, or made things like coffee, or interior décor, or governments, or things of the soul, like love, or relationships.

---

5 Anton Chekhov, *The Seagull*, translated and directed by Stan Lai, premiere November 1990, National Arts Hall, Taipei, Taiwan, translation published in *Drama Quarterly*, Beijing, Aug 2016.
6 Beckett quoted by Driver in *Columbia University Forum*, 23.

Observe the most ordinary thing, like making a cup of tea. In the West, the dilemma is whether to dunk the teabag into hot water or pour hot water onto the teabag. Furthermore, how hot does your water need to be? These may seem unimportant, but they all contribute to your understanding of how a cup of tea works. The simplest of structures, a table, has to work by merely standing up. A house is a large table with walls. It not only has to stand, but its roof also cannot leak, and its walls and windows cannot let in wind. Your project cannot fall apart or leak while people are looking at it. A house is a system in itself, with invisible pipes and insulation and other components that all need to function together to work, just as your creative piece is also a system of parts, seen and unseen, that work together. If you understand how things are built, and built to work, then you have the dormant ability to build something like it.

Working with Time

Time is our canvas if we work in any of the temporal arts. How things work extends into time. To gain an understanding of how time works, we observe sophisticated phenomena, like time itself, or its manifestation, like winter, and watch how it morphs into spring. Careful observation can bring us new insight into these seemingly common things. Then, of course, we must observe works of art themselves. See how any Bach fugue from *The Well-tempered Clavier* works. This is complicated enough. Then see how the fugue works in tandem with its accompanying Prelude. What you thought was a whole now is half of a whole. Then see how the prelude and fugue work within the macro-structure of the grand design itself. We can study or simply feel how each individual piece expands in time and brings out our emotions through this expansion. Then we can see how this one unit is connected to others, to create small scale ebbs and flows that lead to larger movements, and finally to the grand architecture of the unified whole.

The more you observe, the more you will find that the problems facing the artist are similar throughout time. It is all a question of how to make the work work in accordance with how it is envisioned to work. See how Kubrick's *2001: A Space Odyssey* starts with a certain visual motif, then rises and falls in action, ultra-slowly, to its amazing climax where the motif reoccurs, and observe how the viewer's emotions are taken along for the ride.

How does *Hamlet* work? Not really the way a Hollywood film works. That's why adapting Shakespeare into film is not an easy task. I recall studying Shakespeare as a student, kind of in a haze, because though the language was so transcendently beautiful, I didn't quite get what he was doing or how he was doing it. Later, I realized I was using the wrong set of eyes to look at the phenomenon called Shakespeare. A Shakespearean play does have an arc that carries the action and emotions along, like a normal Hollywood film, but there is a deeper element at play that moves the action in a fundamentally different way. Shakespeare used parallel lines to structure many of his plays. In *A Midsummer Night's Dream*, for instance, the theme of love runs in four parallel lines that churn forward and sometimes intersect. The fairies' realm, the lovers, the mechanics, and the play within the play that the mechanics are rehearsing. Yes, there are twists and recognitions that are part of Aristotelian theory, but *A Midsummer Night's Dream* is not ultimately driven by the Aristotelian model. The engine that pushes everything forward in this play is analogy through the use of parallel mirrors that reflect each other, like parallel subway lines that diverge and then intersect, finally meeting together at the terminal station. Once you understand this ingenious principle, you see how it also works in *Hamlet*, with its parallel revenge plots; *King Lear*, with its parallel father/child juxtapositions; and other Shakespearean works. That we consider Shakespeare part of the Renaissance may be misleading.

What Shakespeare did, in my estimation, was to integrate the sprawling nature of the medieval Mystery plays he saw in his youth into the unified structures of the Renaissance aesthetics that were being introduced to England at the time. This grand assimilation reveals another aspect of Shakespeare's genius and is a model of sophisticated method.

A Toolbox for Method

Just as we need a warehouse for content/experience on the other side of the map, on this side we need to assemble a toolbox for method. Our own personal creative toolbox collects technical experience and know-how, all the tricks of our trade, from our practice as well as experience. It not only stores technique, but how to apply the technique in an informed way. It provides all the options when considering how to put a creative work together. We need to consciously collect these tools on a daily basis.

It goes without saying that the more tools we have at our disposal, the more possibilities are at our creative service. The higher grade your toolbox is, the more it can do for you. In simple language, this means that the more "tricks" you have in your magician's box, the more options you have when you weave your spell. It is also equally true that if we don't know how to use our tools properly, they will not do the job. The difference between having just a 2B pencil and having an art kit with 128 gouache colors and markers is obvious. What is also obvious is, there is no guarantee that the fancy art kit will make better art. It's just that you have more choices. A creative project can never succeed just on the basis of quantity of tools used. To know how to use one tool expertly is already enough to help a project succeed. The legendary physicist C. V. Raman said, "When I got my Nobel Prize, I had spent hardly 200 rupees on my equipment."[7]

In assembling our toolbox, we collect experience in our own craft, how we hone our craft, how we watch what others do in our craft, and beyond our craft. It includes the styles, as well as the techniques of our craft. If you are a film director, you note an unusual camera angle as a potential tool to store in your box, or the use of one continuous shot throughout a film, like in *Adolescence*, which Hitchcock pioneered in 1948 (*The Rope*). An artist will note unusual materials in a painting; a graphic designer may spot a new font in an old book; a songwriter may hear a rhyme she has never heard before. Having passed through the filter, they are jotted down in our physical notebook, or stored in our mind's toolbox, ready to be pulled at any moment for use in a creative project.

Like the filter on the left side, the filter for our toolbox keeps things it likes while discarding others. It is linked to habit and our evolving artistic sense. Thus, it can be trained. It influences our artistic sensibilities, and in turn evolves in relation to how our sensibilities change.

Inevitably, we will collect conflicting tools in our toolbox. We should be objective when this happens, because a tool that once worked successfully for one project may destroy another. That is why a carpenter's toolbox has a hammer and a saw, for different jobs or different aspects of a job. Don't use the hammer if you need the saw, and don't use either if they are not called for. I have seen many a theatrical production ruined by the overuse of tools like projections that weren't at all necessary for the production.

A Tool Named Curiosity

Einstein famously said, "I have no special talents. I am only passionately curious."[8] This may be the most potent tool for our toolbox. To stay curious is to continually be interested in anything new.

Artists are always on the lookout for new methods, but we do need to exert some prudence. I know artists who will never let the chance to attend a workshop

---

7 www.brainyquote.com/quotes/c_v_raman_821675?src=t_hard_work
8 Albert Einstein, quoted in *Philsoblog*, philosiblog.com/2012/03/14/in-the-middle-of-difficulty-lies-opportunity/

slip by, in the name of learning something new. But there are so many new things that pop up every day: How can we chase after them all, and when can we decide when enough is enough? Granted, many of these new things sound very enticing. A random web surf yielded workshops on "Chakra Warm-ups for Actors," "Women's Moon Circles," "How to Become Successful in Every Aspect of Your Life" … I am certain that these are beneficial for whoever takes them, but I cannot help but wonder what such practices are based on, and how many years have the teachers spent on mastering the practice? I see that it can take as little as six weeks to gain accreditation as a happiness coach. Again, I cannot comment on the efficacy of such programs, but I personally would prefer to stash my toolbox with methods that come from proven traditions that take longer to master. As Oscar Wilde warns us: "The public have an insatiable curiosity to know everything, except what is worth knowing."[9]

Conceptual Gear

Our creative toolbox is divided into two compartments: practical and conceptual.

If you are a painter, your practical tools are things like the ratio with which you mix your paints, the ways to assemble your canvas, and the quirky things that make your work unique. If you are a marketing director for a new IT product, your practical tools include how to allot a certain part of your budget to social media, and which bloggers to go to for what particular means. A theater director may observe a novel way to warm up actors before a performance, and this becomes part of her routine regimen. Practical tools are the tricks of our trade. They are collected in school or on the job.

A musician's toolbox is first and foremostly filled with very practical things, like your instrument itself, the resin you use for your violin, your guitar strings. Of course, we always hope to have the best practical tools available, and indeed, many artists fuss mightily over their tools. But the more expensive equipment is never guaranteed to deliver a better performance. Charlie Parker played a plastic saxophone on one of the greatest jazz albums ever recorded,[10] after having pawned his regular instrument before the gig. Jimmy Oliver is said to have given a tenor

---

9 Oscar Wilde, *The Soul of Man Under Socialism and Selected Critical Prose*, quoted in *Goodreads* www.goodreads.com/quotes/tag/curiosity
10 The Quintet, *Jazz at Massey Hall*, Debut Records, December 1953.

mouthpiece to John Coltrane, and Coltrane made it sound so good Oliver wanted it back.[11] Tools make the art, but they do not make the art.

The conceptual part of your toolbox stores concepts used in making things, including strategies and styles for building and composing. Stream-of-consciousness, for instance, is a conceptual tool that can be used by a novelist, a songwriter, or a playwright. Twelve-tone and atonal composition are conceptual tools for a composer, as are classical fugue or sonata forms. The resourceful architect will store conceptual tools from other disciplines in his toolbox—musical, literary, culinary, glassblowing, whatever—that may be of use in a certain project. All artists borrow conceptual tools from other disciplines. An installation artist may be inspired by a gourmet wine-pairing menu. The art of juggling may influence the design of a chandelier. Watching a bricklayer lay bricks, you may suddenly be inspired to create a new choreography.

I have noticed how stage directors and designers fiercely study any new practical or conceptual "tricks" or any new technology. Of course, just knowing that someone did something special using halo technology or that there is a new LED screen that is as thin as a piece of paper doesn't mean that you need to use it. But you store it in your toolbox, and it may someday be useful for you. I once witnessed a fireworks competition in China, where the competing groups told stories through their fireworks. It was, to put it mildly, wild, watching the story of *The Little Mermaid* told through ear-shattering, undulating waves of fireworks spanning hundreds of meters in the sky, accompanied by music and narration. Of course, I stored this in my toolbox, but it has never been of any use to me.

Your toolbox should span as many genres as you can fit in. If you are a novelist, you should first know all of the different stratagems of your own craft: how to structure a story. Though you are stocking your technical toolbox, not judging what may be of use to you in the future, you need a discerning wisdom to filter out truly unnecessary things. Otherwise, you may be just transplanting one set of clutter for another.

The Paradox of My Toolbox

My personal toolbox is pretty well stocked after working for four decades professionally. However, I do not actively pursue new tools. Sometimes new technology is shown to me, and I get interested but never really excited. I understand that

---

11 Stephen Cerram, "How John Coltrane Got His Sound," *JazzProfiles*, Oct 22, 2021, https://jazzprofiles.blogspot.com/2021/10/how-john-coltrane-got-his-sound.html

tools are what they are: means to facilitate the construction of your project. That said, I will not bore you with the details of what is in my toolbox. I do want to bring attention to a symbiosis of conflicting tools in my box. One is called improvisation, the other structure.

For many years, I used improvisation as a primary tool for the writing, or as I consider it, "wrighting," of my plays.[12] Working with improvisation with actors is giving them the freedom to take their characters in given situations wherever they want to. How can such freedom be reconciled with the structural demands of a play, which are so important to its integrity? Improvisation is by nature spontaneous, free form. Structure is about limitation, placing things in certain orders that are not free to be moved around. Synchronizing these two has been much of my life's work.

The way I understand it, first you need to be very competent in using both tools. You need to know that improvisation itself, though relying on spontaneity, must happen in a controlled environment. There must be borders set up for an improvisation to be effective. You cannot just ask an actor to improvise on anything and say "go." You can try, but it would just be like the automatic writing of the Surrealists back in the 1920s—certainly revealing, but hard to say what it reveals. These experiments ultimately lacked structure and thus may have been insightful for the artist, but ultimately inaccessible to the reader. Improvisation, in any field, needs parameters. Without boundaries, there is no such thing as freedom. We consider Lionel Messi a great improviser, but in the context of a soccer field. Even the great stand-up comics need topics to improvise on. Of course, it would be fascinating if you asked Kevin Hart or Robin Williams to just start talking with no topic. Improvising on nothing is the same as improvising on anything. You can, and I am sure they would, if they could, accept the challenge to structure anything into meaning. Not to say that stand-up comedy needs structured meaning.

When we think of the preeminent Chinese swordsman novelist Jin Yong (1924–2018), we would not be thinking of improvisation. But once at a dinner where I found myself fortunate enough to be sitting next to him, I asked him what the secret of his writing was. What a crazy question! Who would ever answer that? But he did. He gracefully told me, "I spend a long time developing the characters. Maybe half a year. Then, when they are all fully realized in my mind, I just place them together. They know what to do. They write the novel themselves."[13] I

---

12 Stan Lai, *Selected Plays*, Vol 1, 1–6.
13 Personal conversation, c. 1990, Taipei.

thought that was incredible. Figure out the life stories of all your characters, and their inner nature, and just place them together. They will tell the story. They will take the ball and run. Of course, this was a gross simplification, but it was another master class for me, and it actually reflected and served as confirmation for the way I work.

Improvisation demands structure in order to transcend the element of play and become productive in creative work. In the theater, when I am working on a play, I carefully set up borders for the actors before engaging them in improvisation. These borders include a firm understanding of the character and of the situation. For these two essential elements, I may spend weeks just talking with actors. It is not unlike what Jin Yong described, but I am working with real people. Once they are ready, I can put them into a situation, and they will instinctively know what to do and say. If they can let go of themselves and be in the moment, while being in tune with the goals I have established for the work, amazing things may happen. If they are self-conscious and thinking about how this might work, or how that might be cool, the improvisation is not of much use to me. From the transcripts I get from the sessions, I put together a scene in writing, then an act, then the whole play, myself improvising in the process.

And so, to be able to reconcile these two seemingly conflicting tools, you need a third tool, which is a knowing, of how to put disparate parts together, knowing what is structurally sound. Knowing what spontaneously generated free-form content can survive within a meticulously crafted structure and what cannot.

Knowing what works and what doesn't.

It is not just a mathematical or geometrical formula dealing with ratio and proportion. It is a feel of ebb and flow, how a certain order of the elements in your work creates an emotional response that is different from another order. That said, the math aspect is also indispensable. How a building stands up works on the same principle as how a novel, or a concerto, stands up and doesn't fall apart.

Our toolboxes are assembled not just to have tools on hand to be employed, but on a more sophisticated level, tools in your collection are there to be used together, in any combination. To know how to use all the tools at your disposal for a creative work could be called the wisdom of method.

Exercises and Further Thoughts

1. What are the tools of your field? Make a list. How many do you need to acquire?
2. Review the relationship between wisdom and method. Can you now see how they work together on a deeper basis, not only in creative projects, but in life itself?
3. Consider the adaptation of a classic in the theater or in film. How did the audience receive it? Did it stray far from the original or stay basically faithful? Did it work?
4. Examine what kind of a toolbox you personally have, for creative projects. How well-versed are you in the conceptual ideas in your field? How good are you at the techniques applicable to your field?

CHAPTER FIFTEEN

HOW THINGS WORK

Being Encyclopedic

There are two sides to the spectrum of preparing to undertake a creative work: Do nothing. Study nothing. Let everything come freely into your mind, without references, without context. Or, know everything. Be an encyclopedia of all things, particularly your own field. If you are a guitarist, you know all the guitar music that has ever been played. You know how your guitar is built, how different strings sound, how different pedals create different effects when plugged in to different amplifiers, and so on. I feel that it is good to find a happy balance, not in the middle, but alternating between the two. Sometimes you can find the childlike nature in you and act without any preconceptions, like Hung Tung, letting connections and associations come and go freely. Sometimes you can work on the basis of solid knowledge and references.

To know how to make things, you need to know how things are made. There are two basic things to study for this: phenomena, which is the physical world, and history, what we as a species have done over the centuries. You can call it "how things work," and "what has been done," or "Phenomena" and "History" on the Expanded Map.

Like the guitarist who knows everything about guitars, you should strive to be an encyclopedia in your own field. You need to know everything about how to write a play if you are a playwright, everything about building churches if you are an architect, and everything about soccer if you are a soccer coach.

You should also strive to know as much as you can outside your own field. The more you know, the more you have to assimilate. If you are an encyclopedia, you know phenomena and you know history. You know why Chinese Song Dynasty porcelains are so gentle and refined, and how they differ from Tang aesthetics. You see how the differences between a Porsche and a Ferrari may or may not reflect the differences between the Köln and Milan cathedrals. You know how Noh and Kabuki, the two major traditional theaters of Japan, are totally different from each other, in fact diametrically opposed in terms of storytelling, because they come from different eras, and reflect on these different eras. Your conceptual toolbox is well stocked with all the tricks of all trades. You have knowledge of all the "isms" of art history—expressionism, surrealism, symbolism, postmodernism, and so on, as well as all of the styles—gothic, renaissance, baroque, art nouveau, Gupta and Heian architecture, and so on, which means you not only recognize the styles, but understand the underlying social movements that have created the styles. With such knowledge, all of these become your tools which you can draw from into your work if you so choose. Without this knowledge, these tools are simply not available to you.

A creative master is always a student of creativity. A student of creativity is always a student of life. To study history is to know what we have done. To study phenomena is to know how things work. Together they show you how life, and art, works.

The Past Is a Long Prologue

The next step to becoming an encyclopedia is to know what we as a species have done. Not only the events of history but most pertinently what we have done creatively. This brings us to a study of art history, as well as music, dance, theater, architecture, and so on. You should also include science and philosophy. This is a daunting task, so just start with what interests you. Let the rest expand out naturally from what you find compelling. Let the development of your three views (Chapter Eleven) assist you on your way, to gain breadth and depth in all of it.

What we have done reveals what we can do. The past is a very long prologue for our toolbox. Don't take what others say about history for granted. History is fickle, indeed. The facts are usually written down by the conquerors and today are increasingly abused by misinformation. It is ironic, indeed, that the result of the information explosion in this, the internet age, is that misinformation has also exploded. Develop your own antenna for real and fake. Find your own connections between things. If you are standing at the Acropolis, see for yourself how the Athenians built buildings, and also see that the Parthenon is part of a cluster of buildings that cannot be separated from each other: temple, theater, hospital. This is not a random grouping. All over ancient Greece, you see the same configuration, which presents a holistic urban plan, reflecting a certain philosophy of societal structure.

Then when you visit the Caracalla Baths in Rome, for instance, you will not just stand there going "Wow," but you can start to visualize a teeming society, over a thousand at a time, conducting all aspects of work and play in huge bathtubs.

You begin to understand the difference between ancient Greece and Rome, from the point of bathing.

History is conquerors conquering as well as farmers farming. Through history, we see cause and effect, how shifts in thinking created shifts in the way cities look, or buildings are built, or music is composed. If you study the history of Western art, you can see that the radical shift toward the use of perspective in the Renaissance is actually the result of a paradigm shift in how people viewed the universe and life. Stated simply, a panoramic perch, with infinite points of view, becomes a focused view from a single point. You start to see the inner mechanisms behind the external manifestations.

I remember that every time I visited New York in my student days, my high school pal David Hu, who became an architect, would talk incessantly about every single building we passed by while walking. The "lipstick" building, the Seagram building, Grand Central ... In these crash courses, I was stocking my toolbox while gaining an understanding of the diverse individualities within the whole that is New York. During my personal grand tour of Europe when I was young, I made a point to visit all the greatest hits and strive to be alone with them, but I would spend extra time in places that surprised me. Ravenna, Italy, for instance, slightly off the beaten path, became a refuge for me. My toolbox, as well as my emotional and aesthetic palette, expanded not only with new knowledge of early medieval architecture and the brilliance of the ancient mosaics, but also with the special quietude of these sacred sites that was a different kind of quiet from others. Quietude made its way into my toolbox.

Our Asian cities are often so westernized that we are divorced from our traditions. Understanding the history of Western art actually became an essential tool for my understanding of Asian art. I began to realize that the lack of perspective technique in Chinese painting was not a deficiency, but a result of the Chinese view toward nature and life. There was a oneness and expansiveness that might be hindered by the intrusion of Western perspective technique. This is not to say that Chinese painters had perspective in their toolbox and decided not to use it, but a deeper reflection on the Chinese worldview, in which perspective was not needed or desired.

On a visit to Japan in the 1980s, when I was just starting out as an aspiring artist, I met a friend for lunch, and he suddenly offered, "Are you interested in seeing works of some contemporary artists?" I said, "of course." He checked his watch, and said, "We only have an hour. Let's go." So on his lunch break, instead of having lunch, we went to six different galleries, threading through Ginza, Roppongi, and Harajuku by subway, emerging onto the sidewalk and disappearing into some random building, to find some amazing installation, then rushing off by foot or subway to the next one. I recall vividly each of the works we saw, some with the artist on hand, attending to the empty gallery. I was very grateful for this lunch blitz of contemporary installation art, which connected me to Tokyo through a strange sad sense of disconnection. Nonetheless, everything I saw went into my toolbox.

In learning history, you learn the causes and effects of human glory, as well as depravity and the depths of suffering. You gather stories. You learn which are archetypal, and what their variations are throughout history. You realize that the novel you are writing is actually a rewrite of the Medea story. In learning about the rituals and customs of different peoples, you understand their belief systems. What is sacred to certain people may be sacrilege to others. You learn how and why wars were fought and won or lost. We tend to glorify military strategists like Cao Cao (155–220) of the Three Kingdoms period in China. His stratagems are the stuff of legend and are on display in many feature films and television series. Now that we understand how to analyze motivation, we have a new lens to analyze history and the history of creativity.

Being an Expert

It would be impossible to become an encyclopedia of everything. In fact, if there were such a person, she might be quite boring. To know everything is akin to knowing nothing. The key is in knowing what you know and how to use what you know. The encyclopedia that you are nurturing is, after all, part of your toolbox for method. Therefore, strive to be an encyclopedia in the fields that interest you. Stock your toolbox with things that interest you.

When you get to a certain point, you will be able to see and name all the tricks the magicians are playing, so to speak. If you go to a theater piece, you will say: "Robert Wilson did that in 1972 in Iran." "She is paraphrasing something from Pina Bausch's *Café Müller*." You observe a low camera angle used by a film director and note that it is in homage to Ozu.

If you are a jazz aficionado, like me, you know all the standards and blues forms that the players are improvising to. By knowing the lyrics, you have a deeper understanding of why certain musicians play a certain song in a certain way. And then you are able to identify when jazz artists, in the throes of improvisation, quote lines from other songs, even quote improvisations from other artists, either in homage or in jest. Paul Desmond, for one, did this all the time. Soloists in the all-star bands of Charles Mingus would mime the playing of other artists in the band, like trash talking each other on a concert stage.[1] It is not unlike the

---

1 Listen to *Mingus at Carnegie Hall* (Atlantic Records, 1974) for a good example.

Tang Dynasty Chinese poets, who often quoted each other in an equally highly sophisticated game, and you wouldn't know what they were doing unless you had read everything.

Being an encyclopedia means you can identify all styles, everywhere. A new office building is unveiled in Shenzhen. You look at it and say, oh, this is a retread of a Philip Johnson building. Then, because you are used to looking into cause-and-effect, you start wondering why. Why would someone in southern China want a throwback to that breakthrough era in American architecture? Where is the relevance? The answer may be that the owner did not have much knowledge of the historical context, and may never have even heard of Philip Johnson, but the style was something he wanted.

Being an encyclopedia is not always fun. You enter a Japanese restaurant, look at the décor, and realize that it is Mediterranean with Mexican motifs. Then you listen to the music that no one is listening to, and you realize that it is some random online song list. You hear the waitress speaking with the sushi chef—in Korean. You check the motivation factor for the proprietor. Of course, all businessmen want to make money, but if making money is the major, and perhaps only passion of the proprietor, then what should our motivation for coming to this restaurant be? I have been in such a restaurant in L.A., and later was told it used to be a Mexican cantina that had changed hands to a Korean owner who decided to sell Japanese food.

Big deal. Right. But to know what happened without being told means that you know a few things about interior decoration, food, about music, cultural styles, and business. This doesn't make you a party pooper. You just see more. I have particularly sensitive ears. I hear background music in elevators, lobbies, and restaurants. In restaurants, I have heard playlists that last less than 20 minutes, then loop and loop again, which drives me crazy, but it's not worth making a scene about.

How is any of this relevant to creativity? It is not revealed in a clear way. But when you see more and relate more things together in life, all the details slowly germinate and one day become useful to your creativity, making it richer and more nuanced.

And so, we study, sometimes at a desk, or in an armchair, most of the time just randomly, in life, noticing things, observing things, works of art as well as everyday objects, wondering how a thing is built, always curious about how it works, or why it doesn't work. This all builds toward your knowledge of structure, a knowing of what tools to use when the time comes to use them, and how to use them. I have been playfully using the word "trick," but seriously, if we consider ourselves magicians or sorcerers, it is the correct word to use. All of the tricks in our toolbox are gathered there through our study of phenomena and history, and our everyday observations of the world and life.

Exercises and Further Thoughts

1. Write down a list of everything you think is needed to be an expert in your own field.
2. Write down a list of things in other unrelated fields that you think may help you in your work.
3. Make a list of art forms or genres you would like to know better. Start learning about them.
4. The next time you study something unrelated to your own field, or train in something random, think about how it can contribute to your toolbox.

CHAPTER SIXTEEN

THE PRACTICE OF PRACTICE

To Learn How to Do, You Need to Do

Nothing can take the place of practice. Little can be said about it than to do it. In most disciplines, it is easy to know what to practice. If you are a cellist, you practice the cello. But often, the skill sets are not so clearly defined. Making an animated film, for instance, is a combination of many skills, all of which need to be perfected. It is relatively easy to practice all the various individual skills you need, but it is hard to have the opportunity to put them all together and actually practice how to make an animation. I was fortunate enough to be able to continually practice making plays for public performance while I was learning. After each opportunity, I was able to gain another opportunity, and so I could practice continually. I could viscerally feel how every single new play brought unique creative challenges that were met and solved, and I grew as an artist.

For others, it may not be that easy. For let's say an MFA student in filmmaking, she would only get a few chances to direct a short film. How would this prepare her for a career in the film industry?

If we went by Malcolm Gladwell's famous 10,000 hour rule,[1] such a student would enter the job market with maybe a few hundred hours of work at most. Such a discrepancy is a problem. If you are a painter, you can practice by yourself, as can a computer games designer or player, and accumulate those hours. For disciplines that require a team to function, the chances to practice are precious indeed.

---

[1] The assertion that expertise in any field can only come through practice of at least 10,000 hours. Malcolm Gladwell, *Outliers: The Story of Success* (Little, Brown and Company, 2008), Chapter 2, 35.

The Other Shore

10 years off stage, practicing your craft;
10 minutes on stage, performing.
—rule of thumb for Peking Opera trainees

This may sound a little harsh, but it is a fairly accurate statement about the art of Peking Opera. You need long years of training your body, your voice, even your eye muscles, to be able to make the standard but sophisticated movements and gestures that accompany the difficult vocals.

It takes even longer in the traditional Japanese Bunraku puppet theater, where the trainee may take up to 20 years to gain proficiency as a puppeteer. Necessary? It may seem excessive, but given the precision and subtlety of these arts, perhaps it is. In contrast, the six-week training to be accredited as a "Happiness Coach" seems excessively short.

Gladwell himself has modified his stance on the 10,000-hour rule, saying that it is just a reference, a "useful number, 10 years and 10,000 hours," to attain so-called mastery of a discipline, and that, of course, different people in different environments learn at different speeds.[2]

What is mastery?

It is to know what you are doing, and to be able to do it. In Chinese, one of the adjectives used for the word is *"tong,"* meaning "through," as in "piercing through," or "throughway." To say "her martial-arts techniques are through" doesn't mean she's done. In fact, it means the opposite. She has passed *through* the technique and gotten to the other side of technique. To gauge whether you have attained the mastery of a subject is to see whether you have passed through the field of technique and arrived at the other shore, where technique is no longer an issue. If you are not "through," but still standing on this side, your efforts at whatever you are doing are stumbling and unsure. Confidence is the key word that manifests once you are "through." It is the confidence of a chess player who just keeps making moves and knowing they are all right.

Considered the greatest jazz tenor saxophonist of all time, John Coltrane's practice regimen was legendary. He would practice at any opportunity. It is said that he would board a trans-Atlantic flight with a broomstick, and practice

---

2 Malcolm Gladwell, "Malcolm Gladwell Demystifies 10,000 Hours Rule," *Heavy Chef,* www.youtube.com/watch?v=1uB5PUpGzeY

playing scales throughout the eight-hour flight, using the broomstick.³ It is also said that he would spend 10 hours practicing just one note.⁴

For artists like Coltrane, practice itself was a path to discovery, of sounds, of soundscapes, of scales, and how different scales placed in different contexts would create novel effects. The more you improve through practice, the more possibilities you are able to see. Coltrane said:

> There is never any end. There are always new sounds to imagine; new feelings to get at. And always, there is the need to keep purifying these feelings and sounds so that we can really see what we've discovered in its pure state. So that we can see more and more clearly what we are. In that way, we can give to those who listen the essence, the best of what we are. But to do that at each stage, we have to keep on cleaning the mirror.⁵

The Engine Room

This is how dedicated musicians and painters practice. What about film and theatre directors? What do we practice? I recall a conversation I had with Taiwanese film maestro Hou Hsiao-hsien around 1984 when he had broken through with a unique aesthetic of long shots that was being recognized at film festivals around the world. It was an exciting time when I was creating new plays for the theater. We often visited each other at work, and because we were both creating new works with limited resources and no prior tradition, we talked a lot just about art. We set up the metaphor of creativity being a machine, with us as the pilots of the machine. "I'm in the engine room now," Hou told me. "I can see the whole mechanism. It's just a matter of choosing the right buttons to push." I told him that I could see the door to that engine room, but I was outside, not yet in.

We both understood the metaphor of creativity as a machine with a complex engine room. The beginner doesn't even know of its existence. Soon after, I could feel myself inside, slowly taking command of the controls. After many years, the

---

3 Glen Kostur, "Practicing without your instrument," *Sax On the Web* website, www.saxontheweb.net/threads/practicing-without-your-instrument.46113/

4 Nathan Phelps, "7 Lessons On Practicing Music You Can Take From John Coltrane, the 'Athlete' of Improvisation," *Medium.com*, Dec. 3, 2020, https://nathandavidphelps.medium.com/7-lessons-on-practicing-music-you-can-take-from-john-coltrane-the-athlete-of-improvisation-f296bb3a0915

5 John Coltrane, quoted in Ashley Kahn, "John Coltrane Biography," www.johncoltrane.com/biography

engine room is no longer a place I have to visit. In fact, it no longer exists as an engine room, but just as a natural part of what I do.

A seasoned director many years my junior saw a recent play of mine, *River/Cloud*, at the Wuzhen Theatre Festival in 2024. She said she was emotionally drawn into this story of floating lives, but as a director, she was most amazed at how I had treated every single detail, from text to movement to stage to lights, the timing of it all that created the layers and textures that brought her under the spell of the play. I told her that no matter how many years of experience you have in your art, you still have to attend to each detail one by one. I asked her to note how craft was such an integral part of the final product, and if you are "through" craft, any technique can be employed anywhere with ease.

Where does creative confidence come from? Experience in your craft, of course is crucial, but deeper confidence is built on how you live your life, how you observe life, observe others, and feel compassion for people and things. If your life and emotions are tied to and connected to your society, you must have the confidence that what you care about is what other people care about, and what you feel is what other people feel. There is no other way to be confident that your work can connect with others.

Slowing It All Down

I recall watching an interview of NFL football quarterback Joe Montana in the 1980s, which was a seminal lesson in creativity for me: Montana described the experience of dropping back to pass when he was a rookie as a blur. He could feel the pressure of ferocious 300-pound linemen blitzing in to sack him but couldn't see them clearly.

After some time, Montana said the blurry images began to sharpen, and he could see more and more in the scant 2 or 3 seconds he had to make decisions. After more experience, everything seemed to unfold in slow motion. He could see the defensive ends rushing toward him, getting blocked by his linemen; he could see his primary and secondary receivers clearly, decide which one was open, and throw. Football became easy.[6]

This is an accurate description of the process from layman to master. There is a difference in how fast things open up to reveal themselves. To the beginner, it happens so fast that they cannot see or are not even aware of what is happening.

---

6 This is my recollection of an unidentified TV program, c. 1983.

Another sports story I heard comes from an agent who told me that an NBA rookie, whom he represented, and who turned out to be quite a good player, got on the court with the assignment of guarding Michael Jordan for the first time. Within seconds, Jordan dunked on him. When Jordan trotted past the rookie while going back on defense, he said to him in passing, "It doesn't happen that fast on TV, does it?"[7] I cannot vouch for this story's authenticity and refrained from asking Jordan himself when I met him at an event I directed for him in Taipei,[8] but its message illustrates what I am talking about vividly.

I do believe that the ability to slow things down and see clearly in the moment is an important quality to have for success in creativity. It is obvious in sports that the great ones have this ability. I once watched from behind first base as Barry Bonds smashed a 100-mile fastball off Randy Johnson into San Francisco Bay. I marveled at the moment, as if I were watching two dueling samurais. It was too fast for my layman's eyes, but for the greats, as Mickey Mantle said, the baseball at times is "as big as a grapefruit."[9]

You may wonder why an Asian playwright and director spends his time watching American sports. I do believe an artist gains much by watching masters in any field: a tech wizard, a master tea maker, a neuroscientist, a *qigong* master. I have been blessed to know many of them, and they all have something special to teach you. A close friend of mine was the CFO for the greater Asia operations of a major food corporation. In all my years of knowing her, I had no idea what her actual job was, so one day I asked her, "What does a CFO for a giant corporation actually do?" She said, "I make the budget for the coming year, and then I make sure the budget is executed." Though this had nothing to do with my own work, it seemed that I had learned something important.

I do consider the likes of Jordan, Bird, Magic, Curry, and Montana to be artists, and their art is exemplified not just in the brilliance of their technique, but in the awareness and timing with which this technique is unveiled. In the same vein, Bill Walsh and Steve Kerr, to name two, are directors on the highest level, and when they make decisions, these decisions create results that lead to victory. After a game, you wonder, "How did he know?"

---

7 Personal conversation, Taipei c. 2000.
8 Michael Jordan 2004 Asia Tour Taipei Event, May 22, 2004.
9 Mickey Mantle, quoted by Drake Baer in "Baseball Players See the Ball as Way Bigger Than You Do," *The Cut*, www.thecut.com/2016/10/the-science-of-how-baseball-players-hit-fastballs.html

Getting Dunked on, by Art

Ten thousand hours or 10 years of practice cannot guarantee that everything will slow down and you will attain mastery, but it gives you a better chance. If you have wisdom infused into your method, the practice multiplies in efficiency. Meaning, if you are just going through the motions when you are practicing piano, the 10,000 hours don't really add up. But if your understanding of the art itself deepens as your fingers grow more adept, then the hours multiply quickly. You probably arrive well before 10,000 hours.

In my own work, in the beginning, when working on a new play in rehearsal, I could only see the scene that was set up before me. I had a vague idea of how it might eventually connect to other scenes, but it was all a blur, a fog. It all happened too quickly, and there were too many pieces to keep track of. It was difficult enough to write one scene well; how could I see how it might fit into a larger structure? I was being dunked on, by the art of theater. After the opening night of every new production, I would be sick for a few days, my body mandatorily shutting down after gross overuse.

As the years went on, as in the Montana analogy, the fog lifted, and everything slowed down. I became very efficient at conducting creative rehearsals. I also attained the practical ability to see a whole play when I am working on a piece of it, while it is still in the process of being composed. This isn't easy, but it is a skill that can and must be developed. When you are working on a play, you are necessarily working on parts that eventually fit together into a whole. But if you cannot see the whole, how can you know what the parts should look like? This is a curious paradox because you cannot see the whole unless it is completed. If you are landscaping a Suzhou Garden but don't know the scope of the site, how do you fashion a certain corner? You aren't even sure if it is a corner. It could be the center. This can be frustrating and confusing. The trick is to see both at the same time. This requires lots of practice and awareness, first in fashioning the parts. Once you are adept in making individual parts, you gain an understanding of how they should be crafted in order to fit into the greater whole. At the same time, never stop studying how other artists structure their works, and how all organisms in nature, as well as ecosystems, are whole and complete. Through diligent practice and study, understanding of parts and the whole grows together. It's a bit like connecting the dots or filling in the colors on a painting. The beginner can only can see the dots. Once you are "through," you see the painting and the dots you need to connect, all at once.

Apprenticeship

In all creative fields, the best way to learn is to become an apprentice to a professional, to observe him work, and participate in the work as much as possible. This means mopping the floor, preparing the materials, pouring the tea, taking notes, getting lunch, printing scripts. Any of these tasks will bring you closer to the actual work.

In fact, in many creative workplaces, there is no differentiation between work and all of the things leading up to work. My professor at Berkeley, Dunbar Ogden, once told me the story of going to East Berlin in the 1950s to do research on Bertolt Brecht and his Berliner Ensemble. He found the theater they were working in, entered and sat in the audience. He could see the maestro on stage, smoking, and chatting with one of the actors. Someone else was having a sandwich, and others were moving chairs around. After quite some time, with nothing happening, Dunbar asked someone sitting near him in the audience, "When does the rehearsal start?" The person answered, "It's been going on for quite a while."

This kind of scene became very familiar to me, as throughout my career I have worked in this way (more in Chapter Nineteen). To be an apprentice means to get familiar with the routine of the work, the rhythm of the work, and then see how the creative piece actually materializes. There is no way of replacing this kind of experience with anything you can read in a textbook. The road to becoming a professional, and then a master, is through apprenticeship.

In this day and age, students of creative arts compete for internships, and compare the merits of different intern jobs. My feeling is that there is no good reason to refuse any kind of apprenticeship. You may intern with a great master and learn nothing, and you may intern with a struggling group and have an epiphany. Referring back to John Coltrane, his apprenticeship consisted of roughly 10 years of playing whatever gig he could find. It was an eclectic mix of R&B, big band, small groups, as well as working with masters.[10] The unique style he arrived at later is not reflected in any of these groups he worked with, but in a way it is the sum of all of them, and I would go as far to say that if he left out any of these experiences, he wouldn't get to where he finally was.

I recall the first time I worked with Huang Lei, the Chinese actor. It was the first day of rehearsal for *Secret Love in Peach Blossom Land* with a whole new group of actors in Beijing. I got there early, and to my surprise, found him there also, doing of all things, mopping the floor. At the time, he was already a big

---

10 Kahn.

star. I asked him what he was doing? He said he was just showing respect for the rehearsal room. I realized how his character had set him up for greatness. You don't become a master without understanding what it means to be an apprentice, and how to serve as an apprentice. Many people engage in an apprenticeship because they seek to learn skills from the master, but come away with something more important, which is humility.

Pushing a Burned-out Car Over a Cliff

I once heard that Coco Chanel could make a dress for you without taking your measurements. Mozart could remember whole pieces of music just by listening once, after which he could play them note for note. He also had the special ability to listen to a whole opera of his, not sequentially, but all at once, in his mind.[11] These special abilities are a bit hard to comprehend. One could hope to have such prowess in one's field after whatever number of hours of practice, but you can only hope and wish. In this respect, I have something to share from my own experience.

In the mid-1990s, I spent two years of my life working on one of the most improbable projects you could ever think of: a one-hour daily TV sitcom, written and directed by me, shot by four cameras, and performed on the day of or the day before broadcast, five nights a week. It was called *All in the Family are Human* (*Womenyijia doushiren*), a play on the Chinese words "We are All Family." Think *Friends*, lengthened to an hour, add politics to the script, and change the broadcast schedule from once a week for one season a year to every weeknight, throughout the year.

I undertook this project under the circumstances of a major creative burnout from over a decade of nonstop work, and the commercial failure of my second feature film, *The Red Lotus Society*. I had lost all passion for work and considered everything I had accomplished as meaningless. My colleagues told me to find a beach to lie on for a couple of years to recharge. Out of the blue, a television producer from a new cable company offered to give me a prime-time slot to do anything I wanted. I had no interest in anything, much less television. But I did it. Instead of shutting myself down for a much-needed reboot, I plunged into a whole new field with an impossible challenge. It is hard to understand such a decision, like pushing a burned-out car over a cliff to make sure it goes into the shop totally destroyed for a total rebuild. My persistent producer friend came on very strong,

---

11 Duke.

and after refusing him many times, I gave it a try. I was what Hollywood calls the showrunner, but much more. I was sole writer and director as well as producer.

I worked with theater actors who knew me well, using improvisation to create the daily script, adding the ingredient of Taiwan politics, which on any given day was feisty, surreal, and often comical. Taiwanese democracy was in its youth, as was cable television. From decades of repression, suddenly anything was possible. Censorship had been erased. Nothing was taboo. I created a diverse "family" of eccentric renters in a big house. The show was a wacky but faithful take on the growth of Taiwanese democracy and life in the 1990s. Each episode, the main storyline could go through any of the characters we had designed, but usually, the news of the day would be so interesting that we would use it as the main storyline and incorporate the characters into it while lampooning the president and other politicians. Though it was rough (live shot selection, no chance to edit), we gained a loyal audience.

The characters were designed with contrasting quirkiness and political views, which created the central tension of the show. Though the image of Taiwan internationally is of a "model democracy," it was bitterly divided then, and more so now. We tried to bridge the differences through comedy. The show was an interesting alternative to the normal melodramas that were on the major networks in Taiwan at 8 p.m., after the hourly news at seven. The original plan was for 40 episodes, but we wound up doing 600. Fans look fondly back at the crazy run of this political sitcom that was never imitated, nor could it possibly be. Many of our theater actors became stars, and many stars of the day came in for cameos.

Now that I look back, it was absolute madness, every day! Think of *Doonesbury*, but for an hour, every weeknight! A screenwriting friend from Berkeley days who was working in Hollywood came to watch me work. She said that this could never happen in America. I said, why not? There is no censorship in America, I thought. She said in theory, I was correct, but there is economic censorship, meaning your show needed to be screened by sponsors and the network for subject matter and political correctness, so you probably couldn't do it on the same day. Looking back, I still am amazed that the station in Taiwan gave me full rein over everything. I was the one who decided whether any line would be offensive to any group, and how to handle political correctness throughout the diverse cast of characters and situations. In reality, there wasn't any time for the station to check anything or change anything anyway! They had to trust me. And with that trust came a greater responsibility.

We dealt with the gamut of political and cultural life in Taiwan, often with exceptional boldness. We challenged a known mafia head who was moving into politics and buying votes throughout his district. We targeted corrupt officials, finding the ludicrous side of serious criminal activity. We lampooned corrupt and inept politicians, including the President, often criticizing his policies. One of our main characters was a Taipei City government employee who never had to go to work because he penciled out his office in the architectural blueprint of the new government building, and so, after construction, his department did not exist.

It wasn't all laughter. During the years of the show, there was a big legal case where three young men were accused of murder and sentenced to death, but they all had legitimate proof that they couldn't possibly have been at the site of the crime. They also claimed they were coerced into writing confessions. I did my due diligence, speaking with many experts, and believed in their innocence. We kept their photos on the set and often added the debate about the case into the daily script as a reminder of the possible injustice that could happen. Despite all odds, the case was reopened, and they were found not guilty and freed. We celebrated on the show after we watched the three of them weep at the news conference on their release.

Another instance was when the daughter of a famous TV actress was kidnapped and held for ransom, her finger mailed to the actress. All of Taiwan was gripped by the news. It was hard to write comedy amid such grim reality. Tragically, after days of suspense, the daughter was found killed. The day the news broke, I recall being sick to my stomach and not wanting to write anything. She was, after all, the same age as my own daughter. During the episode, the actors sort of just wandered around the set, in mourning, as was all of Taiwan.

My 10,000

This project is an example of how far creativity can take you, and I hope you can see how it challenged all of the elements in my creative map: life and art, wisdom and method. I was the writer, director, and also news editor. I had to make decisions that pertained equally to life and art. This successful show was never replicated anywhere that I know, and now that I look back at it, I realize that you do need a special skill set to be able to drive this car, a combination of writing, directing, comic sense, timing, political savvy and cynicism, skills in setting up improvisatory scenes, skills in writing a daily outline, skills in creating a show for an exact amount of time, with no chance to edit, skills in making sure each talented cast member got enough exposure each day. To start, I had a dedicated and talented group of five assistants working with me on each show, and I eagerly awaited the day when they could take over the driver's seat to write and direct a whole episode, so the pressure wouldn't be all on me. That day didn't come until after 100 episodes.

By my own count, my 10,000 hours were achieved during those two years, 1995 to 1997. At the time of my burnout, before the TV show, I had already written and directed 12 original plays, including an opera and two original feature films, and received Taiwan's most prestigious National Arts Award, as well as many international film festival awards. So, what did the 10,000 hours give me that I didn't already have? Most noticeably, I attained a solid *knowing* of what I was doing. When I was working on the parts, I knew what they would turn out to look like, and I knew how they would attach to the whole, and I knew what the whole would look like. That is certainly a very empowering feeling because there are no big surprises when you get into final rehearsals. Just like an artist who applies a coat of paint onto a painting, she knows exactly what it will look like when it is dry. That's what I'm talking about. Aside from this general knowing, I developed an uncanny ability to know time. That's why the story about Chanel doesn't seem too strange to me, nor are claims that Wes Montgomery and Chet Baker couldn't read music. They didn't need to read music, because notes are not music, and they knew music, not notes. When I finished writing a certain segment of the daily sit-com, for instance, I knew that after editing and rehearsal, the recorded segment would be 11 minutes and 25 seconds and not 10 minutes and 45 seconds. I had pressure to know this because every day while working in the afternoon, I was given a number, which would be the length of the show, dependent upon the advertising slots sold. Sometimes it was 46'15", sometimes 47'20". Whatever it was, with no chance to edit anything, I had to deliver a show on the dot.

And so I developed this ability to know precise time without a stopwatch. I have retained this ability somewhat to this day. When I do a one-hour lecture, I know when to stop, and it usually is at 59 minutes. This is one of the perks of 10,000 hours. But in all seriousness, it is more than this. More important is simply the deepening of the knowing of your craft. I don't use the word "artist" lightly. Before we are artists, we are craftsmen. Without craft, there is no art. To be a master craftsman in any field is to know this will work, that won't, what can attach to what, what won't, this actor will be able to handle this character, and not that one. You are "through." You have passed through to the other side and no longer struggle with technique. All your energy can be put into the left side of the map, expanding and refining your wisdom, which in turn funnels back into your work. You are ripe for quantum leaps in your art.

If the Beatles attained their 10,000 hours around the time they made their first number one record, this means those hours came mostly from gigs played in their formative years in Liverpool, and in particular, Hamburg.[12] It makes sense

---

12 Gladwell, *Outliers*, 45–47.

that a few years later, after they had achieved their 10,000 hours, their music went to another level, a deeper consciousness, coupled with a deeper artistry. Look at the quantum leaps from "Please Please Me" to "Nowhere Man" (2 years) to "Strawberry Fields Forever" (2 more years).

In retrospect, instead of sputtering out and disappearing after a midlife crisis, which very possibly could have been the case, I came out of the experience with a deepened understanding of my craft and have kept working creatively to this day, hopefully always improving. To note, many of my works that are considered heavyweight came after this stint, including *A Dream Like a Dream, Ago, The Village*, and others. Looking back, I don't think I could have achieved them without this lengthy "internship."

Diligence

Diligence on the right side of the map, near the bottom, is in correspondence with motivation on the left. Diligence needs little explanation. It is the key to practice and study, and practice and study are key to method.

Though diligence is easy to understand, it isn't easy to be diligent. Everyone knows that hard work has its dividends in every discipline. The problem with many who find it hard to be diligent is that diligence doesn't seem to be much fun. The choreographer Twyla Tharp's excellent advice is: "Creativity is a habit, and the best creativity is the result of good work habits."[13] Make diligence a habit. It strengthens focus and upgrades whatever you are doing or studying. There are no negatives with diligence.

I can't help but to think back to John Coltrane. David Crosby tells the story of being totally smashed out in the men's room of a Chicago jazz club, when Coltrane entered the restroom, coming off a set on a break, and continued to play his saxophone, filling the restroom with scales.[14] The greatest don't become the greatest without such dedication, even obsession.

With diligence comes a similar word: discipline. This is another habit that is easy to understand but not so easy to maintain. Disciplined diligence is a formidable quality to have in whatever endeavor you undertake.

---

13 Twyla Tharp, *The Creative Habit: Learn It and Use It for Life* (New York: Simon and Schuster, 2006).
14 Josh Jones, "The Night When John Coltrane Soloed in a Bathroom and David Crosby, High as a Kite, Nearly Lost His Mind," Open Culture website, https://www.openculture.com/2019/10/the-night-when-john-coltrane-soloed-in-a-bathroom.html

Exercises and Further Thoughts

1. Have you accumulated your 10,000 hours in your field? If so, can you feel the tangible difference before and after? Can you list these differences?
2. If not, what skills do you feel are lacking?
3. Choose an artist who has had a traceable long career. Can you identify the period where the artist makes a breakthrough that corresponds with the "10,000 hours" we have been referring to?
4. Can you see that the breakthrough is not just a change in style, but a quantum advancement in craft and confidence?
5. Have you ever served as an apprentice to someone accomplished in their field? Review the experience. What was the most important thing you learned?

CHAPTER SEVENTEEN

CRAFTING STRUCTURE

One cannot help but be in awe when he contemplates the mysteries of eternity, of life, of the marvelous structure of reality.[1]

—*Albert Einstein*

The Key to How Things Work

The key to how things work, and to figuring out all the styles and genres we as human beings have dreamt up, is structure. In method, structure is perhaps the most important element to master.

Everything and anything has structure. A Bach fugue has structure; the blues has structure; Bosch's *The Garden of Earthly Delights* has structure; even the seemingly random stream-of-consciousness of Joyce's *Ulysses* has structure; so does a cloud floating in the sky. So does any combination of these things, if you can see it. With Einstein's eyes, you can see how marvelous the structure of reality is.

If we can visualize the structure of anything, then we know what it is made of and how it is built. Then, we can proceed to figure out how it works, and we can make it work.

The etymology of the word is architectural, but it applies to every organism. Structure is the external manifestation of internal necessity. Micro reflects macro. Where there is structure in a house, there is structure in a cluster of houses, in a community, in a city, in a country. Like many European cities, Paris has its circular structure, with a center and concentric arrondissements around it, unlike New York, which has its unique structure of boroughs, spreading out on three sides and drawn into the magnet of Manhattan. Tokyo is somewhat defined by its circular

---

1 Albert Einstein, quoted in *A-Z Quotes*, www.azquotes.com/quote/455371?ref=structure

JR Yamanote subway route, but within are many subcenters and no actual center. Shanghai is divided by a river. These different configurations create basic differences in how life runs and feels in these cities.

Where we find structure in all physical things, our lives are running in a unique structure called time. A human life is defined by two bookend moments, birth and death, two pillars that support what happens in between: childhood, adolescence, adulthood, middle age, old age, each of which has primal rites of passage, and each of which has its own substructure. This life structure is intersected by and reflected in the unfailing structure of the seasons, and the unfailing structure of day and night. These are the primal structures of life, embedded deep in our consciousness.

Blueprints and architectural drawings are products of logical scientific thinking, which reflect the engineering aspect of structure. Pillars and beams *need to be*, in the context of what a house is *supposed to do*. If a house is not meant for people to live in, if its purpose is to plant trees, then it won't need beams or pillars. It is fine for it to collapse at any time, and in the end, it won't be called a "house."

Behind every structure, there is a why, the motivation that drives the what and how of the structure. The reason for the design of Gothic buildings, such as the Köln Cathedral, is intimately tied to the passion to build it in the first place. It needed to be as tall and bright as possible inside, for the purpose of worshipping a God who is above. This led to the design of Gothic arches and flying buttresses, which were structural and not aesthetic choices.

Similar in motivation to worship the powers beyond yet totally different in structure is the Borobudur temple complex in Indonesia, which is based on the mandala shape, with concentric circles and squares radiating out from the center. The differences in these two structures reflect the differences in their respective cosmologies. Understanding these structural differences reveals the intricate diversity within the often surprising commonality that is humanity.

Structure is the key to form. Form reveals function. Function reveals intention.

The Urge for Unity

> The sparrow, though small, has all five organs complete.
> —*Chinese saying*

Audiences derive pleasure from seeing completeness in creative works and can detect incompleteness or flaws in the structure of plays or films as they watch them. Unity becomes the norm by which works are judged.

What is the definition of "unified"? In life, it is an object or experience that has a clear beginning and end, and functions as intended. A more sophisticated yardstick would not be length, time, shape, or mass, but purpose: how the object relates to its purpose. We can only define a work in relationship to its objective. Therefore, a Kurt Schwitters collage could be deemed complete, even though it looks totally fragmented. Samuel Taylor Coleridge's poem "Kubla Khan" can also be seen as complete, even though it was left by the poet in unfinished form. In contrast, Cao Xueqin only wrote 80 chapters of his masterpiece *Dream of the Red Chamber*, but later writers felt the obligation to complete the work in its current 120-chapter form. We can put asterisks behind both the 80-chapter and 120-chapter versions as being incomplete, for totally different reasons.

In the years when it was a fortress, the Louvre's structure was dictated by the function of its needs, which included fortified walls. The structure changed when the function changed into a palace, and new buildings gradually took the place of the old. After the Revolution, the function of the palace changed to a museum, reflecting the ideological shift from monarchy to republic. The rooms that had been living quarters for the royals became display rooms for art and artifacts. In 1989, I. M. Pei introduced his glass pyramid in the courtyard, and this seemingly incongruous new structure, which visually clashed with the original architecture, created a new and dramatic entrance and touring route for museum-goers, linking the courtyard to a reconfigured underground entrance. Did this monumental new edifice create two separate structures, in conflict? Or a new way of looking at architecture for a new age? As Frank Lloyd Wright said:

> Form follows function—that has been misunderstood. Form and function should be one, joined in a spiritual union.[2]

Critics discuss whether Mozart wrote "too many notes" in a certain symphony, or whether Beckett wrote "too few words" in some of his plays, or whether your living room has an extra chair that doesn't need to be there. In the end, how we decide depends on whether or not we are in agreement with what the necessity is. You cannot say that Versailles has too many chandeliers if its purpose was to showcase the magnificence of the French royalty. You cannot say Antonioni's *L'Avventura* moves too slowly just because you are used to a film

---

2 Frank Lloyd Wright, quoted in *Guggenheim.org*, www.guggenheim.org/teaching-materials/the-architecture-of-the-solomon-r-guggenheim-museum/form-follows-function

moving quickly. If the purpose of a Dadaist performance is to show how meaningless the world is, then the fact that it doesn't make sense gives it meaning and unity.

Structure is the concrete form of need. Need comes from the purpose of the work. The purpose of the work comes from its internal conception/intent and basic function, as defined by the creator. To be complete and structurally sound, we must be in tune with necessity, in terms of what is needed for the project at hand.

Structure creates unity. How deep your knowledge of structure is defines the range of your method.

Searching for Rules

Aristotle and all the theorists who attempted to explain good and bad theater also attempted to set up models for all to follow. But the true model is internal and differs for every artist. This having been said, are there common rules that we can go by?

Beginning writers, and accomplished ones too, for that matter, often spend most of their time agonizing over structure. Staring at a blank page doesn't necessarily mean you don't know what you want to say, but it can mean you don't know how to say it. More often it means you're trying to say it, but it's not coming out right. Inside, it's clear and makes perfect sense, but you don't know how to make that "inside" appear on the outside piece of paper. Certainly, this is the most common problem facing writers.

To me, the process of writing a play is like making a stew. There are a lot of ingredients in my mind, and they are all stirring around in the pot, trying to find the right place to go, while the whole pot is also brewing and seeking to place all the ingredients in their proper place, where they can be cooked to the proper tenderness. In such a situation, you have mature ingredients, but no proper recipe to put it all together. Ingredients in themselves may not make a great stew. There is a proper order and timing to everything to make it work to the best effect. Sometimes, to find that order, you need to calm your mind and let the ingredients settle where they may, which often is where they should be.

Often, writer's block occurs for the simple reason that you don't really know what you want to do or say. Or what you want to say is not yet a complete idea. This is a problem of content, not form. If this is the case, you will have to go back to the conceptual stage to solve it.

Deconstruction in a Shanghai Café

One afternoon in Shanghai, the architect John Yang took me to a quiet coffee shop where I told him I wanted to get some writing done. We sat in an old bookstore café in the former French concession. I wrote my script. He grabbed a recent *Architectural Digest* from the shelf, took pen and paper from his bag, and started sketching the structure of a random building featured in the magazine. He took the whole building apart, floor by floor, including all the piping and wiring until it was stripped to its bare structure. Then he put it all back together, drawing by drawing, just as an exercise, for fun, like a concert pianist practicing scales. I took note that this is how an accomplished architect spends his Sunday afternoons, and how seriously we should approach structure.

To put it simply, structure is order. What comes first, what comes second, what goes last, in time, in space. If it makes sense, it works. A theater is built with a lobby in front, and restrooms usually in the back or sides. Why? Because it works that way. You wouldn't want a theater lobby to be detached from the theater, and the restrooms another block away. A soccer match lasts 60 minutes, with 15 minutes of extra time if the game is tied. It is played on a field of a certain length, with 11 players on each side. Why? Because it makes sense, practically and athletically.

As human beings, we are habitually interested in order and disturbed when order is broken. This seems to be a primal concern. When a total eclipse disrupts the basic structure of day and night, it makes news. When monsoon rains don't come when they should, it disrupts the whole economy of countries. These events also trigger supernatural concerns, bringing forth clairvoyants and soothsayers who predict calamities and prescribe remedies.

Order is also cultural. Soup is served last in China. Salad comes last in Italy. If you consider a meal without dessert incomplete, then most Chinese meals in China would be considered incomplete.

X-Ray Vision

If we had X-ray vision, the structure of things would be revealed naked before us. Too bad most of us don't. But we actually can train to see how things are built, how they create a rationale that makes them work from the inside, and we can get very good at it.

The simplest way to see structure is to see parts of a whole. A tree has a trunk, branches, and leaves. Three parts. Actually, there are also roots, making it four parts. Or two parts if you consider underground and above-ground. You can also say that there are branches and leaves on each side: north, east, south, and west. We still haven't gotten to the veins that draw water from the roots up into the branches, or the photosynthesis function that nourishes the tree. There are so many ways to break a tree down into parts, each giving us a different viewpoint. How can we see structure in a way that is useful for us? Is there an *essential* structure to a tree that we *must* see in order to really understand how it works?

Structure is why something stays together and does not fall apart. When we see a building, we usually first notice its decorative aspects, but what is essential is what keeps it standing, what keeps the rain out, how the utilities flow in, and how waste flows out. These are the building's essential structural secrets, the keys to how it works.

When we work on a creative project, it is the same. We need a way to keep it standing, to keep all the elements together. No one wants to live under a leaking roof, wear a coat that falls apart while walking, or see a play whose plot falls apart in the middle.

Structural engineering is an advanced field that requires a license. We should treat creative structure with the same respect. Structural engineers can calculate whether a certain bridge will be able to hold rush hour traffic. Design and the varying strength of materials all come into play under the engineer's calculations. So it is with creative structure. A symphony is no less structurally complex than the concert hall it is performed in.

Creative ideas have their natural form the moment they are conceived in the mind. In a creative project, the order of things is dictated by the association between things. The sequence of how to tell a story or how to arrange the elements in a painting may be immediately recognized by the artist. Sometimes it takes a long process of work to see it. Once seen, it is a flexible thing that can be altered as the work proceeds toward its final goal. However, just like changing the structure of a building is a massive undertaking, changing the structure of your work is a deeply involved process that may lead you to want to start from scratch, all over again.

If you cannot see the structure of your work, it may be that your work is seriously flawed from the inside. If an architect cannot figure out how to design a proposed building, it may not be that she lacks the proper creative inspiration or technical expertise, but perhaps the project description given to her by the client is flawed or unclear, and so she cannot figure out what goes where.

If there is something wrong with the structure of your project, it has little chance of survival. This is not just true of a filmscript, a musical, or an installation; it includes how companies are organized and how festivals are run. How can we check to see if the structure of our creative endeavor is sound? Let us come back to the concept of parts and whole. How many parts is our whole comprised of? As with our tree above, we can try to see this question from many different angles, each revealing different aspects of structure.

To learn how things work is to see structure. To see structure, you must first see unity. To see unity, you must see what parts are necessary to make up the whole. To see what is necessary, you must see the essence. Structure is the external manifestation of the inner essence.

What is essential becomes structural.

The Numerology of Creativity

To see a tree as having two, three, or four parts is using different sets of eyes to see how the same tree is structured. Your own creative projects may also be seen using these different eyes, but it is important to decide what the natural, essential number of your project is, for what you are attempting to achieve.

The "essential number" of your project is how many parts it is made up of in your mind. Chekhov's major plays are all structured in four acts. This creates a certain rhythm that is conducive to his needs. It goes without saying that if a story should be told in three parts, but you tell it in two parts, it comes across very differently. The question is, how should it be told? That is for you to decide. The magical thing is, there are clues to the answer built into the question. That is what is essential, and hopefully you can find it.

Shakespeare's *The Winter's Tale*, written in 1610, comes down to us today in 5 acts, with a total of 21 scenes. So, it is natural to consider it to have 5 major parts and 21 smaller parts. After a simple reading, however, you will notice that *The Winter's Tale* is clearly a story told in two parts, the first part 16 years before, the second part 16 years later. If you are directing and consider it to have five parts, you will direct it in a certain way, which may cause problems because its essential number is "2," not "5." It would be like building a hotel complex of five villas when the actual instructions call for two towers.

The Winter's Tale was published in the original Folio of 1623. We consider the text authentic. But what is authentic is subject to the reality that Shakespeare never wrote his plays to be published. In fact, he and his company did everything in their power to *prevent* his plays from being published, for in his time, if a script could be found in published form, that would greatly decrease its box office appeal.

The 1623 folio edition was edited by friends, in tribute to Shakespeare. By this time, the great age of Elizabethan/Jacobean theater was coming to an end, and new standards based on Renaissance aesthetics were starting to come into vogue in England, including adherence to Aristotle, who was misinterpreted as having determined that Greek tragedies were all composed of five acts. For this monumental publication, all of Shakespeare's plays were arbitrarily divided into five pieces each, no matter whether this division reflected the original structure of each individual work or not.

If we see *The Winter's Tale* correctly, as essentially two pieces as opposed to five in its whole, it is a two-act play and not a five-act play. The number "2" has a wholly different character than the number "5." "2" is set up for parallels and contrasts; "5" gives a greater sense of sequence and broader sense of variety. Just like a 3/4 waltz beat is different from a march, writing a song in the wrong beat will create discord in your work.

We need to see numbers in creative work, but manageable ones. A 97-part musical composition, in my estimation, is not manageable. It inevitably must be broken down into smaller parts. Anything within five is manageable. Six can become two threes or three twos and therefore potentially confusing. My *A Dream Like a Dream* is written in 12 Acts, but the number 12 is not particularly manageable, so I visualize it as having four parts because that is how it is performed, with three intermissions, including a long dinner break.

We work toward creative unity. But "1" is the most difficult number to visualize and to manage because of the purity of its wholeness. When we are doing the actual work, our focus is always on parts. Rodin could only chisel one part of his sculpture at a time. Kurosawa could only film one shot at a time. If we know how many parts there are in the whole, we have a way to work more sensibly and more efficiently toward the final product.

Hollywood has long advocated a three-act structure for screenplays, even though Hollywood films have no intermissions between acts. The great fourteenth-century Japanese Noh dramatist Zeami wrote an important theoretical work called *Kadensho*. His main theory may seem totally obvious: a good performance has a good beginning, a good middle, and a good end.[3] What a revelation.

Actually, it would be hard to get better practical advice. I have seen many works without beginning or end, which just cannot stand up, as well as seemingly random fragments that are bunched together with amazing unity. I have also seen works that appear not to have a beginning, but actually do. Beckett's *Waiting for Godot*, a two-act structure, seems to have neither beginning nor end, only the middle. It appears to be a run-on structure. But on deeper examination, it has a

---

3 Zeami, *Kadensho* (Kyoto: Sumiya-Shinobe Pub. Institute, 1968), 39.

rich and enclosed structure. *Godot* works on the principle of repetition. Though Act 2 is a variation of the form of the first act, this does not mean that a third act can be added on. Through one repetition and one only, Beckett has shown us what he wants to, and leaves it there, complete in its seeming openness.

To Make a Flower Bloom

Zeami has another important theory, called *yugen*, or "sublime mystery" as I translate it (it has also simply been translated as "grace"[4]). The Noh play aims to blossom, like a subtle flower, bringing forth the beauty of *yugen*. Zeami says:

> A play must always be written with the basic principle of producing the seed that leads to a blooming of the Flower.[5]

This is a beautiful way to look at all creative works. When I listen to Bach's "Fugue in B Minor," the final piece of the monumental *Well-tempered Clavier (Book I)*, that is exactly what I hear, the blossoming and wilting, of life, and how wilting can create the most sublime blossoming. This is how we should write plays: a series of chemical reactions that lead to the ultimate climax, just like flowers that bloom, with the fragrance delivered at the end.

To know structure is wonderful indeed. To know how a flower blossoms is to have the secret tool to create mystery and beauty in your work. The great masters like Bach and Zeami understand how the flower blossoms, and can create blossoming at any moment, in any pattern.

Two Primal Choices

There are as many stories under the sun as there are ways to tell them. In this day and age, stories can be told in any order. The audience member in the theater sitting next to you may suddenly stand up and sing. Or you may be asked, as audience, to decide the order of a dance. Or you may wander into a house, and thereafter, whatever happens happens, and is considered a performance. Whoever creates the show makes the rules.

---

4 Zeami, *On the Art of the Nō Drama: The Major Treatises of Zeami*, trans. J. Thomas Rimer and Yamazaki Masakazu (Princeton: Princeton University Press, 1984), xxiii.
5 Ibid., 161.

At the fountainhead of the Western world's literature stand the *Iliad* and the *Odyssey* (c. 750 BC). Though these two epic poems of Homer are always considered a pair, they surprisingly are diametrically opposed in terms of structure. The *Iliad* uses the literary strategy called *in media res*, meaning "late starting point." Of the ten-year Trojan War, Homer chooses to start at the last two months, focusing on one character, Achilles, ending in his death. This is a very small slice of a very long story, composed in a tight, intricate ring structure.

The *Odyssey* works in a radically opposite way. The story of the travels of Odysseus after the war is over is a ten-year journey across sea and land. Homer starts from the beginning of the travels and ends at the end. There is no late entry point, no ring structure, just straightforward storytelling. Opposed to the tight structure of the *Iliad*, the *Odyssey* is a loose series of adventures that seem to roll on and on, like a bedtime story that can be added to or subtracted from. This is the archetypal epic adventure story, complete with a happy ending.

These two works, among the earliest known in Western literature, serve as the two poles of strategy for how one goes about telling a story: a small slice or a sprawling panorama. Tight or loose. Closed or open. From these two opposing strategies, we also begin to think in terms of the different spirits of tragedy and comedy. One is compressed and ends in death and darkness, the other is expansive and brings life and hope. If you understand the different strategies of the *Iliad* and *Odyssey*, you have a good start on understanding literary structure and compositional strategy.

This is an important lesson from the ancients that may help ground us in this increasingly fragmented age, when people swipe endlessly at their phones to switch content and may no longer even expect things to be whole. A pop artist, for instance, can easily be foiled in her plan to produce a concept album, because once released, the downloaded album can be shuffled on the listener's device in any random way. In the days when vinyl records were the norm, there were two sides to each album, two distinct parts labeled "A" and "B." Since a record player can only play one side at a time, in one single direction, a set order was established and adhered to, and usually was thoroughly thought out. You couldn't play vinyl records randomly, even if you wanted to. Landmark works such as Pink Floyd's *The Wall* and the Beatles' *Sergeant Pepper* couldn't have worked outside of such a framework, which, continuing with Zeami's analogy, allows you to design and manifest when the flower of each side blossoms, even as flowers are blossoming within each individual song.

What to do? We will see what happens. Whether fragmentation and randomness will take over all aspects of life or whether order and unity will make a comeback, this is for the times to tell.

Proportion

Structure manifests as proportion. Everything in nature, and in art, has proportion. Tastes change with the times. What may have been considered a good proportion in a certain age may now not be as appealing. What may have been considered a golden rule or a perfect proportion can also change with time. We don't, for example, build too many pyramids these days, and we might consider there being too many pillars in the Parthenon, or too much empty space in the Forbidden City. In fact, the shape and proportion of the ancient Greek theater changed over time due to the change in the nature of the performances. From nothing but a circle around which an audience gathered, there emerged a scenic house, which became bigger and bigger, infringing upon the circle space and ultimately engulfing it. This would be the prototype of our modern proscenium theater, which favors placing actors and audience facing each other rather than having the audience encircle the performance. This simple geometric difference is actually primordial in its significance, pitting linear against circular, finite against infinite, fragment against whole.

The Grand Hotel in Taipei has a Tang Dynasty roof and may be considered to be inspired by Tang Dynasty architecture. The problem is proportion. Tang Dynasty buildings are low-lying structures with large elaborate roofs. That is how they gain their unique beauty. The Grand Hotel stands at 14 floors tall. It just doesn't work.

What hasn't changed over the centuries is the rhythm of life. The elemental alternation of day and night, the cycles of the seasons, are reflected in the cycles of human life. The rainy season and dry season alternate in cycles in many places. This is rhythm, and it is also proportion. To be in tune with these elemental things means being in tune with rhythms that all people recognize. To be able to replicate these rhythms in our work gives our audience easy access to our creativity.

Arc and Triangle

The temporal arts of filmmaking, songwriting, choreography, fiction, and so on, all work with what is called the arc of the action. I call it a triangle, from the nineteenth-century practice of the "Well-made Play," found in the melodramas of French playwrights Scribe and Sardou, extending to Ibsen, and also written into theory by Freytag.

The well-made play opens with a conflict, usually a misunderstanding between the main characters, which gets complicated by further misunderstandings in what is called the rising action until things get to such an intense point that there must be some resolution. This in the jargon is called the "obligatory scene." It is the denouement, the climax, where the original conflict is resolved. The rest of the play is the tying up of odds and ends as the action winds down. Sound familiar? That's because most films, novels, musicals, pop songs, even theme park rides are designed this way.

Represented by a triangle, the conflict begins, then rises to the high point, the obligatory scene, which occurs around 7/10 in (see Figure 17.1).

Audiences are a bit more restless these days. If you are watching a 100-minute film, expect the climactic scene to come around 85 or 90. Sometimes for action films, it comes in the big fight between the good guy and the bad guy at the very end. There is little patience for falling action. Rolling credits count these days as falling action, I guess.

Of course, this is not the only way to write a story. In particular, the theory that a play or film must always start with a conflict is not a sacred rule. But however you start and proceed, no matter how complex or fragmented your narrative is, you must construct your arc. It is not just a tool for playwriting. It is an archetypal shape that represents an elemental emotional pattern in the viewer's mind. To have a healthy triangle in your script gives the audience a familiar path to journey through, and a map for yourself to gauge when the flowers in your script should blossom.

The structure of the popular song explains the triangle in a micro way. In a normal 32-bar popular song written in "AABA" form—8 bars each, think Cole Porter's "I Get A Kick Out of You," or Lennon/McCartney's "Yesterday," the "B" part, the third verse, or the bridge, shifts into a different melody before coming back to the original "A." That is where the natural emotional high is, on or after

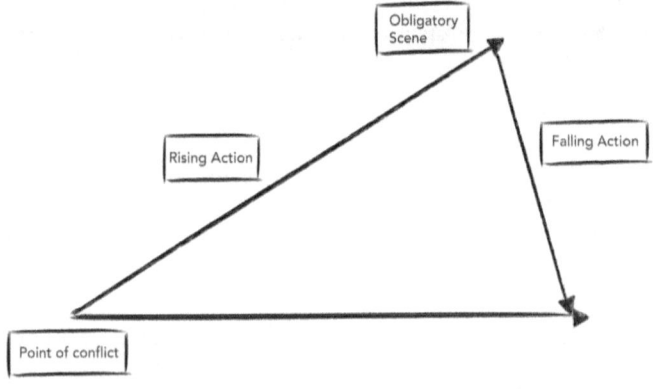

FIGURE 17.1 The well-made play.

the third verse. There are countless examples to study how this works in the Great American Songbook that, in its microcosmic scale, can teach us how drama and emotions rise and fall in a larger work. The well-crafted popular song is like the proverbial Chinese sparrow. All of its organs are intact, and so the same pattern can be enlarged proportionately to create larger structures like novels or films. In fact, the AABA form reflects on how many a Hollywood film works.

One year, on one of my obligatory trips to take my kids to Disneyland, bored, I actually timed the action of Splash Mountain with my stopwatch. It was uncanny. Everything happened exactly like a well-made play, with conflict, small dips in the boat ride that foreshadowed the great climax. The action rose, literally, to the obligatory big scene where you come splashing down the waterfall almost vertically. It all worked in a perfect arc. The ending, however, dragged on, out of proportion, for the practical reason that they needed time to process the photos they took of you in that climactic moment, which they would sell to you at the end of the ride.

The Primordial Pattern

Why is the arc such a primal thing that all recognize? Is the climax of a year in autumn? Is the climax of a day at sunset? Sort of. But why does a story have to end with a bang? Why can't the bang be in the middle, or one third of the way in? Why do we even need a bang? Does a story exist without a climax? My theory is there is something more primal that is mirrored in this triangle, which is the universally experienced act of sex. The arc of the sexual act is something we all recognize: the foreplay, the rising action, leading to the climax, which it is actually called, then the proverbial cigarette at the end. Since this is the structure of the act that creates life itself, it is why we all recognize this triangle at a subconscious level with a sense of awe and mystery and wish to replicate its shape in storytelling. There is nothing more primal to life, and so there is nothing more primal to storytelling.

For an advanced understanding of the triangle/arc and the well-made play, know that the writer, during the course of the rising action, may construct medium-sized triangles on the way up, and on the arc of those medium-sized triangles, may construct even smaller triangles. This is the formula for a serial novel or a Netflix series. The medium segments are episodes, the smaller units each scene that ends in a commercial. Each episode has its rising action and denouement, which contributes to the rising action of the whole series. The viewer is taken on a calculated roller-coaster ride, with ups and downs that gradually reach a designed height (see Figure 17.2).

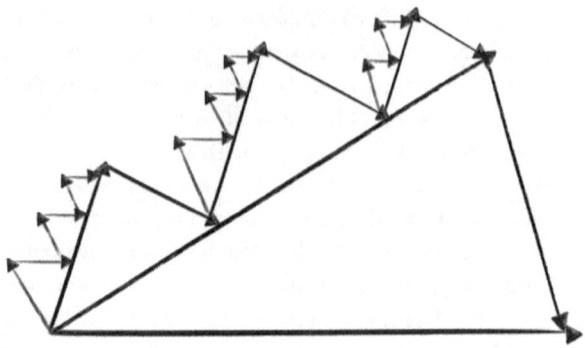

FIGURE 17.2 The elaborately well-made play.

It should go without saying that the triangle, or whatever formula you may learn in playwriting class, is just that, a formula for putting things together. Though time-tested, a formula can never make a good screenplay or novel or song by itself. What you put together, and how you put it together, is the real test. That is where the wisdom element on the left side of the map kicks in to help out.

Ibsen wrote over seventy melodramas before *A Doll's House*. Actually, all of his later masterpieces were based on the well-made play formula. The difference was the spark of wisdom from the left side, which suddenly filled this tried-and-true formula with social consciousness, thus changing the trajectory of modern theater.

Seeing the Forest While Working on the Trees

To create unity, you need to see the whole thing at once. If you can't, it is like working on a jigsaw puzzle where one attempts to connect pieces to pieces and not pieces to the whole. You need to have a way to organize everything into something practically workable. For this, you may not have to learn from artists. There are excellent organizational tools to borrow from businesses or production houses. The key is to allow yourself to see the elements of the whole project in one view. Only when you see the whole can you see all the parts. Only when you see all the parts can you work on each part to create the whole.

You can use post-it stickies to write down and stick all of the components of a project onto a whiteboard, use different colors of paper to write down the names of the different parameters and spread them out on the ground in front of you, or download organizational software that lets you place everything on a screen.

With everything before you, you are in a position to analyze how to put it all together.

My personal method of seeing the whole while seeing the parts developed over the years. A director's script for a play is usually bound page by page in a file folder, but as you direct a play while flipping the pages, you cannot see its entirety. You can only see one page at a time. I developed a simple graph where I notate which character is on stage, minute by minute, scene by scene. I call it a progression chart because it simply shows you the progression of your play, in time, based on the density of characters on stage. Drawn by hand or typed up on a computer, it takes up about two or three pages, depending on the length of the play. Print out the three pages, tape them together, place them before you, and you can see the entire progression of the play. A condensed example, using 2 minutes as a unit, looks like what is presented in Figure 17.3.

This is pure data only, like today's stock market graph, which indicates the rise and fall of the index over time. It shows you the density of characters on stage, which may reveal which scenes are large group scenes with a lot of action, and where there may be less happening. But it is only data. What I do next is turn the chart on its side and annotate it, using colored pencils to mark which parts should go higher emotionally, which parts are plot twists, which parts are music or movement-oriented, and so on. I can also color different parts of the play to show its "density," which may serve as an indicator of how the audience's emotions progress as the performance unfolds over time. Now we have a visual chart of how the progression of the performance should unfold in the director's mind. When you peruse such a chart from the director's seat, you are seeing the whole thing at a glance. The forest is there before you, and you have marked out all the tree clusters and pathways. If you can execute the progression of this chart, you have a very good chance of bringing your audience into the work emotionally, ebbing and flowing with the performance, with the arc rising and falling the way you have designed the flowers in the work to blossom (see Figure 17.4).

With such a chart, I can direct my play in the rehearsal room just by referring to it. I don't need my script.

You should find your own way to create tools that can help you see your work better. If you have a way to see your whole work before you at a glance, you have a handle on how it is made up. You can pinpoint what places aren't working and what are. You can easily see the areas you need to fix.

This is just a tool. Even better is to have it all in your mind. For some, it is possible to visualize the whole work. To be able to see it all on a single piece of paper isn't a bad second choice.

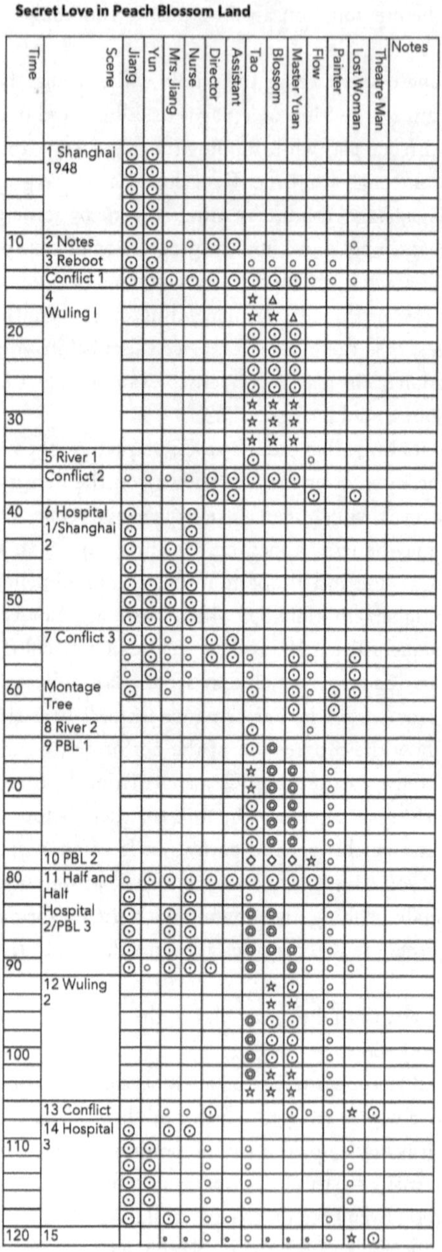

FIGURE 17.3 Progression chart for *Secret Love in Peach Blossom Land*, using 2 minutes as a unit.

Crafting Structure 179

Secret Love in Peach Blossom Land

Time	Scene	Jiang	Yun	Mrs. Jiang	Nurse	Director	Assistant	Tao	Blossom	Master Yuan	Flow	Painter	Lost Woman	Theatre Man	Notes
	1 Shanghai 1948	◉	◉												
		◉	◉												
		◉	◉												
		◉	◉												
10	2 Notes	◉	◉	○	○	◉	◉					○			
	3 Reboot	◉	◉					○	○	○	○	○			
	Conflict 1	◉	◉	◉	◉	◉	◉	◉	◉	◉	◉	○	○		
	4 Wuling I							☆	△						
								☆	☆	△					
20								◉	◉	◉					
								◉	◉	◉					
								◉	◉	◉					
								◉	◉	◉					
								☆	☆	☆					
30								☆	☆	☆					
								☆	☆	☆					
	5 River 1							◉			○				
	Conflict 2	○	○	○	○	◉	◉	◉	◉	◉					
						◉	◉			◉		○			
40	6 Hospital 1/Shanghai 2	◉			◉										
		◉			◉										
		◉		◉	◉										
		◉		◉	◉										
		◉	◉	◉	◉										
50		◉	◉	◉	◉										
		◉	◉	◉	◉										
	7 Conflict 3	◉	◉	○	○	◉	◉								
		○	◉	○	○	◉	◉	○		◉	○		◉		
		○	◉	○	○			○		◉	○		◉		
60	Montage Tree	◉		○				◉		◉	○	◉	◉		
								◉		◉					
	8 River 2							◉			○				
	9 PBL 1							◉	◉						
								☆	◉	◉			○		
70								☆	◉	◉			○		
								◉	◉	◉			○		
								◉	◉	◉			○		
								◉	◉	◉			○		
	10 PBL 2							◇	◇	◇	☆		○		
80	11 Half and Half Hospital 2/PBL 3	○	◉	◉	◉	◉	◉	◉	◉	◉	◉		○		
		◉			◉			○					○		
		◉		◉	◉			◉	◉				○		
		◉		◉	◉			◉	◉				○		
		◉		◉	◉			◉	◉				○		
90		◉	○	◉	◉	◉		◉			◉	○	○		
	12 Wuling 2							☆	◉				○		
								☆	☆				○		
								◉	◉	◉			○		
								◉	◉	◉			○		
100								◉	◉	◉			○		
								◉	☆	☆			○		
								☆	☆	☆			○		
	13 Conflict			○	○	◉					◉	○	○	☆	◉
	14 Hospital 3	◉		◉	◉										
110		◉	◉			○		○				○			
		◉	◉			○		○				○			
		◉	◉			○		○				○			
		◉			○	○									
120	15		●	●	○	●		●	●	●	●		☆	◉	

FIGURE 17.4 Progression chart for *Secret Love in Peach Blossom Land*, annotated.

Whether your work can stand up without falling apart is dependent on your proficiency on the right side of the map. Whether your work is worthy or great, depends on the left side, and more so, on the cooperation between left and right.

Exercises and Further Thoughts

1. Pick any object around you. Now, analyze its structure. How does its structure relate to its function?
2. For the same object, can you perceive what its essential number is?
3. Pick any recent film or play you have seen. How many parts are there? What are the relationships between the parts, in terms of how they push toward an emotional climax?
4. Choose a popular song that you like. Can you perceive its musical structure? How does it repeat, and what does it gain through repetition?
5. Choose a fugue by Bach. Analyze its structure in terms of how it delivers emotionally to the listener. You can use a blank piece of paper, draw a line which represents your timeline, then mark your emotional rise and fall within that timeline as you listen. That is structure.
6. Consider what Zeami says about blossoming and beauty. Can you relate any works you know to this theory?
7. Invent an organizational tool that lets you see your whole project at once.
8. Invent another tool for the same purpose. Note that there is no one way to see your whole work at a glance. Find the one that works for you.

PART SEVEN
Your Creative App

Be space, my friend.

CHAPTER EIGHTEEN

ACTIVATING YOUR APP

Showtime!

We have studied everything on the left and right sides of the map. Now it's time to pull all the wisdom and method together into a creative work!

The small triangle on the upper part of the map represents the Creative App. This is the magical mechanism that, in the moment of inspiration, pulls files from our file warehouse, combines them into new files, then draws tools to work on a project, bringing content and form together, triggering the actual creative work. The simple age-old equation of content plus form begins its incubation.

At the same time, usually a bit later, the app also chooses tools from the toolbox to work together and give shape to the files. Content meets form, initiating an often difficult mating process.

The app represents the actual work done on the creative project, from genesis to the final opus. Everything outside of the small triangle is preparation that happens in life and training. All this preparation is to be used by the app, to be transformed by the app into the final opus.

Look at everything we have done in preparation: We have learned how to de-label objects, and by doing so we free things from the binding that glues them together. They become disconnected, to be reconnected in any way possible. Things that usually have no business being together are now available in our minds to merge and coexist. We have broken down the barrier and connected to the source, which infuses us with fresh creative energy. We have discarded the non-creative mode and are running on creative.

We have developed a mature worldview. The issues that concern us and our opinions toward them carry sufficient weight for a creative project. We understand causes and effects. We have learned how to analyze motivation. We understand how passions morph into behavior and actions, and how we should monitor our own motives when undertaking any creative project. We also know that we should let go, to seek a free and pure expression.

At the same time, we have studied history and witnessed the marvelous things that have been created through human effort that are dazzling in structure, form, and meaning. These buildings, paintings, musical compositions, novels, plays, operas, sculptures, scientific discoveries, business deals, and so on, have all shown us how things can be put together, in what different ways, and what is worthy of being put together.

We have studied nature. We understand how things work, not only on a physical level but the chemical reactions that are created on an intangible level. We have studied the history of art forms and stocked our toolbox with all sorts of *isms* as well as a wealth of technical knowledge. We are aware of the newest technology. We have practiced and practiced our craft, to the point where we are very good at it.

We are at the point of knowing what to do and knowing how to do it. We are ready to connect ideas to form. We are all set. Our app is waiting to be triggered into action.

The app depends on all of the preparation to function, but it is not the sum of all these things. It works on its own logic, the logic of creativity. Its particular functions are association and connection. It makes associations and connects things: stories, characters, impressions, ideas, colors, smells. The simplest type of connectivity is A+B, or "Opposite Placement," two exercises that we have explored in Chapter Six. These simple functions would be a beta version of our app, something to start trying out our app with. Through practice, the app gets more and more sophisticated. The things that can be assimilated become much more complicated. We are capable of building complex structures that have the power to connect. A superior app can connect your wisdom to your method, and the resulting product can connect to your audience and to all existence.

Unfortunately, there is no App Store that offers a download for this app. You have to build it yourself, in your mind. How? By studying everything outside of it. All of the wisdom and method that you accumulate in life and art contribute to the construction of your app. Next, understand how it works, and you can activate it.

Bruce Lee's advice on martial arts practice is "Be water, my friend."[1] For our purpose, we strive to be space.

---

1 Bruce Lee, from film *Enter the Dragon,* Orange Sky Golden Harvest, Warner Bros., 1973.

The Fast Track: Being Space

Creativity is a whimsical thing. Though we have prepared meticulously for it, it still has to happen. We have covered how it all works, and having done our practice on wisdom and method, we are prepared to make it happen.

Unfortunately, the creative app doesn't have a simple on and off button. We must figure out how to turn it on.

Even Mozart, who must have had a top-of-the-line app, didn't seem able to summon inspiration on demand:

> When I am, as it were, completely myself, entirely alone, and of good cheer—say traveling in a carriage, or walking after a good meal, or during the night when I cannot sleep: it is on such occasions that my ideas flow best and most abundantly. Whence and how they come, I know not; nor can I force them. [2]

This reminds me of stanzas coming into the mind of A. E. Housman while walking (Chapter Two), and how so many scientists and artists advocate taking long walks to induce creativity. In fact, Stanford researchers Marily Oppezzo and Daniel Schwartz, as well as others, have conducted experiments that prove walking enhances creativity. As opposed to sitting, "a person's creative output increased by an average of 60 percent when walking."[3] The study also notes the modern myths of Steve Jobs and Mark Zuckerberg conducting meetings while taking walks. I'm not sure about that percentage boost, but if true, we should be walking all the time. To quote Housman again:

> I would go out for a walk of two or three hours. As I went along, thinking of nothing in particular, only looking at things around me and following the progress of the seasons, there would flow into my mind, with sudden and unaccountable emotion, sometimes a line or two of verse, sometimes a whole stanza at once, accompanied, not preceded, by a vague notion of the poem which they were destined to form part of. Then there would usually be a lull of an hour or so, then perhaps the spring would bubble up again. I say bubble up, because, so far as I could make out, the source of the suggestions thus proffered to the brain was an abyss which I have already had occasion to

---

2 Duke.
3 "Stanford Study Finds Walking Improves Creativity," *Stanford Report*, April 24, 2014, news.stanford.edu/stories/2014/04/walking-vs-sitting-042414

mention, the pit of the stomach. When I got home I wrote them down, leaving gaps, and hoping that further inspiration might be forthcoming another day.[4]

This corroborates everything we have talked about in the Wisdom section of this book. Creativity needs space to happen. If your mind's computer hard drive is full, you don't have space to even install the app. If it is always busy running a million other apps, your creative app will lag, and function slowly, or not at all. For any computer, the bigger the hard drive, the more you can do. We need to create space for creativity.

Once activated, the creative app is continuously turned on and working in the background at all times, even when your mind's computer is asleep. When it senses possibilities, it goes to work. How do we activate it? It is not a simple matter of turning on and off. Start by practicing A+B and other exercises to get it going, to get the wheels churning. You have to nurture it, giving it the best environment to wake up and activate. The optimal environment is tranquility. Once your app is running, it is most easily spurred into action when you are doing nothing, and there is ample space in your mind.

Doing nothing also helps clear out space in your mind. In empty space, anything can arise. The essayist Rebecca Solnit explains why walking helps in this respect:

> [...] doing nothing is hard to do. It's best done by disguising it as doing something, and the something closest to doing nothing is walking.[5]

But doing nothing has to go a step further, which is thinking of nothing. This is even harder. Zen practitioner Alan Watts said, "a person who thinks all the time has nothing to think about except thoughts."[6] Thinking does not work for creativity, at least not on this first-tier fast track. Einstein said:

> The intellect has little to do on the road to discovery. There comes a leap in consciousness, call it intuition or what you will, and the solution comes to you and you don't know how or why.[7]

---

4 Housman, *The Name and Nature of Poetry*, 49–50.
5 Rebecca Solnit, *Wanderlust: A History of Walking* (New York: Penguin, 2001).
6 Alan Watts, quoted in www.goodreads.com/quotes/10246506-a-person-who-thinks-all-the-time-has-nothing-to
7 Albert Einstein, in *Forbes Magazine*, September 15, 1974.

In Thoreau's seminal essay "Walking," he explores the idea of "sauntering," "from idle people who roved about the country, in the Middle Ages, and asked for charity, under pretense of going *à la Sainte Terre*, to the Holy Land."[8] He continues:

> Some, however, would derive the word from *sans terre* without land or a home, which, therefore, in the good sense, will mean, having no particular home, but equally at home everywhere. For this is the secret of successful sauntering.[9]

To wander and to saunter. To be going nowhere, but to be going. That is the creative spirit. To wander is to let the mind wander, and the wandering mind may end up in unexpected places. I think of the Franciscan traveling monks who by their code would have no possessions and vowed not to stay under the same roof for two consecutive nights. I also think of the tradition of Buddhist monks begging for their meals. There is a freedom in what they do while constricting themselves. For them, it is not a question of forced poverty, nor is it for the purpose of creativity, but to free the mind from making choices and being judgmental. To accept wherever as a home, to accept whatever as a meal takes real practice, real shedding of labels and concepts. This is the free state, free of judgment and full of space. For the monks, the extra space would be available to be filled with faith and spiritual practice. For us, it is available to be filled with creativity.

The Blank Canvas in Your Mind

Remember, the creative app pulls files from your mind and combines them into new files. We activate our app by using it, by mindfully combining things, visualizing their opposites, and seeing connections between all things. Just as you need a blank piece of paper to start writing, a blank canvas to start doodling, a blank computer screen to start programming, it is a blank mind that readily draws inspiration. Once your app is activated, inspiration is not as sacred or rare as you think. The potential to be inspired should and can always be available. This can be attained through practice. Meditation is the support for this.

There are many different types of meditation, to be used for different purposes. One in particular is the practice outlined in the Exercises after Chapter Eleven, where you think of nothing. It may sound easy, but it is probably one

---

8 See Henry David Thoreau, "Walking," in *The Atlantic*, June 1862, www.theatlantic.com/magazine/archive/1862/06/walking/304674/
9 Ibid.

of the most difficult things to do because our mind is like a river, continually streaming thoughts at a breakneck pace. Our mind is the most powerful streaming device in the world. If through continual practice you can start turning off some channels and quiet that river, you may begin to experience the state of non-thinking, approaching what is known in Buddhism as the empty nature. This is not emptiness in a nihilistic sense but empty of discursive thoughts, creating a platform that can be filled with anything. This type of meditation pertains to the "*shi-ne*" method, and in some practices is called "peaceful abiding." Aside from my rudimentary introduction, there are many excellent books that can explain the practice, which you can and should try, best with a qualified teacher.[10]

This is the essence of the fast-track creative mind. If you can create a state of blank canvas non-thinking in your mind, then you have actually created a master control of the switch to turn on your creative app on demand.

Before you do that, there is another switch that needs to be turned on. That is the basic switch that brings you from non-creative to creative mode. It is everything that we have been dealing with up to here. Keep that machine churning. Always see dogs in the sky. Never draft acceptance speeches before you receive an award. See people and things as they are. Think about the cloud in this book page, how it connects to everything.

The empty state/blank slate is not to be understood as dull or inactive. You must not think of it as an inert space waiting for something to happen. To the contrary, think of it as a bright light that is alert and extremely nimble, able to see and absorb everything around it, and quickly process what is relevant and what is not. It is the opposite of inaction. It is potential itself. It is productive spontaneity.

Spontaneity is key to creativity. Our minds must be flexible and work in a spontaneous way to first let all the relevant elements in, and then let them interact. Do not mistake spontaneity for being unconstrained and impulsive, and just doing whatever you like. Spontaneity, as we have discussed in Chapter Fourteen, is not the ability to act freely at any moment, but a state of mind that takes in everything coming at it and reacts naturally. The old Tibetan saying goes, "To see a painting in a dark room, the candle must be still, and it must be bright."[11] The mind must be still, the mind must be bright. The spontaneous light in the dark room sees everything in all its detail, and makes connections freely.

---

10 Further introduction, amongst many places, can be found at "Shi-ne Meditation (opening awareness)," vajrayananow.com/shi-ne-meditation
11 From a personal conversation with Dzongsar Khyentse Rinpoche.

Spontaneity does not function well in a restless mind, which may be prone to concocting wild things. The restless mind is like a candle that is continually wavering to the drafts that flow through the room. This may produce novel thoughts, but it is also unreliable. To the contrary, spontaneity with a settled mind is a most powerful thing. I believe most of the greatest improvisatory jazz solos and Chinese calligraphy and Abstract Expressionist paintings in history have been created with a settled mind, which may emanate streams of restless energy but is nevertheless settled. See Chapter Twenty for more on the topic.

The Analytical Path

The fast track helps you quickly activate your creative app. It is not easy to get there because you have to release your mind of thoughts while keeping your spontaneity. This is a high-wire balancing act that needs practice to master. If it doesn't work for you, another track is always available, where you actually utilize your thoughts to activate your app. This is the analytical path.

If you are commissioned to do a creative work, the job usually comes with certain parameters. This is what you start your rational analysis with. An architect with a contract to build a museum has a site and a list of the client's needs. These have already defined parameters within which you can work.

If there is no inspiration to start, do not worry. Keep studying the requirements, keep letting all the parameters settle in your cognitive mind. You don't need inspiration now. You need to rationally research the particular type of art to be displayed, trends in museum design, air conditioning systems for museums, audiovisual tools for lecture halls... You need to study the site. What is its history? What kind of buildings are around it, and what kind of people live and work around there? Through analysis, the answers will come logically: Who is the museum for? Where is the entrance? How many stories? Where is the main exhibition hall? Where is the cafeteria? Where is the museum store? What should the building look like? For every question dealt with through such critical analysis, you gain answers, and as the answers add up, the design comes into focus. Some of the iconic architectures of the world, like Frank Gehry's Getty Museum in Bilbao, Spain, look like they came from some spark of inspiration, when they equally could have come from meticulous logical analysis. Kris Yao's Wuzhen Grand Theater is a marvelously conceived double lotus architectural structure with ice-crack patterns particular to the windows of the area as trimming. He solved the original question with a combination of inspiration and rational analysis.

Recently, I have been working with the esteemed Danish architectural firm BIG on a theater in the city of Suzhou, China, dedicated to the performance of plays in the so-called "Lotus Pond" configuration that I pioneered in *A Dream Like a Dream*, which places the audience at the center, with performing space surrounding them. It took a little time for them to understand the concept of the staging, but once they did, I was impressed by the encyclopedic knowledge the talented young team brought to the table, which led to new inspiration for the design of this unique theater.[12]

All the requirements given at the outset equal Michelangelo's statue in the stone. The fast track is to just chisel away and reveal the statue. Equally effective is the analytical way, through which, after careful analysis and rational thought, you pinpoint where to chisel and then work away.

Catch the Wind

When the app kicks in and inspiration does come, capture it. Don't wait until you get back into your working space to write it down or make notes. Do it then, wherever you are. If you are eating, stop eating; if jogging, stop jogging; even if driving, pull to the side of the road and jot it down. The basic quality of inspiration is the same as dreams or random thoughts. They are ethereal, like mist floating in the sun, that can evaporate at a moment's notice. I was fortunate when the massive inspiration for *A Dream Like a Dream* came to me that night in India (Chapter Two). For some unknown reason, I did not write it all down but instead just wrote a few words and went to sleep. Now that I think back, that was quite dangerous. I lucked out the next morning when it was all still there. I could have easily lost the whole inspiration, just like losing the thread of a dream.

For another play of mine, *Sand on a Distant Star*,[13] the inspiration came to me, literally, in a dream, the evening after a transpacific flight. Jet lag made it easy for me to wake up, and I did, following the thread of thought down to the kitchen in my friend's house where I was staying, and I jotted everything down on a note card, then went back to sleep. I do not believe this play would be in existence if I had neglected to make that effort.

---

12 At the time of publication, this theater is under construction as part of a new Suzhou arts complex.
13 See Stan Lai, *Selected Plays, Vol. 2*.

Toolbox Full, Mind Open

At a recent lecture, I was asked how I assimilated so many different things in my work: East and West, comedy and tragedy, monologue and dialogue, conflicting styles, and so on. My answer was that, after all of these decades of creative work, my toolbox has quite a lot of stuff in it. But that doesn't mean that I need to use all or any of it. With a full toolbox, we need to have an open mind. I have seen students of mine come back from training in the Suzuki method, for instance, and this becomes the controlling influence of their next creative work. Though they may have gained precious training, it would seem that they have lost their creative selves. Sometimes training makes us narrower instead of broader. It's not because you spent a long time studying postmodern aesthetics that your work must incorporate this tool, or because you took a special course in the latest lighting technology, and so you have to use it. The optimal way to use our creative app is through the open-minded wisdom that lets us mix and match whatever we think appropriate.

Fullness and openness are not conflicting states.

Be dedicated to your work. If the sculpture is in the stone and you're not ready to chisel away, you have two choices: non-thought and thought. By non-thinking, solutions will come. If they don't, you can resort to rational thinking. Diligence and perseverance help you dig deeper, create cracks, and eventually expose what is inside.

Exercises and Further Thoughts

1. What is the state of your current creative project? Have you figured out the form that goes with the content?
2. While in the creative process, try to do nothing. See what happens.
3. Instead of doing nothing, do everything to analyze every aspect of your project. Ask questions and gather information on everything about the project. See what happens.
4. Can "full" be "open"? How full is your toolbox? How open are you to using your tools in a combination?

CHAPTER NINETEEN

PUTTING IT ALL TOGETHER

Melding Style to Substance

Content has now been pulled together with form into your app. Now the work begins: to meld style to substance, to craft structure, to find the creative solution to the creative question, to figure out all the causes and effects that link the work together, and to install all the details into the project. Usually, it's a struggle for anyone, even the advanced practitioner. More than anything now, you need confidence—confidence in your project, and more importantly, confidence in yourself. As van Gogh said,

> If you hear a voice within you say "you cannot paint," then by all means paint, and that voice will be silenced.[1]

It's now all up to you. You call the shots now. It's time to act. Time to work. Time to do the difficult work.

We can break down any creative work into parts. And so we can envision creative work as putting together all the parts. Assembly. With a clear blueprint, parts are easy to assemble. For the Master, the blueprint is in the mind, inseparable from the parts.

If you know what you want to say, and you know how you want to say it (figuratively, this goes for the visual artist as well), you have a pretty good starting point, and things should go pretty smoothly. But this is usually not the case. What do we really want to say (do)? We have discussed how we often venture into a creative project without truly knowing what it is. The desire is a mystery, a

---

[1] Vincent van Gogh, quoted in www.sarahransomeart.com/blog/motivational-quotes-from-famous-artists

journey to the unknown. This is perfectly legitimate and actually quite normal. It can also be very exciting. At the end of the day, though, you have to discover what you want to do, where you want to go, and what you want to say. I cannot think of too many successful works where the author really didn't know what he wanted to say or do, fumbled around and finally made something to show the public that was worth showing.

Creativity, honestly, isn't easy. How do we get it done? Each artist finds their own way. Over time, you find ways of doing things, and you get better at it. It is a lonely process. The master can teach you and show you everything you need to know about making a masterpiece, everything but instilling the power and ability in you to actually make it. Bill Evans said, "It ends up that if the jazz player—if he is going to be a serious jazz player, teaches himself."[2] This is true of all creativity. There is a point where the teacher can take you no farther and the teaching stops. You must navigate the waters yourself and find your way to the other shore. There is no other way to arrive at your own creativity.

You have to empower yourself.

The 99 Percent

> I don't know much about creative writing programs. But they're not telling the truth if they don't teach, one, that writing is hard work, and, two, that you have to give up a great deal of life, your personal life, to be a writer.[3]
>
> —Doris Lessing

Just because the app is near the top of the map doesn't mean you are close to the goal. Here is where the maddening work of actually writing a novel, or play, or filmscript, or composing a symphony, or an opera, or painting a painting happens.

At this stage I can uplift you with inspirational phrases like "Go with the flow!" "Listen to your inner self!" "Now is where your creative spirit takes over!" And it may all be true, but in the end, you have to face the actual work. Unfortunately, it is the most boring part of the equation, and definitely the most time-consuming. It can also be the most difficult part. For anyone, it only takes a moment to be inspired, but even for the master, it can take long, laborious hours

---

2 Bill Evans, *The Universal Mind of Bill Evans*, Rhapsody Films (DVD), 1991.
3 Doris Lessing, quoted in www.brainyquote.com/topics/hard-work-quotes_2

to actually complete a project. I would say that Edison was close when he said that "genius is 1% inspiration and 99% perspiration."[4] The Chinese phrase for creativity is two words that literally mean "create" and "work"—"*chuangzuo.*" My experience of it is that 10 percent is the "*chuang*" or create part, and 90 percent is the "*zuo*" or work part.

There is no denying that creative work is hard and intense. Even if it is something short, like a poem or a short film, it is still an excruciating labor to give birth to it, perhaps even moreso when it is short and condensed. But that doesn't mean that we can't love it. Most of my friends in the arts are like me. We love to go to work. We can't wait. And there isn't a moment when we don't feel blessed that this is our line of work, even if it is driving us crazy. I guess this is the happy paradox of creative work. It is hard to imagine how all of the scientists and artists of the past, who created all of the great inventions and works of art that have propelled humanity forward, could have defeated all of the challenges along the way without the fervent love of their work.

But the reason why creative work is so difficult is that it is not just a question of putting words down if you are a novelist, or notes down if you are a composer. As mentioned before, we need to create works that are unified. Audiences are not interested in seeing something half done. For a genius like Mozart, it was simple. But for the great majority of us, we figure things out as we go along. We spend a lot of time creating things that eventually don't fit together. Many things ultimately get discarded. But that's OK. That's perfectly normal, in fact, necessary, because they are often the unavoidable missteps that lead to the right things. And once you find those right things, in the right order, you are excited that it all seems right. Then you reevaluate everything, see previous things that you thought were right but now, because of your new discoveries, are wrong, and you have to take it all apart. When this happens, and I'm not trying to jinx you, but it definitely will, truly, it's all good. It happens to all of us. It's the nature of the game. It's the ordeal experienced in all creative work.

Hard work and perseverance is the certain remedy.

Satisfying the Devil

No great work leaves details unattended. Even if the material for a work is very common, the master's attention to detail is always there. The devil is certainly

---

4 Thomas Edison, quoted in www.dictionary.com/browse/genius-is-one-percent-inspiration-and-ninety-nine-percent-perspiration, from *Harper's Magazine*, c. 1932.

in the details, but one way to look at it is that once all of the details have been attended to, the devil is satisfied and leaves.

I would not claim to understand all of the details of all of the different art forms or creative projects. They are for you to uncover and handle. A transcendent dining experience, for instance, hinges on so many details, some to do with food, some to do with presentation. But it all has to do with timing. Only when everything is right is the right effect unleashed, and the devil released.

Perfectionists are obsessed with details. I don't think you have to be a perfectionist to be a successful creative person, but you do have to have a streak of obsessiveness in you. When I am rehearsing a new play, my major tool for details, like for most directors, as well as designers, choreographers, most everyone in performative work, is note-taking and giving. As the rehearsal unfolds before me, I take note of anything that catches my eye that is not right, and after the rehearsal is over, I spend as much time as necessary to give notes and fix things. All of the details are addressed here. An actor should wait for another actor's line before moving. The lighting must fade out in 2.5 seconds and not three. A prop vase is too large. A costume needs to be changed. An actor needs glasses. A word has been pronounced wrong. Every day there is a checklist of maybe 100 things that grows and then diminishes, until luckily, near the end of the rehearsal process, there may be only 10 or 20 things wrong. How to fix these things takes learning, patience, and maybe 10,000 hours. Some details are fixed in an instant; we recognize them as method notes. Others are psychological problems where actors cannot reach the depths or understanding of a character's situation. These are wisdom notes, and take patient coaching with the actors. To know what is wrong doesn't guarantee that you know how to fix it. To know how to fix it also doesn't mean it can be fixed instantly. Some problems can only be fixed over a process of time. This is the wisdom of the director.

Often, I see beginning directors driven crazy by rehearsals. At the end of a rehearsal, they may be shouting or trying to hold in their anger and frustration. One of the simple but hard facts that a director needs to know is that any production needs time to mature. So, one of the greatest qualities a director needs is patience. As a director, you have an image in your mind about what the final product should look like. Unfortunately, that final product will not appear on the first day of rehearsal, or the second. It will take at least four weeks, depending on your efficiency, for this pot of rice to cook. The art of the director is to be able to see how a production is progressing toward its ideal final form, without having any solid reference to that final form. There are not many tangible road markers. You have to be able to assess a day's progress by judging/guessing how you are doing in relation to the completed work. It's like cooking without a timer. You need to know where you are on any given day, in relation to the incubation process, of which length you know. This takes patience and experience.

Schedules, Schedules

Everyone works differently, and we have to find our own way of working.

The fact is, much of the physical work on a creative project is inner work to discover the true soul of your opus, which exists within. Few projects are conceived whole, with perfect planning and scheduling that don't need modification, unless they are part of a corporate system that works like an assembly line and demands a final product, regardless of quality. The Hollywood model production system is designed for efficiency. But there are no guarantees that the true soul of the production can be uncovered through this system. You are guaranteed to create a body, for sure, but not necessarily a soul.

Scheduling is an important factor for the success of any creative endeavor that involves a team. My hard lesson about scheduling came early in my career, when I was commissioned to write and direct a complex opera called *Journey to the West*[5] for the opening of the National Theatre in Taiwan. The orchestral score by Chien-tai Chen was an elaborate composition that included traditional Chinese music elements as well as classical Western opera. The European conductor of the orchestra summoned me to his office to discuss rehearsal schedule. He opened his heavy appointment book, perused it, and pointed to two sessions, a few weeks apart. Exasperated, I said, "What? We are talking about a complex three-hour orchestral score. How could you possibly rehearse it in six hours?" He finally raised his head to look at me, this young Asian director, in the eye. He said, "I'll be ready. Will you?" He continued: "Half of the battle is won through scheduling. Are you up to it?" I swallowed my pride and took in this hard lesson, which in large part is true when you are working in a team with many moving parts.

Now, I make a point to be the schedule maker for my productions. It isn't easy to make an effective schedule for something as complex as a theater production. You have to know the insides of the production, its scope, its complexity, the technical challenges, and all the intangibles, like which actors are committed to other projects and cannot show up on certain dates. Any professional stage manager would be adept at drawing up a feasible schedule, but I do believe that I know how much time needs to be spent on each part of the whole, and so I make

---

5 Stan Lai, *Journey to the West (Xiyouji)* (Taipei: Crown, 1988); collected in *Lai Shengchuan: Juchang, Vol. 2* (Taipei: Meta, 1999).

the first draft of the schedule and leave it to the stage manager to make revisions as necessary.

Having said all this, there can be no timetable or deadline for uncovering the soul of a work. When will magic be revealed? That itself is a mystery. But if you have a deadline, you have to assume that it happens somewhere in the schedule. There is guesswork involved in making schedules, but you have to make the effort to put out the best one possible, which means a balance of enough time, while not being excessively demanding on the cast and crew.

I have developed a style of working in rehearsals that is alternately intense and casual. A session starts on time, but we usually don't start working before engaging in some small talk about anything, usually about everyday life. Food is allowed in my rehearsal rooms, so sometimes we eat or snack before starting. I think this is all necessary, particularly since I believe so strongly in the symbiotic relationship between life and art. My actors understand that the food and small talk are all a warm-up to the work ahead.

The reason to keep a flexible schedule is that no one can tell when the great moments of creativity will happen. You cannot order creativity to happen in the 80 minutes of rehearsal and not to happen during the obligatory 10-minute break mandated by most Equity contracts. I recall when working in America, the actors' union prohibited me, the director, by rule, from even speaking to the actors during a break. A problem with this is that, over my decades of experience, I find that some of the most creative ideas come during the break. When I was composing my play *Millennium Teahouse*[6] in Taipei in 2000, a group of graduate students were in the room to observe my process of using improvisation to write plays. After some intense work, I couldn't break through a crucial creative problem involving the aristocratic intruder. How could I involve him in the crosstalk dialogue? I called a break, and the students all went out of the room for a smoke, or whatever. The actors stayed in the studio with me, and we talked about the problem. Soon we were back on our feet, and we solved the problem with great inspiration. After 10 minutes, the students came back. I told them, you missed it all. If you had stayed during the break, you would have had your thesis.

Perhaps the rules are made to guard against less sensitive directors who would overwork everyone if not regulated and not necessarily produce work efficiently. But I cannot help but feel that the depth and quality of production in America have declined because of this rigidity. I wonder how Shakespeare or Molière

---

6 See Stan Lai, *Selected Plays*, Vol. 2.

would work under union requirements? I do not doubt that they would find ingenious methods to cope, but ultimately, their works would suffer. To be fair, I have worked with American companies that will make exceptions to the rules for run-throughs, but the overall rules neglect the simple fact that artistic creation always defies rules.

Keeping Sanity

When working alone, each of us must find our own creative space where we can work productively. You need a quiet workspace where you can focus and make sense of everything that's bouncing around in your mind. In the early days of my career, it was very hard for me to set up such a space. It was a time when my elder daughter was in preschool, my new theater group rehearsed in my living room, and this same space was being used for dharma teachings by Tibetan masters we had invited to come to Taiwan. On rehearsal nights, we would cook and set a table for over a dozen people. On teaching nights, over 100 people would crowd into our house.

Those were crazy times, and my wife Nai-chu jokingly reprimanded me for not being able to focus within a crowd. I told her it's not as easy as you think. She said, "Look at you. To be able to write, you need the right space, the right table next to the right window, the right chair, the right lamp with the right color temperature light bulb, the right brand of computer, the right music, played through the right sound system, the right food and the right snacks and the right drinks. And even if it is all there, you still might not be able to write your play!" She said she would actually really respect someone who could sit on the side of the road in New Delhi and write. Tough advice, but I took it to heart. I could sometimes see how obsessive and ridiculous I could be, how any given moment on any given day could suddenly become only about me. The stress that accompanies creative work at times can easily transform you into a prima donna. I saw that in many of my creative friends and in myself.

I started observing myself in a stationery store, searching out the best notebook, the best pencil, the best file folder. I agonized over the different merits of a two-hole or three-hole page puncher for loose-leaf pages, so I bought both. In the end, after decades of creative work, you can see the residue of all of these things in the enormous amount of unused stationery I have in my study, the cool pens and pencils I bought but never used, the pretty notebooks that lie blank. I realized that I actually agree with Nai-chu. If you need to erect a palace to be able to write, good luck and may the force be with you. But if the force is with you, you should be able to create anywhere.

Setting a Zone

Whether it is your own palace, a carefully designed studio, your favorite coffee shop, in an airplane, or by the side of the road, you need to erect a zone for yourself. Within the zone, you are completely at ease to do your work. To me, whether I am in my own workspace or on the move, streaming music sets up this zone for me. But it's not just any music. The music you play while doing creative work will certainly have an influence on the work itself. It isn't just some white noise, but an energy and texture that infuses the environment. So choose carefully. My go-to work music comes from a pretty short list: Bach, Mozart, Charlie Parker, Bill Evans, Art Tatum, Sufi Qawwali music… The common feature of these artists is that they are all highly accomplished masters and are proponents of the art of improvisation, which to me releases a freedom in the air around me. When you listen to music that comes from the "zone" of these masters, by playing them, you draw from their zone to help construct your own zone. There is also something pure about them, meaning the music wasn't recorded with the main motivation of making money.

Listen to music you love. If it in itself helps you build or visualize structure, all the better. Though it serves as background to your work, the inherent structure of the music you play remains in the air and influences the zone. Over the years, I have found listening to Bach particularly productive. Perhaps because his works are structurally perfect and highly inventive, having his music in the air erects a sort of invisible structure in the space around you—dotted lines which rub off and help in making sound structural choices. Aside from this, there is a calming effect anyone can hear in his music, a serenity that always creates a good zone to work in.

Listening to Bach when working doesn't mean you become Bach. I wish it were that simple. You are drawing his energy and beauty into your own workspace to help your work become itself.

You may be thinking, there is so much more music out there that I should be exploring, and you are right. But sorry, not when I'm working. The creative workplace needs stable serenity. You don't need to be pumped up and shouting like an athlete before a game when you are writing or designing or sculpting. However, the definition of "calming effect" does differ in different contexts. Sometimes I put on a playlist of Led Zeppelin, Cream, and other hard rock classics. That may seem to be the antithesis of calmness. It is a bit hard to explain. This is music that gave me inspiration when I was younger, so it's always nice to flood your space with known inspiration.

An important note: playing music is not a prerequisite to creativity. Do what works for you. Incense, oils, whatever. If you are a highly advanced creative practitioner, you won't need anything for support. It's all in you.

Retreat

When I am writing a play, I find it always helpful to go into retreat and work in solitude. Either at home, in designated places, or even in unfamiliar places, I will go and write for as long as I feasibly can. Given my normal schedule, a week or two is probably the maximum. In retreat, all of my time can be devoted to writing. This means powering off your phone. For me, I am OK with checking my phone once or twice a day, even though it may draw me away from work for a moment, in retreat it is easy to get back.

The Tibetan word for retreat, *"tsham,"* means "boundary." When you go into retreat, you are setting a boundary. Normally we consider boundaries to be hindrances to our mobility. Here, the boundaries are self-made, meant to keep you within a place where you may concentrate on the task at hand. I believe this is a healthy attitude, to consider retreat as a self-made boundary, which has rules that you keep and disciplines that you follow, for the purpose of fulfilling the one task you have come into retreat for.

When you say you need to "wrap your head around" something, this is literally what you need to do for any creative project. It's hard! And it takes enormous focus. Being in retreat doesn't automatically allow you to wrap your head around your project, but in solitude, you may slowly gather your marbles, to get from the point where everything is scattered to where everything is cohesive, and you have a handle on the work at hand. You know what to do. You know where you're going.

In retreat, it is easy to get into a working rhythm, which you sorely need for creative work. The beginning is always the most difficult. But once you get started, rhythm creates momentum. As you gain momentum, your mind wraps even more tightly around your subject. Your mode changes from input to output. Everything has crystallized in your mind. You spend your days outputting everything onto paper, or computer, or whatever, instead of daydreaming and collecting input. The going gets fast.

It is always fortunate if your project can be started and completed straight from beginning to end within a unified period of time. Normally, we don't have this luxury. A project gets cut up into different phases. Instead of complaining, adjust. It's never easy. It can mean you have to learn how to multitask between two different projects, or between a creative project and obligations from everyday life. Whatever, if you learn to take what is given to you, it is doable, and many people, including myself, do it. The key is to not be frustrated, to accept it as part of the deal, and even to feel blessed that you are able to do any sort of creative work. With this positive state of mind, you may be able to focus even more intently on whichever project you are working on, no matter how short the duration you get to work on it.

To make a creative project is like creating a world. To be in a familiar space to work is always reassuring, but to inhabit an unfamiliar world while working can also be helpful. Retreat changes your view through distance and unfamiliarity. The boundary itself creates perspective.

If you can, arrange a retreat in or close to nature. Nature is the great connector. Nature, including all its seeming imperfections and incongruities, is always showing you how to do it. Be in nature, and let nature be your guide. Whenever in doubt, always go back to nature.

Whatever way you choose to set up your space and how to work, don't lose sight of your motivation. Remember to consider whether you are making gift or garbage.

Eccentricity Is the Norm

The German playwright Friedrich Schiller covered his desk with rotten apples, the smell of which gave him inspiration. Miles Davis improvised on his trumpet with his back to the audience. Georgia O'Keefe painted in the back seat of her Model A Ford. James Joyce wrote with pencils and crayons. Grotowski once asked half of his audience to leave before the performance started, because he wanted less audience that night. Ibsen wrote only in the morning, Kafka mostly after midnight. There is no norm for one's behavior during the creative process. Flaubert said, "Be regular and orderly in your life, so that you may be violent and original in your work."[7]

You are a musician setting up a recording studio to put down some tracks. You are a film director setting up a location. You are a painter setting up her studio. You can be as meticulous as you like, fussing over all the details of everything, but in the end, remember, you have to do it. Meaning, when it all comes down to it, the music must be played, the camera must roll, the paint must go on the canvas.

---

7 Gustave Flaubert, quoted in Brainy Quote. www.brainyquote.com/quotes/gustave_flaubert_109857

Sometimes we spend a little too much time on all the preparatory details because what we are really doing is avoiding the main event, which is actually doing the work! If everything is right, and all the equipment is there, but you aren't, none of it is much use.

I'm sure you have developed your own ecology for creative work, and whatever works for you is fine, as long as you do not infringe on others or cause others pain. There are many examples of artists who are too sensitive to sound or other noises and create hell for their neighbors. Often during creative work, the artist is highly irritable. For some, the burden of creativity is just too much to handle and they may even become violent. If this happens to you or someone close to you, you should really examine: Is it worth it? And by the way, what is causing all of this irritation? The guidelines in this book hopefully have taught you to examine your motives to create. Usually, that's the best place to see what the problem is and fix things.

Creativity is a special time, but do not think yourself so special when you are in the creative process. Try to keep normal mealtimes and get proper sleep. In particular, be kind to everyone around you. The world is the source of everything you create. Be kind to it and the people close to you. You will be rewarded handsomely.

When Stuck

Sometimes during the middle of a project, we suddenly see that everything isn't working as it is supposed to. Something is wrong. Or it just isn't fun anymore. In these cases, we have to go back and figure out how to move forward. If you work alone, this does not affect anyone else, but the process is nevertheless excruciating. This is a lonely time of self-reflection that can take days, even months. It's you versus the work. Sometimes it is so hard as to be insurmountable, and you cancel the project.

If you lead work in a group, the pressure is even more unbearable because you need time to figure out the solution to a question that may not be clear while everyone is waiting. The sculpture in the stone is hiding from you. The more you chisel at it, the more elusive it becomes, until there is not much stone left for you to chisel. It can be a time of great despair but also a time when great courage and wisdom can turn the tide.

When stuck, it may be that the work is calling you to take it to another level, which may take it in another direction. I have been extremely fortunate to have experienced major creative burnout only once, described in Chapter Sixteen. That said, very few works can just be composed from beginning to end without roadblocks. When there is something wrong with the piece, and you don't know how to fix it, it is frustrating indeed. You are stuck. You shut down. You can't even see the problem, how do you find the solution?

Sometimes it helps to pull back a bit, and distance yourself from your work. You need to be in a place where you can see your doubt and your insecurity. Are you holding something back? Are you unable to face some dark place you intended to bring to light? Are you unable to figure out the structure of your work? The most serious doubt comes with the thought: Does your work really have anything to say? In these moments, it is always helpful to check your original intentions. Why did you start this project in the first place? Maybe it is becoming clear now, and this clarity either breaks the ice and you can continue to work, or you can see that it isn't worth it and you cancel the project.

It may bring some consolation to know that this is common and actually part of the game. Even the greatest ones, such as Beethoven, experienced this. You can see it in all of the revisions on his original manuscripts, the fury with which he crosses notes out. This is all a reflection of the hardships he, like all of us, face during creative work.

How to work through these common blockages? There are two ways to go. The first is to just let go. This is difficult if you are working on a schedule with a hard deadline, but you have to find a moment where you just stop and let go of everything. Step away for a bit, even if it means canceling just one meeting or rehearsal to go bowling or do something silly. Get out to get back in.

The Japanese jazz pianist Fumio Itabashi, who composed the beautiful score to my film *The Peach Blossom Land*,[8] was caught playing pachinko at 4 o'clock in the morning in Shibuya the night before he was to turn in and record the theme song, which he hadn't yet written. It turned out he wrote a theme song for the ages.

We now understand that a cluttered mind cannot easily process thoughts, just like a hard disk that is full can no longer store anything new. To let go is to clear space in your mind. Become empty so that you can become full.

---

8 In collaboration with Kazutoki Umezu.

How to Plan a Breakthrough

I recall how earlier in my career, blockages would take weeks or months to fight through. Rehearsals on one of my early works, *The Island and the Other Shore*[9] (1989), had to be halted soon after starting, because I had hit a stone wall, and didn't know how to put together this complex story that was in my mind. The play has three separate storylines that crisscrossed, including one fantasy swordsman world that was actually a novel being written by one of the main characters. I drove all the way from Taipei, in the north of Taiwan, to Kenting, near the southern tip, and stayed in a small hotel by the beach, where I spent my days just walking on the sand. It was a lonely time, and it was winter, so the beach was deserted. Those were the days before mobile phones, and I recall going to a roadside pay phone to call my wife every night and chat about the progress of the story. I recall one night, she broke the news to me that she was pregnant with our second daughter. The elation of that phone call somehow broke through the obstacle. Soon I drove back home, and we resumed rehearsals, working toward what turned out to be a very unique work.

What happened? Hard to say. I knew we needed to stop work. I knew I needed to get away and be alone. But how I became unblocked can only be considered a happy creative mystery.

Now, I do not experience major blockages like I did when I was younger (knock hard on wood), but there are always complex issues to deal with that create work stoppages. Through the simple method of letting go, it takes me as little time as going out for a walk or catching a movie on television (Jason Statham, believe it or not, has the ability to turn off my mind so that it can turn back on again), or getting some good sleep to be able to continue work. Sometimes I do cancel rehearsals to give myself more time to work on a script. I feel sorry for the cast, but I know that if I am not fully confident in the rehearsal room, I will be wasting more of their time.

The first way to work through writer's block is to shut down. By putting things down, you regain the capacity to take up new things. By not thinking, thinking comes. Distance brings new perspective and energy.

The second method I employ, equally effective, is to look at your work straight in the eye, piercingly, down to the last detail. This simply means gathering energy and focus, going through your work carefully, from the beginning, word by word if it is literal, frame by frame if it is a film, and so on. Take notes as you do this.

---

9 See Stan Lai, *Selected Plays*, Vol. 1.

Try to be as objective as possible and see what is happening at every moment: you will see new things when you do this. Where are you taking your audience? Where are you not succeeding in your goals? By being truthful to yourself during this process, the faults will reveal themselves. Then, take up the work again, little bit by little bit, until you get back into a rhythm. One step at a time leads you back. Don't try to solve everything at once.

Compromise Can Be a Blessing

Once I was completing a play written specifically for a particular actor, who was a megastar of Chinese cinema. At the last moment, she pulled out of the production. Since these things do happen in my line of work, I was not particularly perplexed. I kept my patience, and eventually, the situation resolved itself when another actor, even more suited to the role, appeared and joined. I believe things turned out for the better, and I mused that if I had begged the original actor to come back, I don't think the production would have been better.

In art forms such as theater and film, with so many moving parts, there is no such thing as the perfect plan. You have to be flexible at every turn. Recently, for the performance of *I Take Your Hand in Mine*, a play about Chekhov and Olga Knipper by Carol Rocamora which I directed,[10] I designed three movable proscenium arches of varying sizes on the set. When touring to a small town in China, the stage was only big enough for two. To argue would be a waste of time, so I just went with it. I was surprised to see that the play actually works better with just two prosceniums. That's how it is now staged.

In fact, the whole process from beginning to end of a theatrical production is a dance between what can be done and what can't. If you haven't learned the word "compromise," you are in for a lot of headaches and heartaches. I have long learned that the moment an obstacle arises, when someone or something is not letting you do something you want to, and the force is irresistible, you have to learn to go with it. In fact, it really could be some hint that what you originally wanted to do either wouldn't work or wasn't right. Challenges bring unforeseen opportunities. Difficulties may in the end be blessings. Compromise is not surrender; it forces you to find even better solutions. You will never know if you don't hang in there.

---

10 Carol Rocamora, "*I take your hand in mine*" Suggested by the Letters of Anton Chekhov and Olga Knipper (Smith and Kraus, 2000). Translated into Chinese by Stan Lai.

Notes on Giving Notes

As you near completion of your project, it is time to get opinions on your work in progress. But make sure you get them from the right people. The right people may not necessarily be the most informed or the most talented, but the ones who can give you the best advice. You must also avoid those who are only seeking to please you, and those who are only seeking to affirm themselves through giving advice to you.

It might help to think of the other side of the coin. When asked to offer an opinion, you also must tread carefully. Anyone working on a creative project is very vulnerable and fragile. Even the strongest-looking artist, who takes harsh criticism with grace, may actually be destroyed inside if you go too hard, or if the way you say things hints that you do not like the work. It's hard for someone who hasn't done the labor to see how much work has gone into a product, and it's easy to shoot your mouth off and say critical things without the inside knowledge of what is actually being attempted. On the other hand, some artists only respond to hard truths, the harsh critique, so you must tell it like it is.

I always try to be thoughtful and helpful when my opinion is asked for any work that has not been shown to the public. I will always start with encouraging remarks. Of course, if the artist knows me well, they know that something critical will be coming. And well it may, but I tend not to be critical of anything that is not fixable. In other words, any notes I give are, in my estimation doable. I try to see the work from the eyes of the author. Sometimes you might criticize a work and then realize that you are not criticizing it, but actually asking it to be rewritten in the way you want it. That's not constructive. I try not to do that. Always be mindful when asked to give criticism. It is the same when receiving criticism.

During my formative years, aside from my wife, Nai-chu, who has followed the progression of each and every one of my works, the two artists I turned to most for advice and criticism were Danny Yung and the late Edward Yang (1947–2007). My two fellow Scorpio friends were totally opposite in the way they gave criticism to me. Danny's early theater work with his Hong Kong group Zuni Icosahedron was very influential for me, particularly in the way he brought social issues into performance. Danny would be harsh but incisive. It seemed that he leaned toward making my work more of what he wanted to see instead of what I wanted to do. Nevertheless, it was always helpful and pushed me just to be better. Edward, the great filmmaker, was totally different. After seeing a run-through of a new play of mine, he would sit there in the rehearsal room in silence. I would turn to him, my expression asking the question, "Well?" Usually, he would just smile. That was it. I was left with the task of deciphering that smile, which, believe me, was awesomely informative.

Other criticism came to me in my daily back-and-forths with some of the exceptional actors I have had the great fortune to work with, like Lee Li-chun and Chin Shi-chieh, to name two of my closest associates, and Ismene Ting, my sister-in-law who has performed the female lead in many of my works, and is also an accomplished playwright and director. Working with them was always a mixture of love and hate, exhilaration and frustration. They were always willing to challenge me. When I knew I was right, it was always a feisty battle to convince them. When I knew they were right, it was always an excruciating struggle with myself to accept my own faults. Those were beautiful times, because in the end there really was no you or me. There was only the potential wellness and greatness of the work at stake that everyone was focused on.

I recall back in 1998, we were working on a play called *I Me She Him*.[11] A man and a woman meet their selves from 10 years ago when they were lovers, a relationship they have forgotten about. About a third of the way into the composition of the piece, I hit a brick wall and didn't know where we were going. Every day at rehearsal, all I could do was fumble around and work on some improvisations about topics that I thought might help us. But we were going in circles, and the actors knew it. One day, I walked into the rehearsal room still in a fog. After some small talk, I said, "Let's get to work." The two main actors, Chin Shi-chieh and Ismene Ting, suddenly said, "Sit down, Stan. Let us do it. Just watch." And so they made me the observer and started working on the script in a way that I could not have possibly envisioned. It was amazing to see their creative solutions to the brick wall I had smashed against. That one rehearsal opened my mind to what the whole play was about, and I regained control. We went on to create what is considered a very intense and evocative work.

Holistic Creative Healing

When blocked, just like when you seek retreat, find a place near nature. Just like when you are seeking inspiration at the inception of a project, take walks. Just look at a tree, see how it grows, how the leaves flutter in the breeze, and you will feel inspired. Look around and see how everything fits together with such ease, and you will be humbled, while at the same time feel empowered and blessed.

---

11 In Lai, *Selected Plays*, Vol. 2.

Nature can restore your spirits and calm the bouncing elements that are boiling over in your mind. Nature is always healing, and always revealing.

Gradually, try to expand your concept of what nature is. Art is just a label. Nature is everything that happens naturally, which is everything, including art.

Start seeing nature in everything, and you will feel a healing power that draws first from seeing yourself as part of it all. For a moment, see the world as John Cage did: all sounds are music, all sights are art. Most importantly, do not forget: nothing that you do will be in vain, even if you have to tear down everything and start over. All failures eventually bring you to success. Listen to what Miles Davis, who worked in an art form where you could make a hundred mistakes a minute, said:

Do not fear mistakes, there are none.[12]

Exercises and Further Thoughts

1. Make a list of what the details of your particular craft are.
2. Think of the last time you experienced "writer's block," no matter what field you are in. Recall how you got out of it.
3. What does the schedule for your current project look like? Can you see the wisdom of scheduling?
4. How eccentric are you? Does any of your eccentricity bother the people around you? Do they bother you?
5. Have you ever created pain for others because of your creativity? Can you recall the circumstances?
6. What does your perfect creative environment look like? Do you have the opportunity to create a place like that?
7. Have you ever met an obstacle that later turned out to be a blessing?
8. How good are you at compromise? Consider a project you have done, and suppose an essential element was no longer available. What would you do? Can you visualize a new way of doing it?
9. Try working in places you wouldn't ordinarily work in. See if you can make creativity more of a common thing, not something special that has to happen in a special place, not like the scientist who must go to the laboratory in order to conduct an experiment. You can experiment anywhere.

---

12 Miles Davis, quoted in *Goodreads*, www.goodreads.com/author/quotes/54761.Miles_Davis?page=1

CHAPTER TWENTY

WILD CARDS

A Theory of Talent

>Talent is only the starting point.[1]
>
>—Irving Berlin

Nature or nurture? The debate about talent is ages old. From Plato and Aristotle to Kant and Locke, recent studies have reconfirmed that talent is definitely something you are born with, but other recent studies also prove that talent is acquired and that genes morph according to environment. I cannot prove either. Let's just state the fact that we all possess a certain amount of talent, whether it is from our genes or developed in life, or both. But it is common sentiment that talent in itself will take you nowhere. It needs to be developed. Wikipedia says:

> A **talent** (or **aptitude**) is the natural ability to do something better than most people. Talent is often confused with skill. We can develop and improve skill but not talent.[2]

I agree that skill can be improved, but I am not convinced that talent cannot be nurtured, nor is it necessarily specific to a certain field.

When I was growing up in Taiwan, no one was encouraged to be an artist. Our parents' generation, hounded by consecutive wars and displacement, wanted all of us to train as engineers, scientists—something they considered safe, to balance the chaos in their lives. Most of my classmates went on to do these things, many in America. Our generation had a plethora of scientists but almost no artists. Does this mean that artistic talent is dictated by region, and that Taiwan/

---

1 Irving Berlin, quoted in www.brainyquote.com/topics/talent-quotes_3
2 simple.wikipedia.org/wiki/Talent

China got less of it in the post-war years? I find that hard to fathom. I think back on all of my classmates—were they all not talented? Of course they were. And they all excelled at what they did. Could we say that talent is something generic, not specific, and their talent was used in the field of the sciences, or other rational learnings, because the arts were closed to them?

One individual who rebelled against this norm was my dear friend Edward Yang, whom I mentioned earlier. He went down the path that most of his classmates did, excelling in the sciences, going abroad to America to study, getting a degree, and landing a well-paying job in computer programming back in the 1970s. One day, as he told me, he woke up staring at his ceiling in Seattle, where he had settled. It was his 30th birthday. He had achieved everything that he wanted, or was it what his parents wanted? A good education, a good job, a beautiful house, a fast car. I remember when he told me the story, he said, "Stan, you can't understand what was going through my mind. I was gazing at the ceiling and thinking, that's it. I'm seeing the end. This is the same ceiling I will be staring at 30 years from now when I retire and the house is paid off."

Edward quit his job to pursue his true passion, filmmaking. Within a few years, he directed a short film, and soon after, full-length feature films that have become legendary, garnering top honors at Cannes and other international festivals. He died way too early, but as I calculate, he passed exactly 30 years after that ceiling-gazing moment. Life gave him 30 years to choose a path. He heeded the call from his unrealized talent and fulfilled it in a big way.

What talent does one need to be a playwright? A director? It certainly is not as simple as being able to write beautifully. I bow down to Shakespeare. But as we mentioned at the beginning of our exploration, his talent cannot be summed up as mere writing talent. There is so much more. His talent would need to be spread around many different skill sets. There might not be a single stand-alone talent called "playwriting" or "directing." But there may be one single talent that we can just call "talent" that lends itself to all the different aspects needed to master playwriting and directing, and it is this energy, if we may call it that, that unlocks all the other individual talents. In an article surveying studies on gifted children, David Brooks summarizes my thoughts:

> It's nice to know who is good at taking intelligence tests, but it's more important to know who is lit by an inner fire.[3]

---

3 David Brooks, "What Happens to Gifted Children," *New York Times*, June 13, 2024, www.nytimes.com/2024/06/13/opinion/gifted-children-intelligence.html

Maybe "talent" is that inner fire, the drive, plus a heightened aptitude for learning, that is applied to what one is particularly curious about. An abundance of talent helps us learn faster, see more quickly, and know how to do things. At any rate, do not lose track of the fact that talent is essential, but not worth as much as you may think. Without effort and luck, it won't go very far. From my estimation, you need to put in much more effort and have much more luck than you have talent in order to succeed.

Luck

Luck is a slippery thing. Though described as a lady, no one has ever seen what she looks like. The Chinese saying goes, "Fortune moves on four legs. We only have two." Its evasiveness lies in its many forms. It sometimes disguises itself as misfortune. I believe, with little backup evidence, that if you work hard and maintain a positive attitude, luck will come to you. Perhaps it is just positive thinking, but when challenges arise and misfortune comes, I suggest that you consider it just a change in plans. Call it compromise or whatever, maybe someone upstairs is looking after you, and urging you, even forcing you to change. Perhaps this challenge, as we have noted in Chapter Nineteen, is in fact fortuitous. Luck is paying you a visit, but not in the form you are expecting.

Personality

Personality is the combination of traits that make up your character. Though usually very stubborn, personalities can grow and change over life, through changes in habit and how we see, as discussed in Chapter Nine, with great effect on creativity.

Are there certain personalities that are more amenable to creativity? There have been studies correlating the so-called Big Five personality types to creativity. The winners are "openness to experience" and "extroversion."[4] I am not a social scientist, but I can't say I agree. Most of my creative friends are not extroverts. In fact, I even have trouble splitting all personalities into five "Big" types.

From what I have seen of the spectrum of artists and creative people all over the world, I do not believe that certain personality traits give an individual a

---

4 See as an example Sun Young Sung and Jin Nam Choi, "Do Big Five Personality Factors Affect Individual Creativity? The Moderating Role of Extrinsic Motivation," *Social Behavior and Personality*, 2009, 37(7), 941–956.

definitive edge in creativity. Just like there is no astrology sign that is definitively more creative, I do believe that creativity embraces all types of personalities. These personalities in turn bring individuality to your creativity. Just like there are all sorts of people, so are there all sorts of creative works.

What I am certain of is that we all have talent, but we need the opportune moment to harness it, focusing on what we wish to achieve. And we all definitely have our own personality. Combined with talent, this gives you your own unique creative voice.

Sense and Sensitivity

Sense is on the right side of the Expanded Map, opposite from Taste. They both work on the filters of our life experience. Whereas Taste influences How to See, sense works on stocking our creative toolboxes.

Sensitivity is a different thing. It is another wild card. It is the depth of our feelings when we experience. Creative people are usually more highly developed in this area. You could say their experience filter is thinner, letting in more than most people.

Sensitive people see more, feel more, but also can get hurt more because they feel more. A person sensitive to color sees nuances that others cannot, or color triggers strong emotions in them that others cannot feel. A person sensitive to human relationships can read the inner monologues of people involved in a negotiation, see the fine text printed between the lines of what a friend is saying.

Sensitivity is absolutely essential for an artist, to be able to to feel emotions in people, to see the soul of people and other works of art, to feel the energy of a place. Though creative people thrive on sensitivity, do not mistake sensitivity for creativity. True, without sensitivity, one's work may lack flair. But feelings in themselves, not anchored to wisdom or awareness, tend to float. To be able to feel more than others may be a gift, but it may also be a curse. Many sensitive potential artists spend a lot of their time obsessed with their sensitivity. How sensitivity can be translated productively into creative works has little to do with sensitivity itself.

Sensitivity is "openness" or willingness to open oneself up to experience. People who open up are receptive, but that also makes them vulnerable. If one is too open, without perspective, one can be sympathetic/vulnerable to almost anything.

In older cultures, the ultrasensitive person is not only open to the emotions of this world but of other worlds as well. Shamans, mediums, and clairvoyants are all hypersensitive. Other worlds are accessible to them, but with such openness come new challenges, to their everyday lives and how society treats them. Actors, in fact, for centuries, were considered "unclean" by most societies, in part because of these traits.

I work with many sensitive artists and students. Sometimes they cannot handle their own sensitivity. This leads to confusion in personal life. In some cases, the championing of sensitivity can become an alibi to indulge in the strictly sensual, thus legitimizing all sorts of indulgence and obsession. Such persons accumulate rich experiences for their mind's files, but without perspective or reflection, soon the mind is overflowing with sensual impressions, leading to confusion. It is possible to confuse sensitivity with wisdom.

Without a doubt, on the creative path, strong sensitivity reaps a richer experience. The question is whether or not we can harness and process this experience into any deeper meaning. Sensitivity needs a guide. This guide is, again, the always useful habit of self-examination. Is your sensitivity self-serving/self-indulgent, a source of personal pride or pain? How can it be of use to others, or is that not your concern? How can it be harnessed into your creative work, to be shared with others?

In the end, it's not about how much you have seen or known, how many places you have traveled to, how many books you have read, but how deep your feelings are toward any single thing. How deep those feelings are can also sway toward many different directions: intense anger, hatred, or love, and compassion. What for?

You must be sensitive to sensitivity itself.

Perseverance

> Solutions always outnumber problems.[5]
>
> —Xu Chunhua, Chinese entrepreneur

Like discipline, perseverance goes without saying. It is a necessary trait for creative work. You need perseverance throughout the work process. You need extra perseverance when the going gets rough. The closer you get to the finish line, the more you need. The work just gets harder and harder as you shape your final structure and put in all the details that go into making things perfect.

---

5 Xu Chunhua, talk to Theatre Above, May 21, 2024, Shanghai.

The Kung-Fu of Improvisation

We have spoken much of improvisation as a quality you need to be creative. There are many levels of improvisation, including a basic spontaneity toward any opportunities or challenges that arise, and improvisation as a method in itself to create works.

They just played what they liked, as long as it would fit.[6]

This line, from Louis Armstrong's "A Song is Born," is a simple and accurate description of how jazz works, but it can stand for all creativity. Just do what you want, as long as it works. It sounds great, even easy, but what "fits"? And fits what? Who decides what works?

What "fits," and what "works" are key judgments to make in the creative process. You can put an extended Ornette Coleman-esque jazz solo in the middle of a Brahms piano concerto. That's just "A + B." Easy to conceive, but does it fit? Does it work? How about an explicit rap song set to Bach? Goethe's *Faust* on a future colony on Jupiter's moon Io, with AI as the Devil?

Ideas are cheap. Whether they ultimately fit and how to ultimately make them work, this is the kung-fu of creativity. This kung-fu involves all the components in the map and how to connect them all together.

As a jazz aficionado, I try to catch live jazz when I can, and I have been blessed to be able to sit before the likes of Bill Evans, Sonny Rollins, Jim Hall, McCoy Tyner, Stan Getz, and many other luminaries in small jazz clubs around the world. I recall my buddy from my Taipei college days, Gary Chen, who runs the legendary music shop Stein on Vine in Hollywood, taking me around the jazz clubs in L.A. in the 1990s to see his friends, jazz greats, play. I recall the privilege of witnessing transcendence in the presence of Charles Lloyd and Cedar Walton one night at the Catalina Club. Their playing was off the charts. As their solos soared through the air, you could see the musicians and connoisseurs in the audience share wide-eyed glances with each other, nodding in approval, as if to say, "He's got it tonight." But got what? Certainly not scales and arpeggios and theories of improvisation. Those were the techniques, the method, the vocabulary they need to construct their art, but the paradox of jazz is that the jazz artist must let go of his technique, and, in fact, let go of himself, in order to get into an improvisation, at which point all of the technique kicks in. This is the same criteria that

---

6 "A Song Was Born," music by Don Raye, lyrics by Gene de Paul, from the film of the same name, 1948.

kicks in when we are witnessing pedestrian jazz, or ho-hum improvisation. When the artist cannot get into, or will not get into, or does not know how to get into an improvisation, it is quite painful for those who can see, and disrespectful to the art itself.

For artists working with improvisation, the work itself may seem like a snapshot of the deepest layer of the file warehouse. In a creative form such as jazz, where content, form, and inspiration appear instantaneously, wisdom and method are fused together. As Armstrong explained it, "What we play is life."[7] The emotion expressed during the improvisation comes from the wisdom of the artist's life experience. Abstract expressionist painters like Jackson Pollock, who pioneered the form, attempt to paint automatically, without thinking or planning. Not fabricated or preconceived, it is spontaneous. Form is organically decided by content. As the critic Harold Rosenberg said of Pollock: "The big moment came when it was decided to paint 'just to paint.'"[8]

The key to "just painting" is to be in a state where you are thinking of nothing, not unlike trance or meditation. Thus, whatever comes from your brush is more or less a direct expression from a deeper you. Content and form, wisdom and method blend into one in Pollock's way of painting. As a playwright, I maintain a file warehouse where I can pull stories and characters and images. Artists such as Pollock also have an inner file warehouse, but when they paint, they bypass all of the files and seem to draw straight from the source. What comes out from that source are shapes and forms in their undefined state.

In Pollock's way of working, it only works if it is pure—meaning, you are in the painting, painting. At no moment do you jump outside and watch yourself paint, or stop and rationally critique what you are painting. If you attempt to rationally create a work that looks like Pollock's, you are destined to fail because the rational mind stands in the way of such creativity, blocking it, and the exact strokes that were applied during rational thought will stick out like a sore thumb to the sophisticated viewer, making the painting in effect, a fake.

In the improvisatory arts, we can see the direct relationship between art and life, method and wisdom. When viewing Pollock, we are staring at his wisdom, which doesn't come through as some philosophical tract, but as it is: abstract, a snapshot of the contents within the artist's soul that connects directly to our soul.

---

7 Louis Armstrong, quoted in *Louis Armstrong Society.org* www.larmstrongsoc.org/quotes
8 Harold Rosenberg, "The American Action Painters, December 1952," quoted in full in *ArtNews*, www.artnews.com/artnews/news/top-ten-artnews-stories-not-a-picture-but-an-event-181/

As Pollock himself said, "Every good artist paints who he is."[9] AI certainly can produce paintings that look like Pollock's work, but if true abstract expressionism comes directly from the soul, we would have to ask where the direct soul of AI is and what is in it.

It is the same with the Chinese and Japanese free-style calligraphers, who must let go of their formidable technique and bare their souls during improvisation, in this way sharing their souls. The technique displayed is from a lifetime of practice. If your technique is not mature, no matter what your field is, if you want to use improvisation as a creative expression, you will have few resources to improvise with, and the results may seem clumsy or juvenile. If you have achieved a high level of sophisticated technique in your art, but your soul is underdeveloped, the results are easily seen through as shallow. I have seen many a "wild style" Chinese calligraphy work that looks spontaneously brilliant, but for the discerning eye that can see, it is just an ego trip, a showing off of technique, and it actually may be premeditated. To the contrary of baring their souls, such artists do not know how to, or do not have the courage to, bare their souls.

Masters of improvisation are technically supreme, but to perform improvisationally makes them spiritually vulnerable. The jazz master understands this. As the complex notes of the song are being performed, the soul is inching its way into appearance, like paint or blood seeping into the air, to the point where there is no more pretense, no more disguise. The great jazz musician lives for such moments, which in Chinese has the name *wangwo*, or "forgetting self." In these moments, with the self forgotten, the jazz musician, as well as the abstract expressionist or Chinese brush calligrapher, is naked, like the shaman in the throes of possession, bereft of self, soul totally bared, thus showing and sharing their complete self. To improv from a place that is not the soul is a basic dishonesty, a lack of artistic sincerity that may trick the audience, and more seriously, the artist himself.

How do we, the viewers, judge the nakedness? Invariably, technique is on display— method—but more obvious is the wisdom. Such an artist must spend at least as much time cultivating their wisdom as their method. Art such as this demands that the contents be, in essence an "imprint of mind," not to be conceptualized to start, and not to be modified or beautified when done.

---

9 Jackson Pollock, quoted in www.jackson-pollock.org/quotes

The Grand Conspiracy

> Ultimately, it comes down to taste.[10]
>
> —Steve Jobs

Taste informs all of our artistic decisions. You may think that your taste is a unique expression all your own, but on further examination, taste may not be so much the personal choice that you think. Taste is nurtured by habit, and influenced by popular fads and political correctness. To see how one's tastes develop is to see how they can also be modified.

Why are you wearing what you're wearing? You obviously chose it, and so it should reflect your personal taste. But who taught you to choose it? I once asked my friend in the fashion industry what she was up to. She said they were busy working on next fall's designs (14 months away), in which they were installing orange as the fad. As my advertising exec friend said, "We are in the business of creating desire." So fashion is created, in a grand premeditated conspiracy if you may, over a year in advance, then sold to you, who may think you have chosen it because of your own taste, but your taste itself has been subjected to subconscious manipulation from the design world, season after season.

By adhering to what we like and don't like, habit affects our taste and our whole way of looking at the world. When we surf channels on a television set or choose food at a buffet, see how habit plays a big part in what we pick. We pick things that we like. That goes without saying. How could we crave things we dislike? We think we have the ultimate freedom to choose what we want, but the automatic habit of like and dislike immediately cuts the playing field in half.

Taste is something you cannot get around in creative work. All of your decisions, everything you create, are intimately tied to your taste. You cannot create something beyond your taste. Everything in your life goes into nurturing your taste. Jobs' suggestion on cultivating taste is very helpful:

> [...] expose yourself to the best things that humans have done and then try to bring those things into what you're doing.[11]

Since taste is influenced by habit, make it a habit to study tasteful things. Get to know the great things humans have done, in all fields, even if you didn't

---

10 Steve Jobs, Interview on CBS News, 1995, www.youtube.com/watch?v=5y03eFMmOKY
11 Ibid.

previously feel any inclination toward them. If you never loved opera, give it a try. How about Peking Opera? Get past the strangeness of the sound, and there is a wealth of artistry to explore that can enrich your taste and your work. Consider that, for many Asians, the sound of Italian opera is at least as strange as the sound of Chinese opera for a European.

One year I was sharing a meal in Taipei with a renowned international film critic who told me he was going to Hong Kong to interview an up-and-coming young director, whom everyone said was the next great thing. A few weeks later we met again, and I asked him how the interview went. He said that this director would never become great because of the place he took the critic to for dinner. The critic said, seriously, "If that's his go-to food, there isn't any way he can become great." Wow. What a statement. I was in no position to argue, but what he predicted, whatever the complex reasons, turned out to be true. Whether this young director failed because of his taste in food is hard to say. What is true is that everything you accumulate in life builds your taste, and your taste shapes your work. If you are always in touch with greatness, your taste becomes shaped in that way.

Exercises and Further Thoughts

1. On a scale of 1 to 10, rate your talent. Then your luck. Then your work ethic.
2. Make the same rating for some successful creative person. No need for conclusions for this. Just observe.
3. On a scale of 1 to 10, how sensitive are you? Would you wish to be more, or less?
4. If you are not already adept, take some lessons on improvisation. It doesn't matter if it is dance/movement, theatre games, music, painting, stand up …. Examine how the experience of learning improvisation helps your creativity.
5. Assess your own taste. Examine how it affects your decision-making, from the products you buy to artistic choices.
6. Compare your taste with someone whom you consider to have great taste. How can you improve to get to the next level?
7. Make a list of great things you would like to get to know better. Start working on the list.

CHAPTER TWENTY-ONE

COMPLETION

Seeing the Mountain

I once saw the mountain as a mountain, and the river as a river.
Then I saw the mountain was not a mountain, and the river was not a river.
Now I see the mountain as a mountain, and the river as a river.[1]

This simple and poetic Chinese saying expresses the journey of life, and reflects how most of us torment ourselves in the creative process. How sweet it would be to be able to proceed straight from step one to step three, bypassing step two! But that usually is not the case, and we must in some way be blind to our work, and our lives, in order to see it again. We might even experience deep ideological shifts or a religious epiphany, which brings us to a radical reconception of our work. Over time, we may become disillusioned with our new way of thinking, and we are back to the original face of the work, but it no longer looks the same. We need to change it all over again to get back to where we were. Often the torment of the process is not so much in seeing what is wrong with your work but in actually getting into the ditches and fixing it all, which may mean taking the whole thing apart and putting it back together again.

For those who find it hard to make it to the finish line, I can sympathize with the conundrum. It certainly can seem daunting to have to let go of something that has been so close to you for so long, and show it to others, many others. That can be really scary. But if you are a perfectionist, you must learn the value of compromise, which is the very value that perfectionists loathe. Perhaps you are too close to your work, like a parent who is always holding his baby, never letting go. Distance is a necessity for any evaluation. You cannot

---

1 My translation from the Chinese.

evaluate what is sticking to your face, but that is what many artists who are unwilling to let go do. This love or infatuation with your own art may be a powerful factor for its success, but sometimes you need to pull back a bit. If you think your work is so special, you may never get it out. Loosen up, maybe show your work to people you trust. Eventually, you will come to the point where you are willing to let go and let your work shift from the private domain to the public.

The Dreaded Bell

Many people dread deadlines. To me, they are part of my life. I have written and directed plays that are already sold out before opening night, which sometimes means before the play is finished. The designers and composers whom I work with must face these same deadlines, and sometimes deadlines are very helpful because they force you to get to the final line. We all strive for the beauty of a naturally flowing piece. Once you start fooling around with what used to be uncontrived, all the strokes and colors you add are like cutting scars into what was once a perfect statue. A hard deadline can stifle what could be a great work. It is double-sided. You must give deadlines their due respect, and plan diligently to arrive on time and in good shape.

In a recording studio, the professional mixer will always want to correct imperfections in the recording, but often it is those imperfections that make the work great and human. In recent years, I am happy to be able to access online more and more original cuts of music I love, in their original form. For instance, the "naked" version of the Beatles' "The Long and Winding Road." To be honest, I don't know why it needed all of the strings and arrangements of the final version that we have listened to all these years. I thought it had already found a pretty perfect expression. But that was a creative choice that was made, which we must respect. Even in my own work, audiences over time detect changes I have made to a certain play, and they question the reason. To me, these are creative choices that maybe should have been made at the premiere. On the other hand, through performance over the years, the play has revealed more of itself to me, and I make choices to change things. You might consider me a perfectionist who respects deadlines, but doodles on long after a production is in performance.

What kind of final product are we showing the world? Is it worthy of being shown? To you? To the world? Has it met your aspirations? What do you aspire to? What is the mountain that you strive to climb?

Spell Weavers

Every work of art is the creation of a reality. We who are qualified weave spells to bring an audience/viewer/reader in. We are sorcerers. The kung-fu of weaving spells is an external path, learned in conservatories and training programs. It is the "outer kung-fu" of creativity. Learning what to express in your spell, once woven, is an internal path, learned in life. It is "inner kung-fu."

We have all experienced being in that special place while viewing great works, where we are drawn inside the work, into a place where time doesn't exist. As a playwright and director, it is my aspiration to create such a spell, which the audience falls into and doesn't come out until the curtain call.

This is what we should aspire to. Our craft is dedicated to making chemical reactions in our work, flowers that blossom in a certain way, that trigger emotional reactions in our audience. We strive to become alchemists, sorcerers, weavers of spells who mesmerize an audience, bringing them into the work, which in turn connects them to concerns outside the work.

Seamlessness

There is another aspect to creative work that we should aspire to. In the great works in the history of humankind, there are no extraneous pieces that we can break off and discard, no extra paint strokes, no extra notes, no extra words, nor can anything be added. Everything is in the right order. There are no seams that reveal how the work is put together. Like the proverbial Chinese cloak of the sky, or what Zeami speaks of as an "elegance beyond maturity,"[2] these rare works are seamless. Many such works are created in one organic push, where form and content appear simultaneously, and the artist is most likely in a flow state. Like laying an egg. That simple. And that difficult.

There is a natural fluidity in purity that allows one to move seamlessly from concept to concept and to the know-how of executing these concepts. In such works, chemical reactions—the timing of when certain emotions hit the viewer—are not analyzable. These pieces are made through the artist's *knowing*. The work breezes through the app and forms into the final product with seemingly little effort.

There is something vast and intricate here. Connections in the mind that are difficult for novices to grasp are assimilated in the master's mind in an instant.

---

2 Zeami, *Kadensho*, 49.

The master sees with more complexity. The premise of her reality—and creativity—is much more encompassing. The master's starting point assumes connections between things that others may not be aware of.

To know what fits, what works, what is worthy. It all gets clearer as you gain more experience. You gain method in wisdom, and wisdom in method, until there is no longer any differentiation between the two. No line separates left and right on the creative map anymore.

Harvest

You have finished your creative project. Is it a success? In what terms shall we consider the word? How do you feel about yourself? Are you satisfied with your work? Has your journey taken you where you wanted it to? Have you improved in technique? Are you wiser, in art, and in life? How has newfound wisdom informed your newfound method? These are some of the many aspects you can consider when thinking about the word "success." Most importantly, has your work benefited anyone? Yourself? Benefit can come in many ways: healing, sharing, learning, feeling enriched, enriching others, transcending, connecting...

We have already learned that the keenest evaluation for success goes back to the original intention, the motivation to create the work. Are you satisfied with the correlation between the original motivation and the finished product? Is your work a commercial success? Was it meant to be? As we have explored, there are just too many different factors that kick in to create a work's commercial success. Commercial success is something that can only be worked toward and wished for. There can never be guarantees.

I once read an article about a new film by Steven Spielberg that was opening that weekend in theaters. He retreated to a Montana ranch because he wasn't in the mood to entertain box office numbers. Wait a minute. Who was he, I thought? He was Steven Spielberg, who directed so many of the greatest box office hits in history. If even he could not be confident in his commercial success, who else possibly could?

At a forum in Beijing on creativity in the 2010s, I spoke about how unpredictable the box office was for the film industry, and advised filmmakers to pay more attention to what they truly wanted to make instead of what they thought the audience wanted to see. In other words, trust your heart, not what you think other people will like.³ One of the top producers of the day, who had had a long

---

3 *Xinjingbao 2012 Economic Forum*, International Hotel, Beijing, November 30, 2011.

string of box office successes, stood up and rebuked me. He said I was totally wrong, that they had figured out an algorithm through an extensive database that could accurately predict what audiences wanted to see. Before I had a chance to reply, he excused himself and left for another commitment, which I thought was rather rude. I didn't say anything, but in my mind I thought, "If that's what you think, bless you, but just wait and see." Though he did have continued success for a time, ultimately many of his films failed and the company accumulated formidable debt.

Exercises and Further Thoughts

1. How do you handle deadlines? When you find it hard to meet one, what is the problem? Was the time alloted unfair?
2. Think of an instance when you were drawn into a creative work, like a movie or a novel, and completely forgot about time? Would you consider that being absorbed into a spell? Can you understand how the weaving of such a spell demands certain qualifications?
3. Think of a "seamless" recent work of art you have seen. Revisit it, and re-examine the beauty of it. Again, can you understand how the making of such a seamless work demands certain qualifications?
4. Think back to any creative project that you have started and finished. Did the results at the end meet the expectations at the beginning? Did the expectations change during the work?

PART EIGHT
Journey to Transformation

What is the use of art if not to transform?

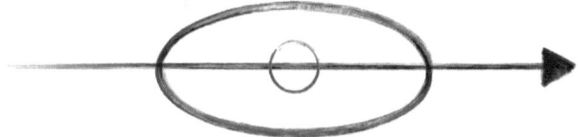

CHAPTER TWENTY-TWO

FROM WHERE TO WHERE?

The Journey

Creative works bring an audience on a journey. A roller coaster at a theme park takes us on a literal ride that has emotional high points programmed into its design. In ancient societies, the performance of rituals brought a people, or a person, from one place to another in a symbolic, but efficacious journey. A whole society could be brought from a place of danger to safety, not by moving the clan, but by pacifying negative spirits and energies. A boy became a man after initiations of passage. An epidemic could be pacified through the successful performance of prescribed rites. A couple would be joined together through sacred rites that were meant to create an actual, albeit invisible bond.

In this day and age, there are no longer any shared universal rituals. The Disneyland ride or Hollywood blockbuster film are the closest we can get to a common universal experience, but they are not built to be transformative, only thrilling. You might argue that Aristotle prescribed purging the audience of pity and fear through performance,[1] but I do not believe he was thinking of a roller coaster ride. Though we deal with the same physical events as the ancients — birth, death, the changing of the seasons—our ways of celebrating or commemorating these events are more and more fragmented and individualized. Today the only link we have to ancient rituals outside of organized religions is through art. There are no functioning temples of unified faith in the center of a modern metropolis, perhaps only government buildings in their stead. A theater, concert hall, and museum will likely be part of the civic center, bearing the load of spiritual nutrition to a modern society. We may not see ourselves as such, but through

---

1 Aristotle, "Poetics," trans. S.H. Butcher, *The Project Gutenberg eBook of The Poetics of Aristotle*, https://www.gutenberg.org/ebooks/1974, Chapter VI.

the creative act, it is we artists who carry forth the previously sacred act of *religere*, connecting. Through these institutions, we manifest transformation.

The Efficacy of Art

In an anthropological sense, ritual must have efficacy. Meaning, if you have a ritual to pray for rain, then, after it is completed, it should rain, otherwise the ritual has failed. The question then is, if creative work has taken over the function of connecting, then what are we connecting to, and from where? What are we transforming from, and into what? Are we able to make a connection from the mundane to the divine? What is the definition of "divine"? If we don't have the capability of the ancients to purify a society, are we able to at least purify an individual? Can we transform ourselves first, to become the proper vehicle to lead others? If we are true sorcerers, we can bring the audience into a place where they are transformed, and they stay there. Transformation, perhaps, is the difference between craft and art. The craftsman can make beautiful things, while the artist, who is a sorcerer, can make beautiful things that have transformative power.

Creativity is a journey, this is for sure. But where is the starting point? What is the destination? Where are you taking me? Where am I taking myself? It seems quite arrogant to think that the work we do can be transformative, because it supposes that we know where the destination is. But if we don't, what are we doing? What is the purpose, the efficacy, of making art?

The Accidental Arsonist

One day at my school in Taipei, I saw two students wandering around campus in a daze. I recognized them as the ones who had just performed a particularly intense version of Sam Shepherd's *Fool for Love* in a student director's project a few days before. I stopped them and asked, "You're still inside?" They nodded. I said, "You shouldn't be. The curtain comes down on the last show, you strike the set, and it's over. You go home." But they couldn't. I found the director, their classmate, and talked to them together. I told the director he was playing with fire, but he didn't know how, so he could bring them into the fire, but not out. It took a little while, but soon they were back to normal.

This is a case where a director is leading his cast through a state of transformation that he doesn't really understand. The dark energies inherent in the work appealed to him, and he was able to bring the cast into that dark place, but he did not have the maturity, in life or in art, to bring them back out. Nor did he realize that it was part of his job. Instead of being a firefighter, he became the arsonist. In such a case, and in many other cases I have seen over the years, many done by professional companies, the audience is put into a difficult position. The director can lead audiences into dark places. This is not that difficult. But without wisdom, or if darkness is the extent of the director's wisdom, then the audience cannot be transported out of that darkness. For many, that may not be the purpose. To conduct a tour of dark places, a brilliant, dazzling tour, takes courage and skill, and may in fact satisfy audiences and critics alike.

Pain, Healing, and Sharing

If you are in a dark place and you have the skill as an artist to bring your audience into that place, that in itself is an accomplishment. But you do have to think about the consequences. I share with you a wasteland full of emotional land mines, the bottom of my well where all the snakes are crawling, then I leave you there, because I do not have the means to bring you out, because I cannot bring myself out. There would be those who recognize that place, empathize with you, and feel a closeness to you. Your work may even be considered a masterpiece. But I still would need to know, where are you taking me? And why? What is your motivation? What do you want me to be transformed into? How has art transformed you?

At a recent talk at Stanford, an audience member asked me if creative work had to come from a place of pain. Though suffering in oneself certainly provides impetus for expression, it is not a prerequisite. I told him in fact, you should not feel guilty if you have *not* suffered as much as others, which I find is one curious way an artist can feel inadequate. Instead, I said, it is sufficient and perhaps even more potent if you can feel the suffering of others. Through the understanding of and empathy with the pain of others, whether it comes from your own personal experience of pain or not, you are powerfully equipped to undertake any meaningful creative work.[2] Through shared experiences of pain, we may find a way of healing, and a way to share the healing with our audience.

To trigger transformation in our audience should be our goal, even though we may not be able to achieve it at our current level of method and wisdom. The fact is many forms of creativity these days are not built to transform. Aspiring artists are entitled to expression, and to express oneself seems to be motivation enough.

---

2 Stan Lai, "Creativity for Scholar-Directors," a seminar at Stanford University, April 18, 2025.

But there is a difference between merely wishing to express and an act of sharing. As artists, we express ourselves, but the expression is meant to be shared, so we should be aware of what we are sharing. We consider whether we are making a gift or garbage, offering or destruction, whether our work can be a transformative experience that makes the world a better place, or is it just a glorified form of self-gratification?

To Forget or Remember?

In the spectrum of creativity, there are works that are made for you to forget, and works that are made for you to remember. Works intended as entertainment may excite you and transport you to somewhere else for a short period of time, where you can forget everything that is troubling you, and sometimes the piece itself soon after is forgotten. On the opposite end of the spectrum are works that have the power to transform built-in. They don't let you forget. They engage you, tackle what is troubling you head on, stay with you, and transport you to a new vantage point.

I recall reading an interview with Arthur Miller on the 50th anniversary of *Death of a Salesman*. He was asked what has changed on Broadway. He said,

> Nothing starts on Broadway. It doesn't have the vigor to initiate anything. So it's really in a decayed position at the moment, and I don't see how it's ever going to improve in our time. What we still do well is musicals, but that's not theatre. That's pure show business.[3]

I have never considered entertainment and art to be mutually exclusive of each other. There is great room for intersection between the two. The difference is, are you making work to forget or remember? To be able to cast a spell that brings an audience totally into your world for two hours demands formidable skills, indeed. With such skills, it would be best to ask oneself whether it would be a waste of one's talents to use such skills as a means of escape only.

---

[3] Peter Applebone, "Arthur Miller: Present at the Birth of a Salesman," *New York Times*, January 29, 1999, archive.nytimes.com/www.nytimes.com/library/arts/012999miller-theatre-profile.html

Destination: Beyond

The highest creative works are works that transform the viewer into connection with greater humanity, with greater concepts, with life itself, into connection with powers and energies greater than life. The great works of mankind elevate the viewer to a higher plane of awareness, where we are connected to something awe-inspiring, something beyond. Through such connection, we are transformed because we have been connected, however briefly, with that something beyond, something mystical, spiritual, divine. This cannot happen unless the artist herself is connected.

The first time I understood this sacred obligation was when I saw Peter Brook's play *The Suit* at the Hong Kong Cultural Centre in 2002.[4] Three African actors performed this simply staged work, with a bare stage and just a few props. The play was performed in French, with Chinese and English supertitles. The audience was multinational. As I watched this simple story from South Africa, I was suddenly overwhelmed by the immense universal humanity it had drawn me into. I felt connected to the story, to these actors from so far away, to the maestro whom I had admired for so many years. I felt deeply connected to all of the other audience members who were sitting in this same large room with me, and the connection went beyond the audience. As I left the theater and walked into the Kowloon night, the connections seemed to multiply and embrace everything. I had been transformed. I was greater than myself, a part of a greater self. I understood why Peter Brook was considered such a master, because his power to connect was so majestic.

That evening, it was as if the artist had successfully taken down the barriers to the source in all of the audience and connected us directly to it, which connected us to each other and everything. This experience gave me immense faith in the creative act. There still are wizards and sorcerers who roam the Earth, who can give the gift of healing, purification, or transformation through the sharing of their art, bringing us back to the primal functions of ritual and the basic essence of being human.

---

4 Peter Brook, director, *Le Costume*, based on story by Can Themba, adapted for stage by Mothobi Mutloatse and Barney Simon, performed by Theatre des Bouffes du Nord, April 18 to 21, 2002, Hong Kong Cultural Centre Studio Theatre.

A Circle

I recall my days studying at Berkeley. Every Tuesday at noon, a circle of people would gather on the grass at the university entrance on Oxford Street. The purpose was to pray for world peace. I would join in if I passed by on that day. I would see students, professors, street people and street artists, all just standing there in a large circle, heads lowered, praying in their own way. When you were done, you left. Others stayed, and new ones joined, until the circle naturally dissipated after 1:00 p.m. when everybody got back to class or work.

How silly? But that's what we did. Did it work? Judging by the state of the world, apparently not. But who knows? To me, the fact that there would be enough people to gather into a large circle in this day and age, and spend a few minutes thinking about world peace, was enough to rekindle my faith in humankind. No matter how naïve you may think it was, who knows about the efficacy of it? That is not for us to comprehend.

Listen, Contemplate, Act

For over 2,000 years, students of Buddhism have been given this essential advice to practice on the path:

> *Cultivate the wisdom of listening, the wisdom of thinking, and the wisdom of action.*[5]

This should be excellent advice for the study of anything, and seems to be tailor-made for those on the path of creativity.

We listen to so many things, but do we listen with wisdom? How much garbage do we let in that is not worthy of our ears? Are we even thinking when we listen, particularly in creative terms? And when we think, are we thinking with wisdom? Or are we letting our thoughts just slide into default mode and let mental habits take over? Then, when we act from this listening and thinking, are our actions conducted with wisdom?

This ancient advice benefits us from the beginning to the end of a creative project. It is also great advice for life, period, particularly in this age of misinformation. And by now, we do understand how life and art are intertwined at the root.

---

5 There are many teachings on the subject. An introduction can be found in Khensur Jampa Tegchok, "Listening, Thinking, and Meditating," imisangha.org/listening-thinking-and-meditating

To be mindful of your listening, thinking, and actions is to be mindful of everything you see, hear, and do. If we have this awareness, we can start to see the interrelatedness of everything. Everything is related to everything, and I am related to everything. To be able to see this is grand indeed. Through mindful practice, this interrelatedness will become firm in our minds, and we will live a fluid and creative existence. Creativity becomes a natural, fluid thing, not something contrived and painful.

The Language of the Soul

At a public dialogue at Wuzhen with the eminent theater practitioner and theoretician Eugenio Barba, he and I asked each other about what the essence of theater was. Eugenio spoke of his concept of "embrace"—that the act of performing theater was an act of embrace, with oneself and with the audience. I spoke of the essence as being the creation of a separate reality that connects and transforms, and when the audience leaves the theater, they have left the separate reality but remain transformed and connected.[6]

To achieve both of these concepts, we must be fluent in a special language—the language of the soul. I noted that masters such as Eugenio Barba, Peter Brook, and Shireen Strooker, like ancient shamans, are wizards, sorcerers, magicians, however you want to describe them. But the description of the artistic sorcerer, in my mind, is one who can bring the audience into the connecting and transforming force, and this can only be done when the soul speaks to the soul.

We must learn the language of the soul speaking to the soul.

It is the most potent language known to humankind. It can only be learned when your wisdom is sufficient, your toolbox has adequate tools, your soul is open, and you are willing and able to channel all the connecting forces to open up the souls of your audience. The speed of communication when the soul speaks to the soul is far faster and deeper than any Ethernet connection.

---

6 Stan Lai and Eugenio Barba, "One Hundred Years of Solitude: A Conversation between Eugenio Barba and Stan Lai," *Wuzhen Dialogues, Wuzhen Theatre Festival*, October 25, 2024.

Sincerity and Humility

"You can play a shoestring if you're sincere" — John Coltrane[7]

I recently gave a talk to high school students who had organized a theater competition in my father's hometown of Huichang, China, which I have helped rebuild into a rural hub for theater. In this once impoverished town, the arts have created new opportunities for young people. A student asked me what was the most important thing for creativity in the theater. I paused and thought about it for a second, looking out at the hungry young faces that had only recently been exposed to the arts and creativity. I said, if you are sincere and you possess certain skills, you surely will attain a level of success.[8]

I guess this is a pretty good formula. It is another way of describing the interplay of wisdom and method. In this day and age of slick production and computer-generated everything, sincerity is a rare commodity. Sincerity is a kind of wisdom. It goes hand-in-hand with humility. Together, they don't sound like anything powerful or ambitious enough to create something great, but actually, they lay the humble foundations for greatness.

Sincerity is a commitment to what you believe in. It is your honest understanding of life and yourself. Sincerity carves a path from your heart to your work. It helps you work from your heart and not your brain. Your brain can play tricks on you, and you can play tricks on your audience. But an audience knows when something is pure and when something is fabricated.

Humility is an undervalued quality. It seems as if one would need the opposite to be the assertive artist making decisions, the brash creative leader shouting orders to her group. But only when you are humble can you become a receptor. The greater your humility, the greater your volume as a vessel. The arrogant person doesn't have much space in his character to contain anything else but arrogance. The humble person is basically empty. She can accommodate anything. With humility comes expansiveness.

If you have an amazing toolbox full of incredible techniques, you can surely play any trick you want on your audience. But if that toolbox has been stocked

---

7 John Coltrane, quoted by Nathan Phelps, "7 Lessons On Practicing Music You Can Take From John Coltrane, the 'Athlete' of Improvisation," *Medium.com*, December 3, 2020. https://nathandavidphelps.medium.com/7-lessons-on-practicing-music-you-can-take-from-john-coltrane-the-athlete-of-improvisation-f296bb3a0915

8 Stan Lai, public lecture, Theatre Converge, Huichang Theatre Village, Huichang, Jiangxi Province, China, July 24, 2024.

through the filter of humility, and used to express something truly sincere, your work will become something special. You have the ability to communicate with an audience directly; you have mastered the language of the soul speaking to the soul, and not mind to mind, or soul to mind. The foundation of this language is sincerity and humility.

Passion and Compassion

I offer another fail-proof formula: passion + compassion. Without passion, it is hard to generate creativity. However, we should understand by now that passion cannot do the job by itself. Is there something called "disciplined passion"? To me, that is a great description of how to get creative work done. But there is one more ingredient to put in your recipe: compassion.

We must have passion for life, for our work, but our work must have compassion to be meaningful to others. We must consider our work a gift to the world. We are not here to show off, but to share. We are not here to take, but to give.

Without compassion, art can become extremely egocentric and perhaps not worthy of the word "art" anymore. If the whole purpose of your artistic endeavor is to be seen doing snazzy stunts and saying outrageous things, then if you can gather an audience, more power to you. But be careful what you wish for. If you can make compassionate works, they will create compassionate effects; if you make egotistic works that support and engender violence and sexist attitudes, they will naturally create violence and sexist attitudes.

By being passionate, you are throwing everything into your work. By being compassionate, you are caring for everything you create, every character you devise, every story you tell, and you are caring about your audience. It's an unbeatable combination.

Exercises and Further Thoughts

1. What is your definition of art? What is your definition of great art? Does great art have to be based on pain and suffering?
2. Have you ever been transformed by a work of art? Have you ever been transformed by a religious act or ceremony? Is there a difference?
3. Have you ever felt connected to a oneness with everything? Do you think that art can make this connection?
4. In everyday life, when you listen to anything, is it done with wisdom or not?

6. Consider the same with thinking. Is your thinking on automatic pilot, or is it true contemplation? Consider the same about practice. If you are not applying wisdom to these essential things, can you change? How does this change affect your life?
7. Rate your humility on a scale of 1 to 10. Can you see how it is a plus and not a minus to your work?
8. Rate and examine your level of compassion in life. Are you only compassionate to those less fortunate than you? Can your compassion grow to a more open level, where you can be compassionate to more and more beings, even the characters you create if you are a writer?

CHAPTER TWENTY-THREE

FURTHER THOUGHTS ON THE CREATIVE ACT

Is Creativity Innately Selfish?

Many people see life as a naturally selfish thing that nature has set up so only the fittest survive. It seems normal that we design our lives and values in a selfish way that can nurture our existential needs. To see motivation as selfish poses no problem for most people.

Deeper investigation will reveal that this is not necessarily the case. Studies have shown how selfish people have an advantage over altruistic people if they are left to survive one on one, but in groups, altruistic people have a definite advantage.[1] For a wolf pack in danger, one individual wolf may sacrifice itself so that the others may survive.

Fra Angelico in art, or Mother Teresa in life, worked with the pure desire to benefit others. This is certainly not the norm. Neither are those at the opposite end of the spectrum who make art that is totally 100 percent for self-gratification. The spectrum of motivation runs the gamut in creative work from altruism to egoism. We usually find ourselves somewhere in between. Can we see that when the needle approaches total egoism, our work is affected in a certain way, and as the needle shifts toward pure altruism, it also has an effect on our final product?

Artists today run the range from the genuine and awe-inspiring to the fake and banal. The essential difference is not in skill level but in their motives for making art. I am often astounded by the astronomical prices contemporary Chinese paintings fetch at auctions. Why am I so seldom moved by these paintings? For one, I learned that in the art market, price is decided by size. It is not unlike going

---

1 See David Sloan Wilson, *Does Altruism Exist?: Culture, Genes, and the Welfare of Others* (New Haven: Yale University Press, 2015).

to the butcher's to buy a certain size cut. You can see how this factors into motivation. If I charged by the minute for each script I wrote, I would certainly make an effort to write a longer script. It is easy to see how this motive will affect the artistic quality and integrity of the work. Fortunately, there are still many who understand that pure motivations bring forth pure works.

Practice and Window

Today, concertgoers go to a recital by Martha Argerich expecting some epiphany; art lovers flock to a well-curated exhibition of Frida Kahlo seeking spiritual guidance on some aspect of life. For many, art has become their religion, and they worship it fervently. This seems fine, acceptable.

One evening, we attended a play in Taipei that plodded through issues the playwright was facing in life. My wife, Nai-chu, remarked that the artist seemed to be using theater as a place for "practice," in the sense of the term "practitioner" in spiritual practice. But theater, with its inherent "show"-ness, she reasoned, would be hard-pressed to become a place for spiritual practice because its nature is a window to showcase the fruits of one's practice. Personal practice should take place privately outside of the theater. To practice within a showcase window would seem a contradiction. By such rationale, art is not a religion but a window through which one can display one's "religion," one's connections to meaning and transcendence.

For many artists today, the quest for art is inseparable from the quest for life. They freely combine experiences from the two. I know artists who engage in romantic relationships for the sake of creativity. This happens more commonly than you might imagine. The workplace becomes a romantic playground. Once the relationship is broken, the artist explores the meaning of the relationship through his next project, which brings along a new relationship. And so on and so forth.

Most people seem to accept this. Artists should be temperamental and passionate, goes the common wisdom. To have an intensely passionate but ultimately destructive love affair can be artistically productive. It is not questioned when artists seek therapy, or even revenge, through their work. In today's world, the artist has been empowered to find himself in art. Or you might say, it has become acceptable for the motivation of the artist to make art her therapy, the way to discover her self, the way to find the meaning of life.

This all sounds acceptable. But can we ask why art is a legitimate realm for the search for one's life? In the past, the church or temple was the center of religious and social activity for the layman, including the artist. For those seeking serious spiritual practice, to search directly for one's life as a full-time job, one would go to a convent or monastery to lead the life of a nun or monk. A key discrepancy between these traditional centers where life is searched for and today's studio/temple theater/meditation center is that practitioners in the former were not expected to produce works to display to the public.

Why do we pay to watch an author's psychotherapy? Would you pay to watch a meditator meditate? And would the meditator's meditation be different if someone had paid to watch?

Artistic License

Many people think that without chaos, confusion, and suffering, there would be no art. Studies have shown that most artists, contrary to public perception, lead relatively content lives that are not highly publicized perhaps because they do not make for juicy stories.[2]

Writers have poetic license to break away from conventional rules of language when they need to. As artists, do we have artistic license to live life away from conventional rules when we need to? My observation is that life and art are highly interrelated, but one must differentiate between the two. In art, one is an artist. In life, one is a person. To think that as an artist, one only needs to work on being an artist and doesn't need to work on being a person means that one has reversed the priorities, and that art is bigger than life.

In fact, life encompasses art, and one is born a person first and an artist second. What kind of a person one is, and what priorities one sets in life, greatly influence one's art. To work the other way around, to be an artist first and a person second means that the kind of an artist one is, the priorities and values one sets in one's art become the major influences on how one lives. What matters is the art one produces, not what kind of a person one is. Does this sound right?

Maybe for the select few, it works. From what I have seen, the majority of artists and aspiring artists who choose to function this way lead a chaotic personal life with much suffering, and they do not necessarily produce good art.

---

2 See among others, Anna Sidelnikova, "Definitely happy: artists who lived in clover. Part 1," *Artsmarts*, April 27, 2018, https://arthive.com/publications/1296-Definitely_happy_artists_who_lived_in_clover_Part_1, and Sidelnikova, "Happy in different ways: artists who lived in clover. Part 2," *Connaissances*, June 8, 2018, https://arthive.com/fr/publications/1393-Happy_in_different_ways_artists_who_lived_in_clover_Part_2.

I recall a heated debate I once had with a dear art historian friend, over how we should regard Picasso's art in light of his personal abusive behavior toward women. My friend, a woman herself, demanded that the sanctity of Picasso's art never be questioned, that whoever can create such work, such beauty, is a genius who is above social norms and can do whatever he wants in life. Art must be separated from the artist.

The debate was laborious. It was like, so what if he destroyed the lives of some women? Look at all the glorious art he gave the world! I don't know. If you could undo the damage done to several human beings in this world, but the price was to forfeit all of Picasso's art, would you?

We called off the debate without a conclusion. We decided we still wanted to be friends.

Is Art Spelled with a Capital "A"?

When I first started my creative career in the theater, it was as if art was always spelled with a capital "A." Art was the supreme goal of my life. This was my world view. As the years passed, once my technique had reached a certain level, my stance began to shift. I recall the year the new technology of *Jurassic Park* took the world by storm, Hou Hsiao-hsien remarked to me that he didn't think it was that big a deal. He asked, "If you have the capability to do anything, then the more pressing question is, what do you want to do?"[3] It was at this time that I was also humbly reminded that Vasari, in his vast work on the lives of the Renaissance painters and sculptors, never used the word "artist" to describe them.[4]

In the twofold training of the artist, wisdom and method are constantly at play with each other, but as one matures as an artist, wisdom or the lack of it becomes the dominant of the two, bringing the artist to greater heights of success or depths of failure. For me, as time went by, "art" naturally no longer needed a capital "A." Work on oneself, in life, was the much more urgent endeavor. Whether or not this work manifested in my art was no longer my primary concern.

The Curse of Originality

We have noted how many creative people are always seeking new methods of expression. For any new work, there seems to be an invisible pressure to do

---

3 Personal conversation with Hou, 1993.
4 Giorgio Vasari, *The Lives of the Artists (Oxford World's Classics)*, Julia Conway Bondanella and Peter Bondanella, trans., Oxford: Oxford University Press, xi.

something original. Every time I unveil a new play, almost invariably the media will ask, "So what's new in this play?" I don't think this is a fair question. Why does any new work always have to have something new in it?

We are infatuated with the new. As artists, we are expected to come up with something new all the time. I have written and directed over 40 original plays. Though most of them do not resemble the others, in content or form, I do not believe that originality is required for creativity. Look at Chekhov, for a simple example. His four major plays, each a masterwork, all resemble each other. But does anyone complain that Chekhov was a copycat of himself? Do we mind that Mozart often borrowed themes and phrases from his own work? Or that Beethoven even confessed that in one of his musical sketches, "This entire passage has been stolen from the Mozart symphony in C."[5] Mozart himself said, "I don't study or aim at originality."[6]

Newness to me is overrated. In the rush to be new, we often forget what it means to be simply good or great. If you wanted me to choose between greatness and newness, I would take greatness any day. And to take the matter further, is there really anything new under the sun?

The jazz baritone saxophonist Gerry Mulligan was once criticized for always sounding the same on his solos. He said he didn't care about being original; he just cared about being good.[7]

Exercises and Further Thoughts

1. What do you expect to gain when you attend a performance or exhibition by an acknowledged master? Try to pinpoint exactly what it is you seek.
2. Would you trade all of Picasso's career for the well-being of a few women?
3. When you go to see a new dance or read a new novel, would you rather it be something original or something good?
4. How about at a restaurant? Would you rather be served something you have never had before, or something you are familiar with, but done very well?

---

5 Stephen M. Klugewicz, "Copying Mozart: Did Beethoven Steal Melodies for His Own Music?" *The Imaginative Conservative*, February 21, 2018, theimaginativeconservative.org/2018/02/copying-mozart-beethoven-steal-melodies-music-stephen-klugewicz.html.
6 Duke.
7 This is from an interview I listened to on the radio in the 1980s, and cannot find the source, so I am paraphrasing.

CHAPTER TWENTY-FOUR

MY PERSONAL JOURNEY

Some References

I thought it might interest some to learn a little bit about my personal creative journey, as a reference to everything that has been laid out in this book.

As I mentioned in Chapter One, I became a playwright rather by accident, having been trained as a scholar and director. With few teaching resources, I went forth building new plays with my students, using improvisation as a creative tool and as actor training itself. My first original play *We All Grew Up This Way* (1984)[1] was collectively created with a class of 15 students, each of whom shared significant experiences in their lives. We performed in a simple hall, with no budget. The actors wore their own clothes. Props and furniture were borrowed from our school. The actors changed all the rudimentary scenery by themselves, without a crew. Lighting was basically switch on and off.

The audience went through key scenes in the lives of the students, who performed themselves in their main scenes while supporting their classmates in others. The play revealed a cross-section of the rapid social changes that Taiwan was experiencing at the time. The performance was deeply moving to all present. It was described by critic Ma Sen as "the birth of a new type of theatre on the Chinese stage."[2]

I continued making new works in this experimental way, without assuming what a play is, what its structure should be, just letting it grow organically through the process, with the motive to discover what modern theater meant to us, in Asia, in Taiwan, in the Chinese language. It was like learning to be a

---

1 *Women doushi zheyang zhangdade* in Chinese, *Stan Lai: Theatre*, Vol. 1 (Taipei: Meta, 1999).
2 Ma Sen, "The Birth of a New Type of Theatre on the Chinese Stage," *China Times*, January 15, 1984.

gardener by watching the seeds you plant grow, not assuming what they would grow into, and not assuming to know what gardening is.

Surprise: Success

In 1985, the first production by the new theater group Performance Workshop that I had formed, *That Evening, We Performed Crosstalk*[3] (1985) became a surprise popular hit, the magnitude of which we were totally unprepared for. This play for just two actors used traditional Chinese "crosstalk" (*xiangsheng*)—a form of stand-up comedy—to comment on its own death as a tradition. We sold out performance after performance, and an audio cassette tape recording of the whole play, two tapes to a set, sold over 1 million sets (Taiwan had a population of 20 million then). The set of cassette audiotapes sold out so fast that the record company didn't have time to print new copies. They were embarrassed to tell me that pirated editions outnumbered the authorized edition 5 to 1.

Crosstalk is the ancient Chinese form of stand-up comedy that gained great popularity in the late Qing Dynasty and the Nationalist Era. It was also very popular in Taiwan. Think Abbott and Costello's "Who's on First?" in a Chinese context. This comic form mysteriously disappeared sometime when I was studying abroad at Berkeley. When I came home in 1983, not only had crosstalk disappeared, it was as if it had never existed! I went to the record store where I used to buy crosstalk cassette tapes and asked the proprietor if there were any new recordings out. His puzzled look was like, "What? What talk?" It was as if he had never heard the name before! I said, "Crosstalk!" He shook his head.

I stepped out onto the street and watched the busy traffic buzzing by me. Yes, the city was vibrant, the economy was flowing. I suddenly realized that something big had happened in the few years I was away. Not only had Taiwan just gone through an economic miracle and become materially prosperous, but this material gain had also unintentionally and unknowingly destroyed many things in the process.

I learned that the most famous crosstalk duo in Taiwan, Masters Wei Longhao and Wu Chao-nan, whom I grew up listening to and idolizing, had broken up because Mr. Wu emigrated to Monterey Park, California where it is said he was selling beef jerky. Wow. One man's decision to leave the country to find a new life killed an entire living artistic tradition!

---

3 *Nayiye, womenshuo xiangsheng* in Chinese. Audio recording UFO records, 1985. Published version Crown Publishing, Taipei, 1986.

Lost Noodles

What other things had we lost in the scramble for economic prosperity? I went to have a bowl of noodles at my favorite noodle shop in downtown Ximending. To my despair, it was gone. The name of the place used to be "Homestyle Noodles." But where was the proprietor's home? I didn't know. I only knew that this noodle maker was just like over 1 million refugees who came to Taiwan from China in 1949, like my parents, from somewhere in China. Well, China is about the same size and as diverse as Europe.

The place had closed down because the landlord raised the rent. I never found that style, that flavor of noodles again, with a spicy but not-too-hot beef-based broth, with thick handmade noodles that had just the right pliability. Judging from the taste, the guy who ran the shop must have been from northern China, which is like saying someone came from South America.

In my imagination, I fantasized that this guy learned to make noodles from his mother, who learned from her mother, and that the soup and spices had a legacy going back 1,000 years. Could a greedy landlord in 1983 in a place called Taipei, Taiwan, have just killed a 1,000-year-old tradition?

Quite possibly. Because in China, the Cultural Revolution destroyed many traditions, and possibly also this style of noodles. Later in life, on performance tours of northern China, I would search for this style of noodles in every different city, to no avail. How fragile is tradition and heritage. It is true that "you don't know what you got till it's gone." Some things disappear, and you can't even name their names. Soon they are as if they never existed, extinct. Perhaps that's the reality we must face, I told myself.

I got together with two well-known television personalities who were interested in theater, Lee Li-chun and the late Li Kuo-hsiu (1955–2013). Together we made this play about the death of crosstalk, which became a metaphor for the death of many things in life, including noodles. What we undertook was no easy task: "Using crosstalk to write crosstalk's elegy" is how I described it. In the play, we performed five crosstalk scenes from different eras in history, each scene commenting on that era. The scenes sounded like they were authentic period stand-up comedy pieces, but they were all new material written by us. The actors had to learn how to perform crosstalk—in different periods of history, no less! It was not unlike Robert De Niro learning how to box for his role in *Raging Bull*, but more, learning to box in different historical styles for scenes set in different eras.

I thought the play was something very experimental. Scholars and students might be interested in this investigation into how culture dies, I thought, but hardly anyone else. I would have been satisfied if we could fill a 100-seat black box theater. Boy, was I wrong. The play was so successful that even today, 40 years later, people come up to me and recite whole passages. For audiences, most coming to the theater for the first time, it was their first taste of modern theater. For others, it was their first taste of crosstalk. They didn't know what to call it and it didn't matter. Another new form of theater had been born on the Chinese-speaking stage in Taiwan. For at least a year, you could hear our play on the radio, in taxis, in restaurants, all sorts of places. Once, in the southern city of Tainan, after a performance, the three of us went to the famous night market for a late meal. We saw different vendors selling seven different types of pirated editions! I wondered, should I be ecstatic or livid?

My two partners, Lee and Li, were comic geniuses. Dark themes emerged from the bright laughter of the audience, who were left in the end to contemplate, what? What did they just see? Was it comedy or tragedy? Was it crosstalk or theater? Did it matter? The famed architect Kris Yao, whom I didn't know then but got to know well later in life, was in the audience, and he laughed so hard that he had to be sent to the emergency room due to an asthma attack. One evening, in a large theater in Taiwan's south, watching from the side of the stage, I swear I actually saw Li Kuo-hsiu brace himself before a punch line. When it came, his body actually flinched as the wave of laughter hit him. Honestly. I asked him about it. He said, "Yea. I need to beef up." Wind velocity from laughter. I know this firsthand.

The Encore, and Beyond

That Evening, We Performed Crosstalk reflected the same values in theater that I have always believed in. Start with a bare stage, and it can become the universe. You don't assume rules, you don't worry about budget, you work with what you have, and you know that the most precious commodity you can possibly have is the human soul. Within the souls of all the people you work with are all the stories, passions, joy, skills, and virtuosity that can convert a bare stage into a unique journey of transformation.

The next year, everyone was waiting for the sequel to *That Evening*, but I kept telling people, we aren't crosstalk performers. We do theater. Our answer to all of the anticipation was the play *Secret Love in Peach Blossom Land*,[4] which became perhaps my most well-known play. It is still being performed today. The play holds the dubious record of having the most unauthorized performances,

---

4 See Stan Lai, *Selected Plays*, Vol. 1.

over 10,000, which I am told is a reliable count, mostly in colleges and high schools in the Chinese world. People ask me my thoughts on why it is still performing, still resounding to audiences today. I really don't know. Maybe the collage form, bundling tragedy and comedy together on stage, telling contemporary and classical stories in fragments, yet achieving a classical unity at the end, has always been a bit ahead of the audience, and audiences always appreciate that.

The rest of the story, I will skim over. Success is a strange thing. I can understand how many artists through history have spoken of the fear of success, how it can eat into you, how you can suddenly have people at your door, wanting you to do things that aren't really you, and soon you become empty. In fact, after the success of *Secret Love in Peach Blossom Land*, a movie company offered me a nice sum to make a film of the play. I said I would think about such an adaptation. They said, "What? No need to think. Just set up a camera in front of the stage and shoot it in two hours." I declined this quick attempt to make a buck. My later film of the play (*The Peach Blossom Land*⁵, 1992) took over a month to shoot, and the aesthetics are quite different from the theater version.

As my career progressed, I was put in a position where I fervently wanted to continue my pure experimental explorations of the theater, but the success of my group gave me pressure to produce new works at a steady pace that were financially viable. I accepted this as my calling and embraced my role in the evolving theater culture of the Chinese-speaking world. The result is a hybrid of these seemingly clashing motivations, which over the decades I have done my best to reconcile.

Creativity Is a Steamed Bun

In 2008, during intense creative rehearsals for a new work *The Village*, a strange idea came to me. *The Village* is about refugees from the Chinese Civil War, who came from all over China to Taiwan, settling in frugal temporary military encampments, and how they survived decades of poverty, discrimination and martial law by learning how to live and work together, despite their diverse backgrounds.⁶ One of the main characters, Mrs. Chu, is a native Taiwanese lady whose family disowned her because she married one of the mainlanders in the village. Mrs.

---

5 Stan Lai, Writer and Director, *The Peach Blossom Land* (film), Performance Workshop Films and Longshong Films, 1992.
6 Stan Lai, *Selected Plays*, Vol. 2.

Chu learned how to make northern mainland steamed buns from her neighbor, a restauranteur from Beijing, who passed the tradition of Tianjin buns on to her in a comic scene where they cannot understand a word of what each other says. Later the Beijing elder passes away, and throughout the play, the buns become a strong symbol of what united them together as one strong society.

My crazy idea was to present a steamed bun to every audience member as they left the theater. My team told me straight up, I was nuts. But I insisted that this would be the very right thing to do. My logic was, we were premiering in December. The play was long. The audience would be leaving the theater near midnight, hungry and cold. How nice if they could hold a warm steamed meat bun in their hands? In the back of my mind, I also thought of Roman comedy, where it is said after a play, the audience was invited to go behind the stage where bread and other food had been set up for them. Theater and food. They have always gone together.

I continued to insist. My team was really put to the task, because the play was to be performed at the National Theatre in Taipei, and was sold out for 10 straight performances, 1,500 audience per performance. Where would we be able to find 1,500 hot steamed buns at 11:30 p.m.? It was logistically impossible, and my team was also worried about issues that the health department might bring up if somebody got sick from any of these buns. That first year, I was so involved in the creation of the work that I was not able to put my mind to solving this problem. In the end, my producing team came up with a compromise, which was to give each of the audience a frozen bun, the type you can buy at 7-Eleven, certified by the health department, which you can microwave. We would package it in a bag with a "Village" motif—the address plate of the main character, which featured the number "99."

It was better than nothing, I thought, and with no other options, I gave in. As it turned out, the buns were an instant hit. Audience left notes saying they either enjoyed the buns at home, or kept them in the freezer as a souvenir of the show. During the second run, my team sourced a vendor who could provide 1,500 buns a night. Hot. And that's how it's been to this day. Every audience member who has attended *The Village* has received a hot bun at the end, including when we performed in New York and California. When we performed in a park in the southern Taiwan city of Kaohsiung in 2011, we were expecting 5,000 people, so we prepared 5,000 buns. But the audience swelled to 12,000 the first night, and expanded to 25,000 the second. My team told me that they had literally bought out all of the buns in Taiwan they could source, which were shipped by express to Kaohsiung so that each and every audience member received a bun on leaving the park.

To get a hot steamed bun as you leave a performance of *The Village* has become part of the tradition of this play, and this play has enjoyed one of the longest running histories of my plays. In fact, when people talk to me about the play, they always mention the bun. My team tells me it is the smartest creative marketing tool they have ever seen. Since then, other theaters have tried to emulate this feat, but so far there has been no gift to the audience so integral to the experience of a play as the hot steamed bun of *The Village*.

An Olympic-sized Elephant

I was lured into feature filmmaking in 1991 and have explained how that led to my creative burnout in 1994, which was miraculously resurrected through a seemingly undoable television project. Since then, I have continued on, in my own way, inventing new ways of doing theater, such as "theatre in the surround," which is how *A Dream Like a Dream* and *Ago*[7] are performed, placing the audience at the center, with the performance revolving around them. I have continued to explore alternate means of theatrical staging, such as the site-specific *Nightwalk in the Chinese Garden* at the Huntington Library Chinese Garden in San Marino, California, and four works of Samuel Beckett in my family's ancestral home in Huichang, China.[8] I also have never veered from my deep belief that the value of theater is not in a production's budget but in simply figuring out the best way to tell a story. I have seen millions spent on incredibly lavish productions that often fail to sell tickets and close. Neither do I despise the benefits that money can bring to a production. But the hard fact is that money itself cannot buy creativity.

There are so many creative challenges and joys that I have experienced over my career. I would like to share this one as perhaps most relevant to the contents of this book. In 2009, I was chosen to stage the opening and closing ceremonies of the Deaflympics, which were to be staged in Taipei. It was a great honor to lead this creative endeavor, the largest public event in Taiwan in 40 years. For 18 months, a team of local artists I had put together worked our tails off to produce this Olympic-sized extravaganza in a stadium. In getting to know the deaf community and the importance of the Deaflympics to them, I formulated the essential concept "Power in Me," which became the slogan of the games and also referred subtly to Taiwan itself, which had become increasingly isolated internationally.

The challenges we faced were enormous. I wanted to fly one of Taiwan's top models, Lin Chia-chi, 200 meters through the air, while a gigantic triangular banner unfurled behind her, on which moving images were to be projected. Since this

---

7 Stan Lai, *Selected Plays*, Vol. 3.
8 *Beckett in the Lai Family Mansion*, dir. Stan Lai, Huichang Theatre Season 003, Huichang Theatre Village, China, May 2025.

was a government project, all of the artists and technicians had to be contracted through the government tendering system, which prevented me from choosing the artistic partners I wanted to work with. For rigging, I was astonished that the company that won the bid was a mountaineering society that had never done anything theatrical. Working patiently with them, we miraculously got the job done, and flew not only Lin, but pop diva Amei safely through the air. One thing that patience could not handle was the fact that the event was scheduled during the typhoon season. As witnessed at the Paris Olympics, rain can really upset such a ceremony. The performances we had devised simply did not have a Plan B for rainfall. My solution, seriously, was to make a sacred vow to the heavens: Please do not rain on September 5, 2009, and I will be a vegetarian for one year, starting from the date of the vow, which was January 1.

It actually worked! Though we had a downpour a few days before, it was all clear on September 5. With 4,000 performers, including 100 hearing-impaired high school students who drummed along with the Zen-inspired U Theatre drummers, we delivered what audiences and athletes together thought was a most amazing and moving performance that brought all of Taiwan together in a special moment. In contrast with the Beijing Olympics opening ceremony of the year before, which showcased majesty and power, we crafted a delicate performance that celebrated the resilience and beauty of the deaf community and reflected on Taiwan.[9] I can't help but refer way back to Sternberg's definition of creativity in Chapter Four, "work that is both novel (i.e., original, unexpected) and appropriate (i.e., useful, adaptive concerning task constraints)."

The torch had been lit. The games were all set to begin. The creative core team and I all sat back, breathed a collective deep sigh of relief, and looked at each other with faint smiles—faint because we were all exhausted to the bone and couldn't even muster a grin. It was then that our only foreign advisor, John Rayment from the Sydney Olympics, who always was the voice of caution and common sense in the room, spoke up. He said, "Ladies and gentlemen, I hate to point out the elephant in the room. The Closing Ceremony is in 10 days and we have done nothing." Silence.

We were too tired to even panic, but it hit us hard. I was down on myself for neglecting this important duty. We had spent 18 months of our lives submerged in the work for the opening ceremony, but for the closing, we only had a few pop stars signed up to perform and some sketchy plans that were never discussed in detail! We realized the predicament we were in and immediately got to work. The

---

9 See National Geographic Channel Documentary, *Inside: Taipei Deaflympics*, dir. Charlene Shih, 2010.

closing ceremony by tradition was scheduled for 7:30 p.m., after the last sporting event, the soccer final, which would end around 5:30 p.m. There was no chance to change venues. I had two hours to set up something. I thought of Super Bowl halftime in America, but we didn't have the time or resources.

The next morning, when we all should have had a day off or a month off, the team was back in the conference room, feebly brainstorming. Here was the moment when my creative app and everything on the left and right sides of my map were being challenged to activate, now! For the opening ceremony, we had erected two large towers on the north and south sides of the stadium. We could use them for musical performances. But what about the whole playing field? We couldn't possibly leave it empty. But what could you do in two hours of setup time?

Pushed to the brink, the solution came. I thought of the extravagant feasts in front of the temples in Taiwan at festival time, where whole pigs are roasted and displayed spread out on tables with pineapples stuffed in their mouths, Taiwanese opera is performed in front of the temple, and tables are set for thousands of people, who do not need an invitation to sit down and eat. I asked the team if they knew any caterer who did this sort of thing. We identified a culinary school in Taipei as a possibility and called the principal. My first question to him was, how long would it take him to set up 400 tables, on plastic canvas, on a football field, including table settings? Soon he called back with the answer: half an hour. I couldn't believe it. The next question: How could we prepare food for 4,000 people at the stadium? His answer: not a problem, because at festivals the food is prepared continually for three days. We could set up four kitchens in tents on four sides of the stadium and start cooking three days before the closing.

We had our answer. The closing ceremony was a 10-course feast for all of the athletes, featuring the greatest hits of Taiwanese cuisine, as well as beer and beverages. The 400 round tables took up the whole football field. The audience was given bento dinner boxes so as not to feel left out. The athletes, from all over the world, were in tears, as were the organizers. Never in their wildest dreams did they think that there would be a closing ceremony like this!

There is a ritual quality to food. To have all the competitors sharing a meal together, on the field where they competed, I admit, was beautiful. We really lucked out with this solution.

New Horizons

This is just one example of the many challenges I have faced over the years, but it is true that the flip side of a challenge is opportunity. The only way to prepare for it is through the cultivation of your personal wisdom and method.

In recent years, I have been blessed with a surge of creative energy. In the last seven years I have written and directed nine full-length plays, including *Ago, One One Zero Eight* and *River/Cloud*, which I consider some of my best work. In 2024, I inaugurated the Huichang Theatre Village in commemoration of my father, Lai Chia-chiu, at his hometown, a small town far away from any metropolitan area. Here, I premiered a new work called *Flower in the Mirror, Moon in the Water*. I chose an ancient ancestral shrine for the play, using only a six-meter square for the stage, with the audience on three sides. I asked the community to donate chairs for the audience, so there were 100 different looking chairs to sit on.

Flower is a complex work about the lives of two women, spanning 60 years. There is a large cast of characters, and there are also characters who are not human, creatures from the ancient Chinese encyclopedia of magical beings, the *Scripture of Mountain and Sea* (*Shanhaijing*). All of this happens within the six-meter square, where I adhered to the Chinese opera tradition of using just one table and two chairs to represent everything in the universe. *Flower* premiered exactly 40 years to the day after my first play, *We All Grew Up This Way*, and exactly 55 years to the day of my father's passing. In my cyclic journey you can find a thematic link back to the values of my first production. Simplicity as the platform for complexity. A bare space can create a universe. That universe can take you through a journey that transforms, through journeys that are often cyclical.

One day at my Theatre Above studio in Shanghai, while I was rehearsing *Flower* with my ensemble, a graduate student writing about me attended the rehearsal and later interviewed me. As she spoke, she had a slip of the tongue and said, "I don't know if this comes through as impolite, but may I say that in these, your late works, your style has changed in a certain way?" We had a great laugh. I said, what could be impolite about that? I'm 70. I've been working continuously since I was 30. Of course you can call this my late stage.

In every way, I know I have been blessed. Very few artists are recognized in their own time. I don't take it lightly. I cherish every new opportunity to do new work, assuming the responsibility that comes with it, always checking my motivation, the initial passion to do the work. If it isn't there, or isn't right, why do it?

Exercises and Further Thoughts

1. Relax. We're done.

CLOSING THOUGHTS

I recall meeting the classical Noh master Shoroku Sekine (1930–2017) in Taipei one year when he was approaching the later stages of his acting career. I asked him over tea, how he trained at this stage? His answer was poignant, and moved me deeply. He said:

"My teachers are all gone. Now my only teachers are the wind, the leaves, the clouds …"[1]

In a way, that's how I feel these days. But my view of "nature" includes everything. Before creativity, all phenomena are equal. Everything is our teacher.

Be well. In life. In art.

---

1 Personal conversation with Shoroku Sekine, 1989, Taipei.

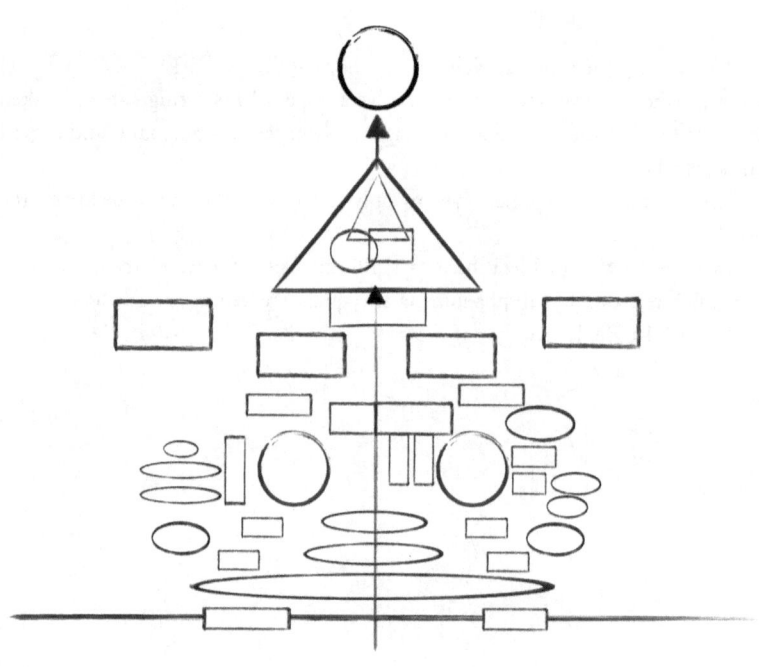

AFTERWORD BY EUGENIO BARBA

Holstebro, December 28, 2024

Dear Stan,

By what means do directors and actors render their private behavior and speech as art on stage? My experience tells me that each of us is creatively alive thanks to a metaphorical lung whose two parts confront each other in an embrace of opposites.

The right part of this vital organ consists of our knowledge, the people we have met, the books we have read, the legacy of the past that we want to embrace or reject, and the memories and experiences of travel and encounters in the face of diversity and the unexpected. This dimension allows us to reflect, calculate, and apply principles and logic to direct our artistic processes toward a goal with responsibility and freedom of choice.

The left part of the lung, on the other hand, is fantasy and imagination, the ability to be in one place and at the same time elsewhere, the fictive condition of dreaming and depicting a life that does not exist in reality, of changing geographical and historical conditions at will, of inventing what cannot be found, but also grasping something ineffable, which we could call Beauty.

For every breath in our creative process, our lungs' left and right parts challenge our knowledge and our imagination, nourishing our certainties and decisions, doubts and aspirations, compromises and obstinacy.

We struggle to give life to a story on stage with the desire to change evil into good, pain into joy, and shadow into light. But a part of our lung pushes us toward another theatrical efficacy in the form of a double effect: to plant a seed in the spectator that time will unconsciously make grow into awareness; and to give the same spectator a sensorial experience of the unspeakable—Beauty. For this, technique is necessary, a deeply embodied know-how. One needs the humble patience of the farmer who knows the art of sowing the appropriate seed in the right soil and in the right season.

Learning to be creative farmers of theater means to persevere and be rigorous and tenacious, sometimes stubborn. There is no Beauty without rules. No new Beauty is born without breaking the rules. Whatever path we follow, we must have the vocation to evoke the maximum through the minimum. And discover the coincidences among the differences. We should never forget that the emotional concern for another's plight, combined with a desire to provide help and relief, is the nobility of our craft.

Let me share with you the physicist Jorge Wagensberg's operative definition: creativity is the alchemic attempt to transform suffering into beauty and fear into knowledge.

In friendship and with all my best wishes for your book,

Eugenio Barba

Eugenio Barba is one of the preeminent theater artists in the world.

REFERENCES

Adolescence. Created by Jack Thorne and Steven Graham. Directed by Philip Barantini. Warp Films, 2025. Aired on *Netflix.*
Ads OK Plz. "Ribbon Bottle (2016)." facebook.com/reel/1654289622191720
Allison, Rebecca. "9/11 Wicked but a Work of Art, Says Damien Hirst." www.theguardian.com/uk/2002/sep/11/arts.september11
Amabile, Teresa. "Freakonomics Radio Podcast." www.wnyc.org/widgets/ondemand_player/freakonomics/#file=json/906997
Applebone, Peter. "Arthur Miller: Present at the Birth of a Salesman." *New York Times,* January 29, 1999. archive.nytimes.com/www.nytimes.com/library/arts/012999miller-theatre-profile.html
Apthorp, Shirley. "Shock Tactics Getting Dirtier," *Financial Times,* July 3/4, 2004.
Aristotle. "Poetics." Translated by S.H. Butcher. *The Project Gutenberg eBook of The Poetics of Aristotle.* www.gutenberg.org/ebooks/1974
Armstrong, Louis. "A Song Was Born." *Live at the Hollywood Empire.* Composers Raye, Don, and de Paul, Gene. 1949. CD recording, Storyville, 2001.
———. Quoted in *Louis Armstrong Society.org.* www.larmstrongsoc.org/quotes
Atisha, Dipamkarashrijnana. *Atisha's Lamp for the Path to Enlightenment.* New York: Snow Lion Publications, 1997.
Awbery, Charlie. "Shi-ne Meditation (opening awareness)." *Vajrayana Now.* vajrayananow.com/shi-ne-meditation
Baer, Drake. "Baseball Players See the Ball as Way Bigger Than You Do." *The Cut.* www.thecut.com/2016/10/the-science-of-how-baseball-players-hit-fastballs.html
Barboza, David. "Painting that Hints at Past Turbulence." *International Herald Tribune,* September 5, 2005.
Beatles. "I am the Walrus." *Magical Mystery Tour.* EMI Records, 1967.
———. "The Long and Winding Road." *Let it Be.* EMI Records, 1970.
———. "Nowhere Man." *Rubber Soul.* EMI Records, 1965.
———. "Please Please Me." *The Beatles.* EMI Records, 1963.
———. *Sergeant Pepper's Lonely Hearts Club Band.* EMI Records, 1967.
———. "Strawberry Fields Forever." *Magical Mystery Tour.* EMI Records, 1967.
———. "Yesterday." Capitol Records, 1965.
Beckett, Samuel. *Molloy.* Translated by Patrick Bowles in collaboration with the author. Grove Press, 1955.

———. *Proust.* Grove Press, 1957.
Berlin, Irving. Quoted in *Brainy Quote.* www.brainyquote.com/topics/talent-quotes_3
Blake, William. *The Marriage of Heaven and Hell.* www.gutenberg.org/files/45315/45315-h/45315-h.htm
Bradbury, Ray. Quoted in *Brainy Quote.* www.brainyquote.com/quotes/ray_bradbury_154628?src=t_hard_work
Brook, Peter. *Le Costume.* Based on story by Can Themba. Adapted for stage by Mothobi Mutloatse and Barney Simon. Performed by Theatre des Bouffes du Nord. April 18 to 21, 2002. Hong Kong Cultural Centre Studio Theatre.
Brooks, David. "What Happens to Gifted Children." *New York Times*, June 13, 2024. www.nytimes.com/2024/06/13/opinion/gifted-children-intelligence.html
Cambridge Dictionary. dictionary.cambridge.org/
Carter, Ronald. Interview "Creativity and Language." *Interalia Magazine*, July 2016. www.interaliamag.org/interviews/ronald-carter/
Cerram, Stephen. "How John Coltrane Got His Sound." *JazzProfiles.* October 22, 2021. https://jazzprofiles.blogspot.com/2021/10/how-john-coltrane-got-his-sound.html
Cezanne, Paul. Quoted in *Brainy Quote.* www.brainyquote.com/quotes/paul_cezanne_134682
Chekhov, Anton Pavlovich. *Four Plays.* Translated by Carol Rocamora. Hanover, N.H.: Smith & Kraus, 1996.
Coltrane, John. "Giant Steps." *Giant Steps.* Atlantic Records, 1960.
Confucius. *The Analects.* Chapter 2, Verse 17. Chinese Text Project, ctext.org/analects/wei-zheng
Covarrubias, Miguel. *Island of Bali.* New York: Alfred A. Knopf, 1937.
Csikszentmihalyi, Mihaly. *Flow: The Psychology of Optimal Experience.* New York: Harper Perennial Modern Classics, 2008.
Davis, Miles. Quoted in *Goodreads.* www.goodreads.com/author/quotes/54761.Miles_Davis?page=1
Disch, Thomas. Quoted in *Notable Quotes.* www.notable-quotes.com/c/creativity_quotes_v.html
Driver, Tom F. "Beckett by the Madeleine." *Columbia University Forum.* 4, Summer 1961, 21–25.
Duchamp, Marcel. Quoted in Wolf, Alexander. "Duchamp's Bicycle Wheel." *Gagosian.* gagosian.com/quarterly/2014/08/15/duchamps-bicycle-wheel-timeline/
Duke, Craig. *VI Control: Musicians Helping Musicians.* vi-control.net/community/threads/mozart-easy-as-that.3264/
Edison, Thomas. Quoted in *Dictionary.com.* www.dictionary.com/browse/genius-is-one-percent-inspiration-and-ninety-nine-percent-perspiration
Einstein, Albert. Quoted in *A-Z Quotes*, www.azquotes.com/quote/455371?ref=structure
———. Quoted in *Forbes Magazine*, September 15, 1974.
———. Quoted in *Goodreads.* www.goodreads.com/quotes/tag/curiosity
———. Quoted in *Philsoblog.* philosiblog.com/2012/03/14/in-the-middle-of-difficulty-lies-opportunity/
Evans, Bill. *The Universal Mind of Bill Evans*, Rhapsody Films (DVD), 1991.
Flaubert, Gustave. Quoted in *Brainy Quote.* www.brainyquote.com/quotes/gustave_flaubert_109857

Four Books and Five Classics. en.wikipedia.org/wiki/Four_Books_and_Five_Classics
Gaudi, Antonio. Quoted in *Goodreads.* www.goodreads.com/quotes/8991736-the-creation-continues-incessantly-through-the-media-of-man-but
Gershwin, George and Ira. "But Not for Me." New World Music, 1930.
Gladwell, Malcolm. "Malcolm Gladwell Demystifies 10,000 Hours Rule." *Heavy Chef.* www.youtube.com/watch?v=1uB5PUpGzeY
———. *Outliers: The Story of Success.* Little, Brown and Company, 2008.
Guoyuribao. English *Mandarin Daily.* Founded Taipei, Taiwan, 1947.
Hall, Stephen S. *Wisdom: From Philosophy to Neuroscience.* New York: Alfred A. Knopf, 2010.
Henderson, Jennifer. "Developing Students' Creative Skills for 21st Century Success." *ASCD.* www.ascd.org/el/articles/developing-students-creative-skills-for-21st-century-success
Hentoff, Nat and Nat Shapiro, Editors. *Hear Me Talkin' to Ya.* Garden City, NY: Dover Press, 1966.
Hesiod. *Theogeny.* Translated by H.G. Evelyn-White, www.theoi.com/Text/Hesiod Theogony.html
History of Bali." *Wikipedia.* en.wikipedia.org/wiki/History_of_Bali
Homer. *The Iliad of Homer.* Translated by Richmond Lattimore. Chicago: University of Chicago Press, 1982.
———. *The Odyssey of Homer.* Translated by Richmond Lattimore. HarperCollins, 1991.
Housman, A.E. *The Name and Nature of Poetry: The Leslie Stephen Lecture Delivered at Cambridge, 9 May 1933.* Cambridge: Cambridge University Press, 1933.
"Japan's Miyazaki gets Golden Lion at Venice." *ABC* (Australia). www.abc.net.au/news/2005-09-10/japans-miyazaki-gets-golden-lion-at-venice
Jobs, Steve. Interview in *Wired Magazine*, 1996.
———. Interview on *CBS News*, 1995. www.youtube.com/watch?v=5y03eFMmOKY
———. Quoted in *Goodreads.* www.goodreads.com/quotes/455762-i-would-trade-all-of-my-technology-for-an-afternoon
Johnson, Heather. "Madame Butterfly, The Flower Duet." *Opera Daily.* www.youroperadaily.com/p/opera-daily-madame-butterfly-the
Jones, Josh. "The Night When John Coltrane Soloed in a Bathroom and David Crosby, High as a Kite, Nearly Lost His Mind." *Open Culture.* www.openculture.com/2019/10/the-night-when-john-coltrane-soloed-in-a-bathroom.html
Jung, C.G. *Collected Works*, Vol. 9, Part I. "The Archetypes of the Collective Unconscious." Edited and translated by Gerhard Adler and R.F.C. Hull. Princeton University Press, 1954.
Kahn, Ashley. "John Coltrane Biography." www.johncoltrane.com/biography
Khensur Jampa Tegchok. "Listening, Thinking, and Meditating." *Imisangha.* imisangha.org/listening-thinking-and-meditating/
Khyentse, Dzongsar Jamyang. *What Makes You Not a Buddhist.* Shambhala, 2008.
Klugewicz, Stephen M. "Copying Mozart: Did Beethoven Steal Melodies for His Own Music?" *The Imaginative Conservative*, February 21, 2018. theimaginativeconservative.org/2018/02/copying-mozart-beethoven-steal-melodies-music-stephen-klugewicz.html
Koestler, Arthur. *The Act of Creation.* New York: Macmillan, 1964.

Kostur, Glen. "Practicing without your instrument." *Sax On the Web*. www.saxontheweb.net/threads/practicing-without-your-instrument.46113/

Kotler, Steven. "Flow States and Creativity: Can you Train People to be More Creative?" www.psychologytoday.com/us/blog/the-playing-field/201402/flow-states-and-creativity

Lai, Stan. *A Dream Like a Dream. Selected Plays of Stan Lai, Vol. 3*. Edited by Lissa Tyler Renaud. Ann Arbor: University of Michigan Press, 2022.

———. *Ago. Selected Plays of Stan Lai, Vol. 3*.

———. *All in the Family are Human (Womenyijia doushiren)*. Television series. Super TV, Taiwan, 1995-97.

———. "Creativity for Scholar-Directors." Seminar, Stanford University. April 18, 2025.

———. *Crosstalk Travelers (Nayiye zai Lvtuzhong Shuoxiangsheng)*. Beijing: CITIC, 2020.

———. "Director's Notes." *Rumengzhimeng* [*A Dream Like a Dream* Theatre Program], Hong Kong Repertory Theatre, Hong Kong, 2002.

———. *Flower in the Mirror, Moon in the Water (Jinghua shuiyue)*. Stage play first performed January 10, 2024, Huichang Theatre Village, China.

———. "General Theory of Creativity." Talk at Princeton University. April 20, 2025.

———. "How I 'Wright' Plays." *Selected Plays of Stan Lai*, Vol 1. Edited by Lissa Tyler Renaud. Ann Arbor: University of Michigan Press, 2022. 1–6.

———. *I Me She Him. Selected Plays of Stan Lai, Vol. 1*.

———. *The Island and the Other Shore. Selected Plays of Stan Lai, Vol. 1*.

———. *Journey to the West (Xiyouji)*. Taipei: Crown, 1988. Collected in *Lai Shengchuan: Juchang*, Vol. 2. Taipei: Meta, 1999.

———. *Lai Shengchuan de Chuangyixue*. (Chinese version of *Creativitry*) Taipei: Commonwealth, 2006; Beijing: CITIC, 2006; Guangxi Normal University Press, 2007.

———. *One One Zero Eight (Yaoyao dongba)*. Beijing: CITIC, 2010.

———. *The Peach Blossom Land*. Film. Performance Workshop Films and Longshong Films, 1992.

———. *The Red Lotus Society*. Film. Performance Workshop Films and Longshong Films, 1994.

———. *River/Cloud (Jiang Yun Zhijian)*. Stage play first performed April 21, 2021, National Theatre, Taipei, Taiwan.

———. *Sand on a Distant Star. Selected Plays of Stan Lai, Vol. 2*. Edited by Lissa Tyler Renaud. Ann Arbor: University of Michigan Press, 2022.

———. *Secret Love in Peach Blossom Land. Selected Plays of Stan Lai, Vol. 1*.

———. *Secrets of Theatrical Creativity*. Public lecture at Theatre Converge, Huichang Theatre Village, Huichang, Jiangxi Province, China, July 24, 2024.

———. *That Evening, We Performed Crosstalk (Nayiye, womenshuo xiangsheng)*. Audio recording UFO records, 1985.

———. *That Evening, We Performed Crosstalk (Nayiye, womenshuo xiangsheng)*. Taipei: Crown Publishing, 1986.

———. *The Village. Selected Plays of Stan Lai, Vol. 2*.

———. *We All Grew Up This Way (Women doushi zheyang zhangdade)*. *Stan Lai: Theatre*, vol. 1. Taipei: Meta, 1999.

——— and Eugenio Barba. "One Hundred Years of Solitude: A Conversation between Eugenio Barba and Stan Lai." Wuzhen Dialogues. Wuzhen Theatre Festival, October 25, 2024.

Lao Tzu. *Tao Te Ching Online Translation*.Translated by Derek Lin. taoism.net/tao-te-ching-online-translation/

———. *Tao Te Ching, The Taoism of Lao Tzu*. Translated by Stefan Senudd. www.taoistic.com/taoteching-laotzu/

———. *Tao Te Ching*. Translated by Stephen Mitchell. New York: Harper Perennial, 1988.

Lee, Bruce. *Enter the Dragon*. (film) Orange Sky Golden Harvest, Warner Bros., 1973.

Lessing, Doris. Quoted in *Brainy Quote*. https://www.brainyquote.com/topics/hard-work-quotes_2

Lhadrepa, Konchog. "Sacred Art." Lecture at Shechen Institute. Bodh Gaya, India, December 10, 2003. Translated from the Tibetan by Matthieu Ricard.

Lorca, Frederico Garcia. "Theory and Play of the Duende." *Poetry in Translation*. www.poetryintranslation.com/PITBR/Spanish/LorcaDuende.php

Ma Sen. "The Birth of a New Type of Theatre on the Chinese Stage." *China Times*, January 15, 1984.

Maddocks, Fiona. "Mitsuko Uchida: 'You Have to Risk Your Life on Stage." *The Guardian*, August 12, 2018. www.theguardian.com/music/2018/dec/04/mitsuko-uchida-pianist-schubert-mozart-70th-birthday-interview

Michelangelo. Quoted in *Goodreads*. www.goodreads.com/quotes/1191114-the-sculpture-is-already-complete-within-the-marble-block-before

———. "Quotes." *Michelangelo.org*. www.michelangelo.org/michelangelo-quotes.jsp #google_vignette

Mill, John Stuart. *Utilitarianism, A Public Domain Book reprinted from Fraser's Magazine*. Seventh Edition, London: Longmans, Green, and Co., 1879.

Mingus, Charles. *Mingus at Carnegie Hall*. Atlantic Records, 1974.

Naiman, Linda. "Why CEOs Say Creativity is the Most Crucial Factor for Future Success." www.creativityatwork.com/ceo-creativity-leadership-ibm-global-report/

Newsweek Special Edition "Issues 2004," December 2003.

Nin, Anaïs. *Seduction of the Minotaur*. Chicago: Swallow Press, 1961.

———. Quoted in *Goodreads*, www.goodreads.com/quotes/tag/chaos?page=1

Orgyen, Tulku. *As It Is*, Vols. 1-2, Translated and edited by Erik Pema Kunsang and Marcia Binder Schmidt. Rangjung Yeshe Publications, 1999.

Phelps, Nathan. "7 Lessons On Practicing Music You Can Take From John Coltrane, the 'Athlete' of Improvisation." *Medium.com*. December 3, 2020. https://nathandavidphelps.medium.com/7-lessons-on-practicing-music-you-can-take-from-john-coltrane-the-athlete-of-improvisation-f296bb3a0915

Planck, Max. Quoted in www.goodreads.com/quotes/1246159-when-you-change-the-way-you-look-at-things-the

Plato. Quoted in *Wikipedia*. en.wikipedia.org/wiki/The_unexamined_life_is_not_worth_living

Pollock, Jackson. Quoted in *Goodreads*. www.goodreads.com/author/quotes/96360.Jackson_Pollock

Proust, Marcel. *Remembrances of Things Past*. Translated by C.K. Scott Moncrief. New York: Modern Library, 1929.

The Quintet. *Jazz at Massey Hall*. Debut Records. December 1953.

Raman, C.V. Quoted in *Brainy Quote*. www.brainyquote.com/quotes/c_v_raman_821675?src=t_hard_work

Ricard, Matthieu. "On Consciousness." https://medium.com/@matthieu_ricard/on-consciousness-38d7e6a84ed

———. *Why Mediate?* Translated by Sherab Chödzin Kohn. Hay House, 2010.

Rinpoche, Jigme Khyentse. Public Teaching. Taipei, Taiwan. December 3, 2005.

Rinpoche, Ringu Tulku. "Wisdom." *WikiRigpa*. www.rigpawiki.org/index.php?title=Wisdom

Rinpoche, Sogyal. *The Tibetan Book of Living and Dying*. San Francisco: Harper, 1994.

Rocamora, Carol. *"I take your hand in mine" Suggested by the Letters of Anton Chekhov and Olga Knipper*. Smith and Kraus, 2000.

Rosenberg, Harold. "The American Action Painters, December 1952." *ArtNews*. www.artnews.com/artnews/news/top-ten-artnews-stories-not-a-picture-but-an-event-181/

Rothenberg, Albert. *The Emerging Goddess: The Creative Process in Art, Science, and Other Fields*. Chicago: University of Chicago Press, 1979.

Sarah Ransome Art, website. "Motivational Quotes from 25 Famous Artists." www.sarahransomeart.com/blog/motivational-quotes-from-famous-artists

Schechner, Richard. "9/11 as Avant Garde Art?" *Cambridge University Press*, October 23, 2020. www.cambridge.org/core/journals/pmla/article/abs/9-11-as-avantgarde-art

Schmermann, Serge. "The Gruesome Creativity of Assassinations Enters a New Phase." *New York Times*, September 18, 2024.

Sidelnikova, Anna. "Definitely happy: artists who lived in clover. Part 1." *Artsmarts*, April 27, 2018. www.arthive.com/publications/1296~Definitely_happy_artists_who_lived_in_clover_Part_1

———. "Happy in different ways: artists who lived in clover. Part 2." *Connaissances*, June 8, 2018. https://arthive.com/fr/publications/1393~Happy_in_different_ways_artists_who_lived_in_clover_Part_2

Shakespeare, William. *A Midsummer Night's Dream*. www.folger.edu/explore/shakespeares-works/a-midsummer-nights-dream/

———. *As You Like It*. www.folger.edu/explore/shakespeares-works/as-you-like-it/

———. *Hamlet*. www.folger.edu/explore/shakespeares-works/hamlet/read/

———. *King Lear*. www.folger.edu/explore/shakespeares-works/king-lear/

———. *The Winter's Tale*. www.folger.edu/explore/shakespeares-works/a-winter'stale/

Shih, Charlene, Director. *Inside: Taipei Deaflympics*. National Geograhic Channel Documentary, 2010.

Simon, Paul. "The Boxer." *Paul Simon in Concert: Live Rhymin'*. Columbia, 1974.

Simple English Wikipedia. simple.wikipedia.org/wiki/Talent

Solnit, Rebecca. *Wanderlust: A History of Walking*. New York: Penguin, 2001.

Sondheim, Stephen. Quoted in *Brainy Quote*. www.brainyquote.com/quotes/stephen_sondheim_331419?src=t_chaos

Spies, Walter. Quoted in "History of Bali." *Wikipedia.* en.wikipedia.org/wiki/History_of_Bali

Spinola, Julia. "Monstrous Art." *Frankfurter Allgemeine Zeitung.* Sept. 25, 2001.

Sternberg, Robert J. and Todd I. Lubart. "The Concept of Creativity: Prospects and Paradigms." *Handbook of Creativity.* Edited by Robert J. Sternberg. Cambridge: Cambridge University Press, 1999.

Strindberg, August. *Inferno/From an Occult Diary.* Edited by Torsten Eklund and Translated by Mary Sandbach. London: Penguin Classics, 1979.

Sung, Sun Young and Jin Nam Choi. "Do Big Five Personality Factors Affect Individual Creativity? The Moderating Role Of Extrinsic Motivation." *Social Behavior and Personality,* 2009, 37(7), 941–956.

Suzuki, Shunryu. *Zen Mind, Beginner's Mind: Informal Talks on Zen Meditation and Practice.* Trumble, CT: Weatherhill, 1970.

Tharp, Twyla. *The Creative Habit: Learn It and Use It for Life.* New York: Simon and Schuster, 2006.

Thich Nhat Hahn. *The Heart of Understanding: Commentaries on the Prajnaparamita Heart Sutra.* Berkeley: Parallax Press, 1988.

———. *Old Path, White Clouds.* Berkeley: Parallax Press, 1991.

Thoreau, Henry David. "Walking." *The Atlantic,* June 1862. www.theatlantic.com/magazine/archive/1862/06/walking/304674/

Toklas, Alice B. *What is Remembered.* New York: Holt, Rinehart and Winston, 1963.

Vasari, Giorgio. *The Lives of the Artists (Oxford World's Classics).* Bondanella, Julia Conway and Bondanella, Peter, Trans. Oxford: Oxford University Press, 1998.

Watts, Alan. Quoted in Goodreads. www.goodreads.com/quotes/10246506-a-person-who-thinks-all-the-time-has-nothing-to

Webster's New Universal Unabridged Dictionary. New York: Barnes and Noble, 2003.

Wells, Rachel. "70% Of Employers Say Creative Thinking Is Most In-Demand Skill In 2024." *Forbes.* www.forbes.com/sites/rachelwells/2024/01/28/70-of-employers-say-creative-thinking-is-most-in-demand-skill-in-2024/?sh=4192aa7d391d

Wikipedia.com. en.wikipedia.org/wiki/Eight_Consciousnesses

———. en.wikipedia.org/wiki/Dunning%E2%80%93Kruger_effect

———. en.wikipedia.org/wiki/Vijñāna

Wilde, Oscar. Quoted in *Goodreads.* www.goodreads.com/quotes/tag/curiosity

Wilson, David Sloan. *Does Altruism Exist?: Culture, Genes, and the Welfare of Others.* New Haven: Yale University Press, 2015.

Wolf, Alexander. "Duchamp's Bicycle Wheel." *Gagosian.* gagosian.com/quarterly/2014/08/15/duchamps-bicycle-wheel-timeline/

Wong, May. "Stanford study finds walking improves creativity." *Stanford Report,* April 24, 2014. news.stanford.edu/stories/2014/04/walking-vs-sitting-042414

Wright, Frank Lloyd. Quoted in *Guggenheim.org.* www.guggenheim.org/teaching-materials/the-architecture-of-the-solomon-r-guggenheim-museum/form-follows-function

Xinjingbao 2012 Economic Forum. International Hotel, Beijing. November 11, 2011.

Xu, Chunhua. "Talk to Theatre Above." May 21, 2024, Shanghai.

Zeami. *Kadensho.* Kyoto: Sumiya-Shinobe Pub. Institute, 1968.
———. *On the Art of the Nō Drama: The Major Treatises of Zeami.* Translated by J. Thomas Rimer and Yamazaki Masakazu. Princeton: Princeton University Press, 1984.
Zhou, Raymond. "Cosmic Dream Drama," *China Daily,* April 15, 2013.

INDEX

9-11 59, 60

A+B 72–74, 90, 114, 184, 186, 216
A+B+C 73, 74
Abbott and Costello 246; "Who's on First?" 246
abstract expressionism 189, 217, 218
Academy Award i
Achilles 172
Acropolis 144
acting 6, 41, 108, 113, 255
actor 5–7, 13, 17, 36, 47, 51, 52, 92, 103, 106, 108, 112 137, 139, 140, 155, 157–59, 173, 196, 208, 233, 245–47, 257
actor training 7, 245
Adolescence 136
Aeschylus 80
aesthetics 135, 143, 170, 191, 249
AI 31, 53, 78, 216, 218
alchemy 52
Amabile, Teresa 30
Amei 252
America 157, 198, 211, 212, 253
anatomy 9, 19
Anouilh, Jean 50; Ondine 50
Antonioni, Michelangelo 165; *L'Avventura* 165
Apthorp, Shirley 58
architect 138, 143, 145, 167, 168, 189, 248
architecture 76, 134, 144, 145, 147, 158, 163–65, 173, 189
Architectural Digest 167

Argerich, Martha 240
Aristotle 166, 170, 211, 229
Armstrong, Louis 216, 217; "A Song is Born" 216
art i, ii, xxiii, 5, 12, 14, 15, 19, 28, 29, 31, 32, 35, 36, 41, 50, 51, 55–63, 66, 67, 77, 80, 82, 83, 90, 91, 93, 98, 100, 101, 111–15, 120, 126, 129, 134–36, 138, 144–48, 150–54, 158, 159, 165, 171, 173, 184, 189, 195, 196, 198, 200, 206, 209, 214, 216–18, 222–25, 227, 229–34, 237, 239–42, 255, 257, 258
Artaud, Antonin 30
artist i, ii, iii, xvii, 6–8, 11, 13, 27–30, 54–63, 66, 69, 70, 73, 78, 98, 101, 105, 111, 112, 114, 122, 127, 130, 131, 134, 136–39, 145, 146, 149, 151–53, 159, 161, 166, 168, 172, 176, 185, 193–95, 200, 203, 207, 211, 213–18, 222, 223, 230–34, 236, 239–43, 249, 251, 252, 254, 258
artistic ii, iii, 6, 16, 20, 29, 43, 50, 62, 99, 132, 136, 199, 211, 218–20, 235, 237, 240, 241, 246, 252, 257
artistry xxv, 57, 63, 93, 104, 160, 220
as is 90, 91, 97, 104–6, 108, 109
Asia xxiii, 14, 21, 87, 153, 245
Asian 6, 22, 50, 102, 145, 153, 197, 220
Athens 45
Atisha, Dipamkarashrijnana 27, 28, 32, 42
avant-garde 16, 65, 133

267

Bach, Johann Sebastian 134, 163, 171, 180, 200, 216; "Fugue in B Minor" 171; *Well-tempered Clavier* 134, 171
Baker, Chet 159
Bali 56, 57
Balinese 56, 57, 66
BAM 60
Barba, Eugenio 235, 257, 258
Barong 56
barrier i, 3, 35, 36, 119–26, 183
baseball 153
Bausch, Pina 146; *Café Müller* 146
Beatles 63, 70, 131, 159, 172, 222; "I Am the Walrus" 70; *Magical Mystery Tour* 70; "Nowhere Man" 160; "Please Please Me" 160; *Sergeant Pepper's Lonely Hearts Club Band* 172; "Strawberry Fields Forever" 160; "The Long and Winding Road" 222; "Yesterday" 174
beauty 44, 51, 56, 80, 88, 93, 120, 130, 171, 173, 180, 200, 223, 225, 242, 252, 257, 258
bebop 30
Beckett, Samuel 72, 81, 127, 133, 165, 171, 251; *Waiting for Godot* 170
Beethoven, Ludwig van 54, 73, 204, 243; "Für Elise" 73
beginner 49, 104, 106, 130, 151, 152, 154
Beijing xxiii, 4, 14, 17, 97, 133, 155, 224, 250, 252; Forbidden City 173
Berkeley ii, xxiv, 6, 16, 45, 50, 70, 92, 105, 155, 157, 234, 246
Berlin (Germany) 58, 122, 155
Berlin, Irving 211
Berliner Ensemble 155
Beyonce 107
Bhutan 16, 100
Bieito, Calixto 58
BIG 189
bin Laden, Osama 61
Bird, Larry 153
Blake, William 11, 18, 68
Bodh Gaya 13, 17, 18, 27, 114
Bodhicitta 112
Bonds, Barry 153

Borobudur 164
Bosch, Hieronymus 163; *The Garden of Earthly Delights* 163
the box 4, 21, 67, 68, 120, 224
Bradbury, Ray 71
brainstorming 6, 67, 73, 253
Brecht, Bertolt 132, 155
breakthrough xxiv, 7, 20, 27, 28, 75, 147, 161, 205
British Council 4
Brittany (France) 14
Broadway 232
Brook, Peter 212, 233, 235; *The Suit* 233
Brooks, David 212
Brueghel, Jan the Elder 15, 76; *Allegory of Sight and Smell* 15
Buddha 14, 31, 45, 46, 65, 113, 114
Buddhism i, 64, 65, 89, 90, 188, 234; Mahayana Buddhism 89; Tibetan Buddhism 90; Yogācāra school 90
Buddhist ii, xxii, 13, 17, 21, 27, 29, 64, 65, 89, 109, 121, 187
Buffet, Warren 81
Bunraku 150
Burning Lake 16

Cage, John 93, 94, 121, 209
Cambridge 4, 12, 30, 42, 60
Cannes 113, 212
Cao, Cao 146
Cao, Xueqin 165; *Dream of the Red Chamber* 165
capitalism 21, 73
Captain Marvel 73
Caracalla Baths 144
Catalina Club 216
Catholicism 65
cause-and-effect 16, 97, 99–104, 108, 147
censorship 6, 157
Cezanne, Paul 55
Chanel, Coco 156, 159
Chang, Eileen 5
chaos 93, 120–22, 125, 211, 241
character 13, 15, 16, 76, 79, 80, 100–102, 104, 106, 113, 133, 139, 140, 156, 158, 159, 170, 172, 173,

Index

177, 184, 196, 205, 213, 217, 236–38, 249, 250, 254
Chartres Cathedral 62
Chekhov, Anton 6, 102, 132, 133, 169, 206, 243; *The Seagull* 133
Chen, Gary 216; Stein on Vine 216
childhood 3, 67, 77, 78, 81, 120, 162
Chin, Shi-chieh 208
China i, iii, 6, 7, 13, 17, 23, 24, 43, 60, 79, 88, 93, 103, 133, 138, 146, 147, 167, 189, 206, 212, 236, 245, 247, 249, 251
Chinese i, xxiii, xxiv, 5, 6, 13, 16, 17, 21, 23, 29, 48, 50, 58, 88, 93, 94, 98, 102, 132, 133, 139, 143, 145, 147, 150, 155, 156, 164, 167, 175, 189, 195, 197, 206, 213, 215, 218, 220, 221, 223, 233, 239, 245, 246, 248, 249, 251, 254
Chinese calligraphy 189, 218
Chinese culture i
Chinese painting 145, 239
Chinese poetry 5
Chinese speaking world 5, 6, 17, 249
choreography 94, 138, 173
Coca Cola 72
Coleridge, Samuel Taylor 165; "Kubla Kahn" 165
collage 165, 249
color 11, 47, 61, 75, 79, 98, 154, 176, 177, 184, 199, 214, 222
Coltrane, John 92, 138, 150, 151, 155, 160, 236; "Giant Steps"92
comedy 62, 139, 157, 158, 172, 191, 246–50
commercial xxi, 57, 62, 113, 156, 175, 224
compassion iii, 99, 113, 114, 126, 152, 215, 237, 238
compose 12, 20, 62
composer 59, 93, 120, 138, 195, 222
composition 57, 61, 105, 138, 170, 172, 184, 197, 208
concept ii, 14–16, 19, 30, 35, 37, 41, 44, 45, 61, 62, 72–77, 79, 87–93, 95, 99, 102, 107, 121, 126, 129, 138, 169, 172, 187, 190, 209, 218, 221, 223, 233, 235, 251
concept album 172
conceptual 16, 30, 52, 75, 88, 90–92, 114, 129, 137, 136, 138, 141, 144, 166, 218
confidence 8, 23, 36, 105, 108, 150, 152, 161, 193
consciousness 76, 89, 90, 94, 104, 106, 121, 138, 160, 163, 164, 176, 186
Confucianism 21
Confucius 43, 45, 46, 50, 87
connections 16, 46, 52, 68–71, 73–75, 79, 107, 122, 123, 143, 144, 184, 187, 188, 223, 224, 230, 233, 235, 237, 240
connectivity 36, 66, 69, 79, 119, 184
content 4, 12, 14, 17, 22, 30, 35, 36, 76, 80, 129, 130, 135, 140, 166, 172, 183, 191, 197, 217, 218, 223, 243, 251
cosmology 21, 120
Covarrubias, Miguel 56
craft 31, 35–37, 115, 129, 131, 136, 138, 150, 152, 159–61, 184, 193, 209, 223, 230, 258
craftsman 159, 230
Cream 200
creative app 35, 72, 75, 77, 79, 181, 183, 185–89, 191, 253
Creative Cultural Industries 4
Creative Map xxii, 34, 37, 55, 61, 67, 119, 129, 158, 224; Expanded Map 81, 84, 87, 97, 137, 143, 214
creativity i, ii, iii, xxi, xxiii, xxiv, xxv, 1, 3–8, 11, 13, 18, 19, 22, 24, 25, 27–30, 35–37, 41, 42, 46–50, 52–55, 57, 60, 61, 64, 66–72, 75–82, 84, 87–91, 94, 97–99, 104–6, 111, 112, 115, 119–22, 129, 144, 146, 147, 151–53, 158, 160, 169, 173, 184–87, 194, 195, 198, 201, 203, 209, 213, 214, 216, 217, 220, 224, 230–32, 234–37, 239, 240, 243, 249, 251, 252, 255, 258
Crosby, David 160
crosstalk 97, 198, 246–48
Csikszentmihalyi, Mihaly 105
culture i, ii, 6, 7, 16, 24, 73, 100, 160, 239, 247, 249

curiosity xxi, 120, 136, 137
Curry, Stephen 153
Cunningham, Merce 93, 94

da Vinci, Leonardo 5
Dadaist performance 166
dance ii, xxiii, 30, 56, 94, 115, 144, 171, 206, 220, 243
Davis, Miles 12, 202, 209
De Niro, Robert 247
Deaflympics 251, 252; Closing Ceremony 252, 253; Opening Ceremony 252, 253
decision-making 105, 106, 220
de-labeling 87–89, 93, 94, 104, 122, 123, 183
democracy 7, 44, 157
design xvii, 76, 131, 134, 138, 164, 168, 172, 189, 190, 219, 229, 239
designer 17, 76, 122, 136, 138, 149, 196, 222
Desmond, Paul 146
devil 195, 196
Dickinson, Emily 63, 111
dictionary 4, 44
diligence 160, 191
Ding Nai-chu xvii, 199, 207, 240
directing 6, 7, 17, 29, 31, 51, 103, 132, 158, 169, 212
director i, ii, iii, 5, 29, 36, 49, 50, 58, 60, 63, 108, 112, 113, 132, 136–38, 146, 151–53, 157, 158, 177, 196–98, 202, 208, 212, 220, 223, 230, 231, 233, 245, 249, 257
discipline 160, 215
discovery 67, 70, 71, 151, 186
Disneyland 175, 229; Splash Mountain 175
Doonesbury 157
Doyle, Christopher 15
Dramatic Art 6
Dratz, Peter 15
Duchamp, Marcel 114; Bicycle Wheel 114
Dunning-Kruger Effect 53
Duende 11
Dzogchen 90

ecology 46, 203
Edison, Thomas 195
Einstein, Albert 29, 31, 75, 120, 136, 163, 186
English i, 29, 67, 68, 94, 95, 117, 233
equality 79–81
Europe 14, 145, 247
European 23, 56, 163, 197, 220
Evans, Bill 194, 200, 216
exorcism 63, 111
experience i, ii, 3, 6, 8, 13, 15, 16, 18, 19, 22, 35, 68, 76–81, 92, 98, 99, 103, 105, 107–9, 119–21, 124, 126, 130, 131, 133, 135, 136, 152, 155, 156, 160, 161, 165, 175, 188, 195–98, 203–5, 209, 213–15, 217, 220, 221, 223, 224, 229, 231–33, 240, 245, 251, 257
extraction 11, 15

fashion 120, 131, 154, 219
Feng, Lun iii
fiction 104, 133, 173
files 16, 19, 35, 72, 75–80, 183, 187, 215, 217
film xxiii, 4, 12, 17, 32, 47, 49, 61, 63, 66, 76, 77, 80, 103, 104, 113, 134–36, 141, 146, 149, 151, 156, 159, 164, 165, 168, 170, 173–75, 180, 184, 194, 195, 202, 204–6, 212, 216, 220, 224, 225, 229, 249
filmmaker xxii, 207, 224
filmmaking 149, 173, 212, 251
filmscript 168, 194
filter 35, 77–79, 82, 136, 138, 214, 237
Financial Times 58
Five Classics 43
flow 17, 90, 94, 104–6, 109, 120, 122, 125, 126, 185, 189, 194, 223, 248, 249, 257
Forbes 5, 186
form 4, 13, 17, 30, 36, 43, 71, 73, 107, 127, 129–31, 133, 139, 140, 164–66, 168, 169, 172, 174, 175, 183–85, 191, 193, 196, 209, 213, 217, 222, 223, 232, 243, 246
football 152, 253
Fou, Ts'ong 29

Four Books 43
Fra Angelico 60, 61, 66, 239; *The Annunciation* 60
freeway to creativity 55, 81
French 14, 16, 165, 167, 173, 233
Freytag, Gustav 173
Friends 156
fugue 134, 138, 163, 171, 180

gap 88–91, 109, 122, 123, 186
garbage 57–59, 61, 71, 73, 112, 202, 232, 234
Gaudi, Antonio 71
Gaza 79
Gehry, Frank 189
genius 5, 18, 54, 62, 112, 130, 131, 135, 164, 195, 242, 248
Gershwin, George 131; "But Not For Me" 131
Getz, Stan 216
Getty Museum 189
gift 112, 202, 214, 232, 233, 237, 251
Gladwell, Malcolm 149, 150; 10,000 hour rule 149, 150
Globe Theatre 62
God xxi, 11, 19, 61, 164
Goethe, J.W.V. 216; *Faust* 216
Golden Bear 113
Gould, Glenn 63
Grand Hotel, Taipei 173
Great American Songbook 131, 175
Greece 144, 145
Grotowski, Jerzy 203
guitar 137, 143

habit 78, 81–83, 87, 112, 114, 122, 126, 136, 160, 213, 215, 219, 234
Hall, Jim 216
Hall, Stephen S. 45, 47
Hamilton 72
Hangzhou xxiii
Hanoi xxi
Harry Potter 72
Harvard 30, 46, 64; Harvard Business School 30
Hart, Kevin 139
Hawkins, John 4
Hesiod 9

Himalayas 100
Hinduism 65
Hirst, Damien 59
Hitchcock, Alfred 136; *The Rope* 136
history ii, iii, 11, 56, 87, 95, 98, 102, 115, 131, 132, 143–46, 148, 184, 186, 190, 223, 224, 247, 249, 251
Hoffman, Bruce 59
Hollywood xxi, 134, 135, 157, 170, 175, 197, 216, 229
Homer 172; *Iliad* 172; *Odyssey* 172
Hong Kong 13, 17, 207, 220, 233
Hou, Hsiao-hsien 151, 242
Housman, A.E. 11, 12, 185, 186; "A Shropshire Lad" 11
How to Do i, 130, 149
How to See i, 3, 55, 67–69, 87, 90, 91, 97, 122, 214
Hsu, Joyce 80
Hu, Ge 17
Huang, Jensen 46
Huang, Lei 155
Huichang Theatre Village 236, 251, 254
humility 156, 236–38
Hung, Tung 129, 141
Huntington Library Chinese Garden 251
Hwang, David Henry i

Ibsen, Henrik 6, 173, 176, 202; *A Doll's House* 173
image 15, 19, 35, 75–79, 121, 152, 157, 196, 217, 251
imagination ii, 129, 247, 257
improvisation 6, 7, 13, 47, 50, 139, 140, 146, 151, 157, 198, 200, 208, 216–18, 220, 236, 245
India 13, 15, 16, 27, 31, 35, 114, 190
Indian 15, 65
individuality 77, 82, 214
Indonesia 164
Industrial Revolution 46
infusion 11, 15, 20, 124
inspiration i, xvii, 4, 8, 9, 11–13, 15–20, 23, 30, 35, 36, 68, 70, 75–77, 122, 129, 130, 168, 183, 185–87, 189, 190, 194, 195, 198, 200, 202, 208, 217
instant replay 18

interconnected 17, 70, 103
International Herald Tribune 16, 58
Invisible Cities 72
Iran 146
Irish ballad 58
Israel 60
Itabashi, Fumio 204

Jackson, Michael 130
Jackson, Shannon ii
Japan 76, 143, 145
Japanese 76, 131, 147, 150, 170, 204, 218
jazz 30, 137, 146, 150, 160, 189, 194, 204, 216–18, 245
Jin Yong 139, 140
Jiufen 76
Jobs, Steve 42, 72, 185, 219
Johnson, Philip 147
Johnson, Randy 153
Jordan, Michael 153
journey xxiv, 5, 7, 31, 35, 36, 52, 63, 65, 71, 75, 125, 126, 172, 174, 183, 194, 197, 221, 224, 227, 229, 230, 245, 248, 254
Joyce, James 163, 202, 233; *Ulysses* 163
Jung, C.G. 121

Kafka, Franz 202
Kahlo, Frida 240
Kant, Immanuel 211
Kapilavastu 31
karma 16, 100, 103
Kenting 205
Kerr, Steve 153
Khyentse, Dzongsar Jamyang xxii, 21, 188
Knipper, Olga 206
know-how xxv, 135, 223, 257
knowing xxii, 6, 8, 19, 23, 28, 31, 42, 47–49, 51–53, 55, 70, 71, 106, 125, 130, 132, 137, 138, 140, 146, 147, 150, 153, 159, 184, 193, 223
knowledge i, 37, 45–48, 53, 104, 120, 125, 129, 143–45, 147, 166, 184, 190, 207, 257, 258
Koestler, Arthur 19
Köln Cathedral 143, 164

Konchog Lhadrepa 113, 114
Korean 147
Kubrick, Stanley 134; 2001, *A Space Odyssey* 134
kunqu 5
Kung-fu 216, 223
Kurosawa, Akira 170

labels 72, 77, 87–91, 93, 94, 104, 107, 125, 187, 209
labeling 58, 60, 87, 90, 91
Lai, Lingling xvii
Lai, Stan i, ii, iii, xxii, xxiii, xxiv, 13, 29, 114, 132, 206, 235, 236; *A Dream Like a Dream* 13, 14, 16, 17, 19, 27, 160, 170, 190, 251; *Ago* 69, 105, 160, 251, 254; *All in the Family are Human* 156; *Beckett in the Lai Family Mansion* 251; *Chuangyixue*, xxiii; *Crosstalk Travelers* 97; "Creativity for Scholars Directors" 231; Deaflympics 251, 252; *Flower in the Mirror, Moon in the Water* 254; "General Theory of Creativity" 29; "How I 'Wright' Plays" 7, 139; *I Me She Him* 208; *Journey to the West* 197; *The Island and the Other Shore* 205; *Nightwalk in the Chinese Garden* 251; *One One Zero Eight* 254; *The Peach Blossom Land*, film 103, 204, 249; *River/Cloud* 254; *Sand on a Distant Star* 190; *Secret Love in Peach Blossom Land* 155, 178, 179, 248, 249; *Selected Plays, Vol. 1* 7, 50, 139, 205, 248; *Selected Plays, Vol. 2* 190, 198, 249; *Selected Plays, Vol. 3* 13, 69, 251; *That Evening, We Performed Crosstalk* 246, 248; *The Red Lotus Society*, film 156; *The Seagull* 133; *The Village* 160, 249–51; *We All Grew Up This Way* 245, 254
Laozi (Lao Tzu) 45, 87–89, 95, 117, 119; *Taoteching* 87–89, 95, 119
Latin 120
Lebanon 60
Led Zeppelin 200
Lee, Ang i
Lee, Bruce 184

Lee, Li-chun 208, 247
Lee, Spike 62
Lennon, John 5, 70, 174
Li, Kuo-hsiu 247, 248
Li, Po 54
Li, Yuchun 17
lie detector 106, 108
The Little Mermaid 138
Lin, Chia-chi 251, 252
Lin, Ching-hsia 103
Lin, Huowang 44, 46
Lin, Hwai-Min ii
Lloyd, Charles 216
Locke, John 211
London 7, 14, 16
Lorca, Frederico Garcia 11; Duende 11
Louvre 165
Lyon 16

Ma, Jack ii
Ma, Sen 245
magician 135, 146, 147, 235
Mahabodhi Stupa 14
Malcolm X 43
mandala 17, 164
Manet, Edouard 57, 58; *Le Dejeuner sur l'Herbe* 57
Mantle, Mickey 153
Manzoni, Pietro 114; *Merda d'artista* 114
martial law 6, 249
Maruo, Suehiro 43
master iii, xxii, 27, 36, 45, 49–51, 61, 65, 103, 104, 113, 131, 137, 144, 152, 153, 155, 156, 159, 163, 171, 188, 189, 193–95, 199, 200, 212, 218, 223, 224, 233, 235, 237, 243, 246, 255
master class 50, 51, 93, 130, 140
masterpiece 5, 130, 165, 176, 194, 231, 243
mastery xxv, 5, 36, 131, 150, 154
McCartney, Paul 5, 174
Mead, Margaret 56
meditation 90, 95, 104–6, 109, 126, 187, 188, 217, 241
medium 48, 80, 214
melodrama 80, 157, 173, 176

memory i, 19, 76, 77, 94, 129
memories 35, 60, 76, 77, 257
mentor 7, 50, 106
Messi, Lionel 139
method i, iii, 27–32, 36, 37, 41, 42, 44, 46, 49, 52, 72, 89, 92, 101, 113, 119, 122, 129, 130, 132, 133, 136, 137, 140, 141, 146, 154, 158, 160, 163, 166, 177, 183–85, 188, 191, 196, 199, 205, 216–18, 224, 231, 236, 242, 253
Mexican 147
Miao folded cloth piecework 131
Michelangelo 62, 63, 71, 72, 190; Medici Tombs 62; Sistine Chapel 62
Mill, John Stuart 44
Miller, Arthur 232; *Death of a Salesman* 232
mindful 69, 90, 187, 207, 235
Mingus, Charles 146
Miranda, Lin, Manuel 62
Miyazaki Hayao 76; Ghibli Studio 76; *Kiki's Delivery Service* 76; *Spirited Away* 76
Molière 198
monk i, 27, 69, 187, 241
Montana, Joe 152–54
Monterey Park, California 246
Montgomery, Wes 159
Mother Mary 61, 63
motivation ii, 54–58, 60–67, 111–15, 132, 133, 146, 147, 160, 164, 183, 200, 202, 213, 224, 231, 239, 240, 249, 254
Mozart, Wolfgang Amadeus 58, 129, 130, 156, 165, 185, 195, 200, 243; *Die Einführung aus dem Serail* 58
Mulligan, Gerry 243
muse 11, 12
museum 3, 114, 165, 189, 229
music xxi, 11, 12, 29, 30, 50, 54, 56, 58, 63, 73, 93, 130, 138, 143–45, 147, 151, 156, 159, 160, 177, 197, 199–202, 209, 216, 222, 236, 243
musical 5, 31, 72, 94, 105, 138, 168, 170, 174, 180, 184, 232, 243, 253
musician 56, 66, 92, 94, 129, 137, 146, 151, 202, 216, 218

National Institute of the Arts 6, 13
National Palace Museum 93
National Taiwan University 44
Nationalist era 246
nature 6, 12, 56, 63, 79, 99, 100, 103, 119, 120, 126, 135, 139, 140, 143, 145, 154, 173, 184, 186, 188, 195, 202, 208, 209, 211, 239, 240, 255
NBA 153
neuroscience 45, 89
New Age 45
New Delhi 199
New York 7, 50, 59, 60, 145, 163, 184, 250
New York Times i, 60, 212, 236
Newsweek 59
Ni, Ni 17
Nick Fury 73
Nobel Prize 136
Noh Theatre 143, 170, 171, 255
non-creative mode 3, 22, 24, 52, 67, 183
non-thinking 92, 188, 191
noodles 76, 247
notebook i, 15, 78, 79, 83, 136, 199
novel 17, 30, 61, 63, 78, 81, 104, 133, 137, 139, 140, 146, 151, 174–76, 184, 189, 194, 205, 225, 243, 252
novelist 21, 36, 63, 71, 108, 138, 139, 195

Ogden, Dunbar 153
O'Keefe, Georgia 202
Old Testament 19
Oliver, Jimmy 137
One Hundred Years of Solitude 49, 235
opera 11, 58, 150, 156, 159, 194, 197, 220, 253, 254
Oppenheimer, J. Robert 60
Oppezzo, Marily 185
opposite placement 73, 74, 184
order 6, 16, 21, 24, 46, 56, 87, 92, 115, 120, 122, 123, 125, 139, 140, 154, 166–68, 171, 172, 195, 198, 202, 209, 213, 216, 221, 223
organic 7, 52, 92, 223
original xxiv, 4, 7, 17, 30, 32, 50, 55, 57, 81, 82, 88, 95, 108, 133, 139, 141, 157, 159, 165, 169, 170, 174, 189, 202, 204, 206, 221, 222, 224, 242, 243, 245, 252
Oscar 113
Ozu Yasujiro 80, 146

pachinko 204
painting 15, 16, 47, 58, 61, 76, 80, 113, 114, 121, 131, 136, 145, 154, 159, 168, 188, 194, 217, 220
painter 58, 60, 62, 68, 78, 92, 131, 137, 149, 202
Palazzo delle Exposizioni 15
Palme d'Or 113
Paris 14, 15, 57, 163, 252
Parker, Charlie 30, 137, 200
Parthenon 144, 173
Partnership for 21st Century Skills 5
passion 36, 55, 57, 58, 60, 62–64, 80, 81, 114, 136, 147, 156, 164, 183, 212, 237, 240, 248, 254
Pei, I.M. 165
Peking Opera 150, 220
The Peony Pavilion 5
perception 19, 67, 68, 69, 89–92, 123, 241
performance iii, 13, 17, 50, 52, 56, 57, 60, 63, 94, 137, 149, 166, 170, 171, 173, 177, 189, 206, 207, 222, 229, 242, 243, 245–48, 250-52
Performance Workshop xvii, 246, 249
perseverance 191, 195, 215
personality ii, 81, 213, 214
phenomena 18, 79, 81, 91, 134, 135, 143, 144, 148, 255
philosophy 29, 44, 45, 100, 144
Picasso, Pablo 242, 243
Pink Floyd 172; *The Wall* 172
Planck, Max 69
Plato 211
playwright i, ii, 6, 36, 49, 50, 62, 63, 80, 101, 102, 112, 143, 153, 202, 208, 212, 217, 223, 240, 245
playwriting i, 7, 29, 174, 177, 212
poet 16, 50, 63, 68, 70, 165
poetry 5, 12, 43, 54, 94, 186
Pollock, Jackson 121, 217, 218
Porter, Cole 174; "I Get A Kick Out of You" 174

postmodern 46, 144, 191
practice ii, iii, xxv, 5–7, 27, 29, 37, 42,
  45, 49, 65, 72, 74, 90, 92, 95, 105–7,
  130, 135, 137, 149–51, 154, 156, 160,
  173, 184, 185, 187–89, 218, 234, 235,
  238, 240
practitioner i, 27, 90, 105, 193, 201, 235,
  240
prejudice 77, 81, 82, 92
Preston, Travis iii
Pride and Prejudice 72
Princeton 29
proscenium 17, 173, 206
Proust, Marcel 67
Puccini, Giacomo 11, 18; *Madame Butterfly* 11
Putin, Vladimir 101

Qing Dynasty 60, 246
Quantum Physics 65

Raging Bull 247
Raman, C.V. 136
Rangda 57
Ravenna 145
Rayment, John 252
reality 42, 65, 87, 91, 157, 158, 163, 169,
  223, 224, 235, 247, 257
religion 46, 120, 240
Religious Studies 45
Renaissance 60, 61, 135, 144, 145, 170
retreat xxiii, 201, 202, 208
Revolution 46, 165, 247
Ricard, Matthieu i, 27, 89, 106, 114;
  "On Consciousness" 89; *Why Mediate?* 106
Rinpoche, Gyatrul 108
Rinpoche, Jigme Khyentse 53
Rinpoche, Ringu Tulku 106
Rinpoche, Sogyal 14; *The Tibetan Book of Living and Dying* 14
rites 43, 56, 164, 229
ritual 17, 56, 57, 144, 230, 233, 253
Rocamora, Carol 206; *I Take Your Hand in Mine* 206
Rodin, Auguste 170
Rollins, Sonny 216
Rome 15, 16, 143

Rosenberg, Harold 217
Rothenberg, Albert 18, 19
Rothko, Mark 58
rules 7, 77, 122, 131, 166, 171, 198, 199,
  201, 241, 248, 258
Saiu, Octavian ii, xvii
San Francisco 153
San Marino, California 251
Sappho 43
Sardou, Victorien 173
Schechner, Richard 60
Schiller, Friedrich 202
Schwartz, Daniel 185
Schwitters, Kurt 165
science xxiii, 5, 60, 69, 144, 212
Scribe, Eugène 173
script 12, 17, 103, 156–58, 167, 169,
  174, 177, 205, 208, 240
Scripture of Mountain and Sea 254
sculptor 71
sculpture 71, 80, 114, 170, 191, 203
self-discovery ii, 63, 64
Senger, Chris 130
sensitivity 214, 215
Senudd, Stefan 95
seventh consciousness 89, 121
Shakespeare, William 5, 6, 12, 62,
  88, 133–35, 169, 198, 212; *A Midsummer Night's Dream* 135;
  As You Like It 62; *Hamlet* 5, 88,
  133–35; *King Lear* 62, 135; *The Winter's Tale* 169, 170
Shakyamuni 14, 31, 46
Shaman iii, 214, 218, 235
Shanghai xvii, 14, 17, 21–24, 164, 167,
  215, 254; French Concession 167
shape 42, 57, 71, 77, 79, 82, 89, 97, 101,
  131, 164, 165, 173–75, 183, 215, 217,
  220, 222
Shenzhen 17, 79, 147
Shepherd, Sam 230; *Fool for Love* 230
Shibuya 204
Shih, Judy xvii
Shoroku Sekine 255
sincerity 115, 218, 236, 237
Singapore 17
Singye Dzong 100

sixth consciousness 89, 121
skills 4, 5, 12, 27, 28, 31, 41, 46, 51, 53, 57, 60, 61, 63, 114, 122, 129, 149, 154, 156, 158, 161, 211, 212, 231, 232, 236, 239, 248
slow motion 12, 152
soccer 100, 139, 143, 167, 253
Socrates 42, 43, 45, 46
Solnit, Rebecca 186
sorcerer 52, 230, 235
sorcery xxv
source ii, xvii, 3, 16, 18, 20, 35, 36, 70, 117, 119–26, 183, 185, 203, 215, 217, 233, 243, 250
South Africa 233
Southeby's 112
space 12, 13, 61, 70, 75, 76, 79, 89, 91, 94, 95, 98, 107, 113, 119, 122, 123, 134, 167, 173, 181, 184, 185, 186–88, 190, 199, 200, 202, 204, 236, 254
spell 56, 131, 135, 152, 223, 225, 233
Spielberg, Steven 224; *Jurassic Park* 242
Spies, Walter 56
spiritual i, iii, 27, 79, 107, 165, 187, 229, 233, 240, 241
spirituality 45
spontaneity 132, 139, 188, 189, 216
Stanford xxiv, 185, 231
Starbucks 72
Stein, Gertrude 31
Sternberg, Robert 30, 45
sticom 156, 157
Stockhausen, Karlheinz 59
storehouse 12, 19, 76
stream-of-consciousness 94, 138, 163
Strindberg, August 63
Strooker, Shireen 50, 106, 235
structure 14, 21, 49, 92, 100, 129, 134, 135, 138–40, 144, 147, 154, 163–65, 167–75, 180, 184, 189, 193, 200, 204, 215, 245
stupa 14, 17
style 30, 61, 93, 99, 132, 136, 138, 144, 147, 155, 161, 163, 191, 193, 198, 218, 247, 254
Sufi Qawwali music 200
Super Bowl 253
surrealism 144

Surrealists 139
Suzhou 154, 189, 190
Suzhou garden 154
Suzuki method 191
Suzuki, Shunryu 49
Swift, Taylor 63
Sydney 252
symphony 12, 92, 165, 169, 194, 243

Tainan 248
Taipei xvii, xxiii, 6, 13–15, 17, 31, 53, 73, 81, 93, 94, 108, 121, 133, 139, 153, 158, 173, 197, 198, 205, 216, 220, 230, 240, 245–47, 250–53, 255
Taiwan 5–7, 14, 15, 22, 44, 53, 76, 93, 94, 131, 133, 157, 158, 197, 199, 205, 211, 245–53
Taiwanese 73, 131, 151, 153, 157, 249, 253
Tan, Amy 21
Tang Dynasty 147, 173
Tang Xianzu 5
Tao 88, 89, 95, 117, 119
Tarantino, Quentin 80
Tatum, Art 200
Television 106, 146, 156, 157, 205, 219, 247, 251
temple 11, 27, 144, 164, 220, 241, 253
Tharp, Twyla 160
theater i, iii, xxiii, 5–7, 17, 23, 30, 36, 50–52, 58, 62, 72, 92, 94, 104, 130–32, 137, 140, 141, 144, 146, 150, 151, 154, 155, 157, 166, 167, 169, 171, 173, 176, 189, 190, 197, 199, 206, 207, 229, 233, 235, 236, 240–42, 245–51, 258
Theatre Above xvii, 23, 24, 215, 254
Theory of Relativity 31, 87, 88
Thich Nhat Hanh 69, 70, 92
Thoreau, Henry David 187; "Walking" 187
Thunberg, Greta 46
Tibetan 14, 16, 62, 64, 90, 106, 108, 113, 114, 188, 199, 201
TikTok 46
Ting, Ismene 208
Ting, Susan xvii
Toklas, Alice 31

Tokyo 7, 21, 76, 80, 146, 163
Tony Award i
toolbox 35, 60, 132, 135–39, 141, 144–46, 148, 183, 184, 191, 235, 236
tragedy iii, 172, 191, 248, 249
training i, iii, 5–7, 12, 28, 29, 31, 41, 42, 50, 60, 90, 106, 121, 122, 150, 183, 191, 223, 242, 245
transformation 36, 52, 227, 230, 231, 233, 248
Trojan War 80, 172
truth xxi, 31, 65, 91, 92, 106, 194
Tyner, McCoy 216

U Theatre 252
U.C. Berkeley ii, xxiv, 6, 16, 45, 50, 155, 157, 234
ugly 81, 88
Ukraine 101
Umezu, Kazutoki 204
unity iii, 164, 166, 169, 170, 172, 176, 249
United Kingdom 100

Vajrayana 64, 90
Van Gogh, Vincent 193
Vasari, Giogio 61, 242
Vijñāna 89
vinyl record 172
Visby, Sweden 76
vison ii, 37, 51, 68, 97, 130, 167

walking 22, 145, 168, 185–87, 205
Walton, Cedar 216
Walsh, Bill 153
War and Peace 72
warehouse 35, 36, 75–80, 82, 135, 183, 217

Washington 59
Watts, Alan 186
Webster's Dictionary 44
Wei, Long-hao 246
well-made play 173–76
West, Kanye 111
Western ii, xxiv, 6, 145, 172, 197
Wikipedia 42, 53, 56, 89, 121, 211
Williams, Robin 139
Wilson, Robert i, 146
wisdom i, 14, 27–32, 36, 37, 39, 41–56, 62, 64–67, 72, 82, 91, 97, 98, 101, 106, 108, 111, 113, 119, 120, 122, 124, 129, 130, 132, 138, 140, 141, 154, 158, 159, 176, 183–86, 191, 196, 203, 209, 214, 215, 217, 218, 224, 226, 231, 234–38, 240, 242, 253
world view 97–99, 108, 109, 242
Wright, Frank Lloyd 91, 165
Wu, Chao-nan 246
Wuzhen Theatre Festival 17, 58, 235

Xixi wetland xxiii
Xu Chunhua 215

Yang, Edward 207, 212
Yang, John 167
Yao, Kris 189, 248
yeshe 106
Yu, Qiuyu iii
yugen 171
Yung, Danny 207

Zeami Motokiyo 170, 171, 180, 223; *Kadensho* 170
Zen 49, 131, 186, 252
Zhang, Xiaogang 58
Zuckerberg, Mark 185

www.ingramcontent.com/pod-product-compliance
Lightning Source LLC
Chambersburg PA
CBHW030135170426
43199CB00008B/75